Good Enough

Cynthia Nappa Bitter

HopeLines
P.O. Box 306
Penfield, New York 14526

Published in the United States of America.

Bitter, Cynthia J. Nappa, 1953—
    Good Enough: A story of hope in a world where losing is winning,
perfection becomes obsession, and thin enough can never be achieved/
Cynthia Nappa Bitter.

1. Eating Disorders.   2. Anorexia nervosa.   3. Bulimia.   4. Psychology.
I.   Bitter, Nappa Cynthia J.   II. Title.

ISBN 9656655-6-9

Library of Congress Catalog Card Number: 97-93354

Cover Design: Brian Manning
Author Photo: Thomas E. Bitter

This book is intended for education and/or entertainment purposes only.
Readers should use their own judgment or consult a medical expert or their
personal physicians for specific applications to their individual situations.

Many of the names and other identifying details, other than author's
immediate family, have been changed in order to protect privacy. Any
resemblance to an actual person is purely coincidental.

To Dr. Stephen M.,
you started me on the long journey back,
and stayed by my side the entire way.

And to my husband, Tom,
because without your love, I would still be searching.
ILYEIYAAPITA

Dad

SONG FOR CINDY

It seems so many years.
It seems so many tears.

I remember before,
the way our love used to be.
I remember the closeness,
Between you and me.

But as times grew older,
and fortunes passed.
I could tell that our true love,
would no longer last.

I thought there would be no end to this terrible thing.
I thought there would be no end.
I thought forever it would ring.

Sickness entered our lives so mean
and it changed your personality.
I began to feel painful hate,
resentment came too.
It seemed stinkin' fate,
on what happened to you.

I thought there would be no end to this terrible thing.
I thought there would be no end.
I thought forever it would ring.

But then I didn't understand.
So I've written this song to sing.
I'm with you all the way.
Success is in our view.
And if you're not healed today,
then tomorrow will be the day for you.

Jon S. Nappa

Acknowledgments

This book wouldn't have happened if it had not been for the patient support of my family and friends. Tom, you never doubted my success, even as you gave constructive criticism and sent me back to the keyboard—over and over again! You fueled my determination to prove that I could complete the enormous project I had taken on. You always believed in my mission. Honey, I couldn't have done it without your love, your continuous reassurance whenever my self-doubts threatened my self-confidence, and, especially, the "technology" you filled my office with!

Mom, Dad, this story says it all. Your love gave me life. Jonny, your writing expertise and brotherly advice were invaluable. The message was always there. Thank you for helping me to "see" it. Debbie, heroes together—the courage is yours, too.

Barb Ferriter, I promised and here it is. You spent countless hours guiding my initial attempts to put these words on paper. Those early beginnings now fill two boxes, and will forever be a part of my personal and professional growth. I have learned how to "start." Chris Votraw, your editorial support taught me the basics, our phone marathons supplied even more. Your patience with my need to talk . . . and talk . . . and talk . . . was priceless. Pat, Carmen, and John Viglucci, thank you for your willingness to help me understand the oft-confusing steps involved beyond the writing of this story. Your sincere caring shone throughout your editorial and technical assistance.

Renee, Dee, Paul, Lucille, Evie, Tami, and Sharon. You each supported my efforts in your own way. Your willingness to be my sounding board, your patience to listen to my many ideas (on the phone, during shared dinners, in the car), and your belief in my goal fueled my enthusiasm and encouraged me to not give up.

And my heartfelt thanks to those who provided me the benefit of their time, their experiences, and their expertise as I pursued bringing this book to market. Your genuine support was appreciated more than you'll ever know.

Preface

Years ago, at the age of seventeen, I sat down to write my life story. I wrote four pages (yes, I still have them) and proceeded to give that story a title: *I Was A Seventeen-Year-Old Problem.* Frustrated, though unsure why, I set those papers aside . . . for the next twenty-two years. Only then, after concluding the most intense journey of my life, could I finally understand the beginning, and return to writing this story. Though I have changed many of the names and other identifying details in order to protect privacy, all events happened as written in this true account of my seemingly innocent descent into the destructive world of anorexia nervosa and bulimia. This is a world in which losing is winning, perfection becomes an obsession, and thin enough can never be achieved. It is a world that continues to lure too many people and claim too many lives.

Over the past two decades, there have been countless books written about the numerous factors involved in developing an eating disorder, as well as the different approaches to treatment. All of these books play an important role in helping us to further understand the many complex issues behind anorexia, bulimia, and compulsive over-eating. Today, there is more knowledge and more advanced pharmaceutical treatment available then when I first developed an eating disorder. However, what hasn't changed is the obsessive mindset, the relentless grip, the endless cycle, the hopelessness that accompanies these disorders. Maybe you will see yourself, or someone you know, as you read through the following pages. Keep in mind that the medical crises depicted within may or may not happen. Yet their occurrence must be shared, as too many believe that "thin" is the only result of eating disorders. That if the person would just eat, then everything would be "okay." If this were true, there would be no need for this or other books written on this subject. The illusions of eating disorders must be shattered, for the devastation and destruction to life is physical, emotional, and sometimes, life-long. However, just as we are individuals with our own unique factors that contribute to the flourishing of these disorders, so is the information and healing approach that will best work for each one of us. That is why this story is neither a clinically focused nor a medical advice book. This story isn't about a magic wand that we sometimes look for when seeking difficult answers, nor is it about following steps one through five. But it *is* about the grim reality of what can happen when we view our bodies as the measurement of self-worth.

Good Enough was not written to take the place of professional guidance or treatment. After all, it is nearly impossible to have a "one-size-fits-all" cure. Rather, it is a story of hope, written to encourage recognition of our inner strength, and the guiding role that it plays in overcoming these illnesses or other adversities we may encounter as we travel the roads of life. This inner strength is your will to live, your spiritual beliefs, and, especially, the hope that you can get better. Because without hope there can be no beginning or no end.

The following condensed story centers around the reasons I developed eating disorders. But, most important, it reveals how I was able to step out of the dark, vicious cycle of anorexia and bulimia and into a bright, beautiful world. The lessons learned were vital in allowing me to take the necessary steps toward health. They enabled me to open my eyes and see myself, but only after I stopped believing the distorted view of my internal self-critical mirror.

Breaking free from anorexia, bulimia, or compulsive overeating requires more than a change in eating habits; it requires a change in attitude towards you. It's about giving you a chance—a chance to try life differently. If the following story helps just one person recognize that, and starts them on their own journey to a healthier, happier life, how can I not share it?

The price of an eating disorder is high. Only you can determine how much you are willing to pay.

As long as you try,
you are not a failure.

cjb

Chapter 1

The Beginning

I turned on the light in the tiny, hospital bathroom, walked over to the sink and looked down into the white porcelain basin, too afraid to look in the mirror. Too afraid to see what I had done . . . of my own free will. I raised my eyes, slowly, and stared into my face. *Oh God, my face!* Gaunt, sunken-in eyes. Hollow-cheeks; scrawny chicken-neck. Parched yellowish skin that called out for hydration, for nutrition . . . for food. *How had this happened? What monster had I become?* I snapped off the light and went back to bed. *Okay, I'm scared. I'm scared because I'm not getting any better. This merry-go-round won't slow down, or let me get off. I wish I could go back to the beginning and start over. But I can't. And I can't stop. Not until I'm thin. Not until my breastbone rests on my backbone. Only then will I be assured that all is safe . . . that I am thin.*

How had my body become a paper cutout of life?

To eat, is to be fat, is to be feared. I'm not sure where it came from, or even when it all started. Yet I know I didn't always feel this way, or feel this lost. In fact, my dad used to say that if he couldn't find me, all he had to do was to look up—at the treetops. And sure enough there I'd be, my face poking out among the vast greenness of the sheltering limbs of the big old oak tree that lived out behind the garage. I was usually off on some great adventure limited only by my imagination, or by my mom calling me into supper.

My mom said I should have been a boy, especially since I preferred blue jeans to dresses. I think it was because I was so different from my older sister, Debbie. She was so darn prim and proper, always worried about getting a speck of dirt on her clothes or a hair out of place that I sometimes wondered if Debbie was right when she said I was adopted.

I wasn't. It was just her big sister disdain that *she* could possibly be related to such a rumpled person like myself.

My little brother, Jonny, believed me to be the next best thing to peanut butter and Ritz crackers dunked in milk. Despite our five years difference in age, I was his favorite playmate and best friend. He was Bullwinkle to my Rocky, Tonto to my Lone Ranger, and Penny to my Sky King—hey, when you're a four-year-old, what's most important is that your big sister is playing with you. Jonny never tired of playing a role in our escapades, and was *always* willing to go first when an idea needed to be tested out. Well, maybe not always quite so willingly. I thought it had been a wonderful idea for Jonny to push me up our long, hilly driveway in his old carriage buggy. It wasn't my fault that Aunt Carol and Uncle Pat had come to visit, and that they just *happened* to choose that particular moment to drive in off the street. And it wasn't *my* fault that Jonny let go of the buggy and ran onto the lawn while I was still in the carriage. Okay, so I was a *little* worried when I sat up and realized I was a passenger without a driver. But I still don't understand why Mom and Dad got so upset. After all, Uncle Pat slammed on the brakes, and the carriage bounced— *gently*—off his car bumper. Could I help it that the buggy tipped over and got kind of dented when I climbed out?

Okay, so not all of my adventures ended that easily back then. Like the time I was ten, when we had moved into a new neighborhood, and I got stuck in the mud. That time, it was with my newest and best pal, Sandy. . . .

Sandy stood on the cement floor of my front porch, shivering, and rang the doorbell.

Dad came to the door. "Sandy, is everything okay?" He was puzzled to find Sandy standing alone, in front of him, covered with dried mud. It had been only hours before that the two of us had left to explore the fields behind our homes.

"W-w-w-e were s-s-stuck in the mud *a-a-nd n-n-n-obody* was helping us. A b-b-oy pulled us out *a-a-and* Cindy wants you to go pick her up. Mr. Nappa, *s-s-she can't walk!"* Sandy wailed.

"What do you mean, Cindy *can't* walk?" Dad looked down at the disheveled little girl and could only imagine what condition I was in. "Sandy, where *is* Cindy?"

"At the *w-w-hite* house," she pointed vaguely in the direction from which she had just come, "on the corner." Sandy bravely swallowed a sob. "Her f-f-eet are *c-c-old.* Cindy *s-s-*aid that you have to come get her."

Dad suppressed a smile, and reached for his jacket. My penchant for predicaments always seemed to result in a need to be rescued. "Let me give you a ride home," he offered as he headed towards his car.

"No thank you, Mr. Nappa. I *c-c-an* w-w-alk," Sandy said bravely. "You *b-*better go get Cindy. She's waiting for you." Sandy lifted her hand in a forlorn wave and continued on her way.

Where was Dad? Sandy should have gotten to my house by now.

"Cindy, would you like this cup of cocoa?" The kindly woman, who had opened her door to Sandy and me, handed me a steaming mug of hot chocolate. I pulled my feet—now encased in dry, woolly socks—up underneath me and snuggled more comfortably on the chintz-covered sofa. It had been *soooo cold* out in those woods! A recent spring thaw had made our hike a bit treacherous as we tramped along numerous muddy trails. How were we supposed to know that under the right conditions, mud becomes *quicksand?* It was a good thing that a big boy had heard us yelling; otherwise Sandy and I might have *frozed* to death! I sipped the warm liquid and anxiously watched the front hallway.

Several minutes passed before the doorbell rang and my father was led into the woman's parlor. I set the cup aside as he hurried over to the sofa. His worried face relaxed in light of my rosy red cheeks and chocolate mustache. "Pocahontas, what am I going to do with you?" he chuckled affectionately, and lifted me up into his strong arms.

"Keep the socks," the woman offered, and she tucked the bag containing my wet, muddy ones underneath my father's arm. He thanked her for the both of us and carried me out to the car. Somehow he suspected this would not be my last call for help.

After the mud incident, I was a bit more cautious, but not less daring in my play. Mom and Dad continued to rescue me from minor mishaps. They brushed the dirt from my knees and encouraged me to play safer. I nodded my head in agreement, though I was already planning which tree I'd climb next or which trail I'd be hiking. After all, when you are the kickball champion of your fifth grade class, and voted most popular at eleven years old, one didn't have time to worry about banged knees, or dented carriages.

But maybe it all started the summer I was twelve. That's the last time I remember *not* thinking about food all the time, or worrying about how much I weighed. The most important thing on my agenda—and my mind—that summer, was trying to decide between riding my new bike, playing Barbie dolls with Sandy, hiking in the nearby woods, or reading the latest Trixie Belden mystery book. That summer promised to be a hot one.

The days were already sticky. . . . The early morning air was still. The bedroom curtains hung listlessly, with not even a hint of a cool breeze. It was going to be another steamy day. I opened my eyes and glanced across the room at Debbie, still asleep in the matching twin bed to mine. Her sheets lay twisted in a tangle at the foot of her bed. Nighttime had brought little reprieve from the oppressing heat.

I yawned and got out of bed, stumbling on the pile of clothes I had discarded the night before. I picked up a pair of wrinkled red cotton shorts, gave them a quick inspection and determined them still wearable. I brushed past Debbie's denim blue skirt and pink blouse neatly folded across a desk chair. I reached out, tempted to muss them up *just* a little. But instead, I pulled on the red shorts, my mind already jumping ahead to planning that day's activities. Half-dressed, I padded barefoot over to the dresser, picked up a hairbrush and ran it through my long, thick, chestnut-colored hair. "A tomboy," Debbie always said. "A happy little girl," everyone often remarked. "Just me," I proclaimed silently, and stuck out my tongue at the mirrored reflection.

I rummaged through the top dresser drawer in search of barrettes and settled for rubberbands. I gathered my hair into two long pigtails and giggled softly at how much I looked like an Indian. Even Dad thought so and nicknamed me Pocahontas. With a smattering of freckles across my sunburned nose, olive-toned skin—courtesy of an Italian-born heritage—round rosy cheeks, sparkling brown eyes, and friendly nature, I enjoyed my comparison to the young Indian princess.

I peered back at Debbie—still asleep—and considered calling Janey, a girlfriend who lived across the street. It had been weeks since we had spent any time together. That's because I spent most of my time with three other friends—Mary Jean, Ellen, and Sandy. Whenever I played with them, Janey was never invited. *Oh,* not because I didn't want to. I liked Janey. In fact, I liked everyone and wished we could all be friends. It was just the other girls who didn't always want to include Janey in our games. And since they did not like to always play together, I forever had to decide whom I wanted to play with. Gosh, it was difficult being twelve!

I kicked the pile of clothes on the floor and uncovered

yesterday's yellow T-shirt. I yanked my baby-doll pajama top over my head and paused to examine my newly blossoming chest. *Hmmm, did Mom need to buy me a bra yet? Naaah!* With one quick swoop, I pulled on the T-shirt and covered those tiny buds of puberty. Bras were not a subject I was ready to discuss. I gave one last look over at Debbie's lifeless body then tiptoed out of the bedroom, closing the door not too quietly behind me.

I sauntered lazily downstairs, my bare feet enjoying the cool ceramic tile as I stepped down onto the front foyer floor. Out of habit, I glanced out the screen door and over at Janey's house. If she were already outside, I'd ask her if she wanted to ride our bikes down to the lake. That was always fun to do . . . *but wait! What's this?* I stared at a very long truck that was parked in Janey's driveway. People—*strange people*—were unloading furniture and boxes and carrying them into the house. "Why, that's weird?" I frowned, puzzled by the activity, and pressed my nose up against the screen door. *Maybe Janey's parents had bought new furniture?* But Janey and her family were nowhere in sight. In fact, none of the people going in and out of the house looked familiar. The scene across the street made no sense. What was going on?

I pushed harder into the screen, my nose flattening against its wire mesh. The truck, emptied of its belongings, pulled out of the driveway. I watched as it turned the corner and read the name scrawled in big block letters on its side: ACE MOVING CO., INC.

"Janey moved?" *While I slept? Without telling me?* "But she hadn't said anything?" I stared at the now unfamiliar house, certain if I looked long enough, or hard enough, Janey would re-appear. But she didn't. And my vision blurred, but not as much by the mesh-screened door as by the tears that filled my eyes.

Janey, an only child whose parents often indulged her, had given no indication of this impending move. Only occasionally had her parent's mentioned a desire to live elsewhere so Janey could have her own horses. Her mom talked of all the fun things Janey and I would do, *if* they were to ever move. She said I would be their guest on weekends, and ride the horses . . . with Janey . . .

together. And then Janey's mom would laugh, give me a hug, and tell me I was like her second daughter. Oh, how I reveled in feeling so special!

I swallowed glumly. How could a friend—*especially* a friend with whom you had pricked your finger with a needle until a drop of blood appeared, and you'd become cross-your-heart-and-hope-to-die blood-sisters—move away without telling you? Blood-sisters didn't just slip away in the middle of the night. *Maybe she was mad at me?* But the only thing I ever did was to be friends with people. Why . . . I never even argued with anyone! Could it be because I played with my other friends without Janey? I know that Janey and I hadn't played together too much over the past few months. But I had tried. *Really, I had!* I had called her on the phone, and gone over to her house. I had told her that I missed playing with her and wanted us to spend more time together. Maybe if I could just figure this out, Janey will come back.

But I couldn't, and she wasn't.

My lower lip trembled, and I choked back tears. In spite of my rambunctious ways, I was extremely sensitive. That's what Dad said. He said he only had to look at me cross-eyed and I would be devastated. Because of that sensitivity, Dad chose his words carefully whenever I needed to be corrected, or be pulled back, as my adventurous spirit sometimes led me into undesirable places. My feelings were easily hurt, and it was at a young age that Mom and Dad had sensed my greater need for reassurance. They recognized that, for me, changes were more difficult challenges than the hidden dangers in the trees and fields that I loved to explore.

My eyes sorrowful, I struggled to comprehend the mysterious happenings across the street as the new family claimed Janey's house for their own. I slid to the floor and huddled against the rigid aluminum door, sobbing. Janey had left without saying good-bye.

And it had to be all my fault.

Chapter 2

Empty Spaces

In September, I entered eighth grade, still questioning the where and why of Janey's move, but never out loud or to anyone else. I was much too ashamed to let anyone know that I might have had something to do with Janey's mysterious move. I did manage to find out Janey's new address from a mutual classmate, though no explanation was given as to why she had known of Janey's move and I had not. I even got up enough courage to write Janey a letter, but she never responded, and my questions remained unanswered.

It didn't help when Sandy told me that she had seen and talked with Janey at a local horse show one weekend. And it was Sandy who finally confirmed my earlier suspicions of Janey being mad at me. "Why?" I asked, and put down the book I had been reading. We were lying under a big apple tree in my backyard, each reading the latest Trixie mystery.

"Because . . ." and Sandy looked down at her book, clearly uncomfortable as she relayed Janey's reason. "She said you had not been a good friend to her."

Oh! Her words delivered a swift jab to my stomach. I

mumbled an excuse about needing to leave and quickly walked away; frantically searching my memory for the something, the *anything* that I had done. *But of course!* How could I be so stupid! It was just as I had thought! It was my choosing to play with the other girls when I *should* have played with Janey.

Janey was right. I had failed as a friend. And with that experience, I celebrated my thirteenth birthday with a bit less confidence and plagued by a vague uneasiness. The sentence Janey had bestowed upon me felt far crueler than I deserved. After all, I had never meant to hurt her. That was not a part of me. I *liked* people. All I ever wanted was for them to like me, too. The only comforting thought was that at least I would no longer have to choose between her and the other girls. Mary Jean, Ellen, Sandy, and I were left to truly be the four musketeers we often called ourselves.

Mary Jean and I were the oldest of our quartet—well, actually, I was, by ten days—but Mary Jean was clearly the leader. She was the mother when we played house, the teacher when we played school, the president of our club. I, along with Sandy, one year younger and Ellen, two years younger, willingly followed Mary Jean's commands. Yet it was Sandy's knack for adventure that I gravitated toward. Together, we romped in the hills behind our homes, playing horses. Or we rode our bikes down to the nearby lake to explore the old French fort. We took turns playing with our Barbie dolls and Barbie's little sister, Skipper. We shared a mutual love for animals, Trixie Belden mysteries, and even planned for our future as we decided to be veterinarians and go into practice together. Why, we were destined to be best friends *forever!*

"Gin!" Debbie announced triumphantly. "And that makes my score five-hundred-and-thirty-four. I win!" I handed her my cards, and stretched out on the floor.

"Cin, don't you think it's time you started wearing a bra?" Debbie teased.

My face reddened, and I quickly folded my arms across

my chest. "I don't need one *yet*!" I snapped and walked out of the room in a huff. But Debbie's remark wasn't as off base as I wished it to be. My body had developed curves and bumps where there used to be none, *and* my period had started. Mom had gone through her spiel, pointed out the Kotex box on the floor in the bathroom closet, patted me on the shoulder with a knowing smile—*ha!*—and welcomed me to womanhood. Half-woman, half-child. Wear a pad, climb a tree. I begrudged the former, preferred the latter. How had Pocahontas survived this wilderness of puberty?

"Cindy!" Debbie yelled. "Sandy's on the phone. And make it quick," she added impatiently, handing the receiver to me. "I'm expecting a phone call."

"Cindy, can you come up to my house?" Sandy's excitement carried through the phone line. "I've got some really great news to tell you."

"Sure. I'll be right there." I hung up the phone and ran out of the house. What in the world could her surprise be? Maybe her mom had agreed to the horseback riding lessons? If she had, then maybe Mom and Dad would give me their approval, too.

Sandy was already halfway down the street. "What's up?" I asked, breathlessly, when we met face-to-face.

"We're moving to Rochester when school lets out in June!" Sandy exclaimed, and she danced around in circles. "My dad got transferred, and we're going to have a new house built. I'm going to have my own room and I get to pick out what color I want it painted!" She paused, thought for a moment, then added, "yellow. I think I'll pick yellow."

Moving? But what about our riding lessons? And exploring the French fort? We were best friends! Who was I supposed to share Trixie Belden books, horses, and adventures with now? The searing pain of Janey's departure came rushing back. I struggled to put a smile on my face as Sandy giddily described her house, her soon-to-be-yellow room, and a nearby riding stable. I said nothing, but my eyes spoke volumes. Only Sandy was too caught up in her newest adventure—one that didn't include me—to notice the tears that I tried valiantly to blink back. It was with a long face that I left her and walked home. The uneasiness of the past year deepened.

June came much too quickly and with it, Sandy's departure. I waited until the last possible moment to say good-bye. With dragging feet and a heavy heart, I walked one last time to her house at the top of the street. I fingered a folded piece of paper in my hand and hesitated in giving it to my friend. I had spent the better part of the previous evening putting into words how much I was going to miss her. Sandy was my best friend. She shared my interests and my dreams. Expressing that had not come easily, even on paper.

"I'll write you every week," Sandy promised, and turned to get into her family car. I shoved the wad of paper into her hand. "Read that on the way to your new home," I said huskily, and hugged her tightly. *Please don't forget me!* I waved bravely to my departing friend until the car disappeared around the corner . . . until she was gone.

That was to be a summer of other changes as well. In August, Grandma Nappa passed away. A few weeks later, Dad took ill himself and was hospitalized. Grandma's death I understood. Old people died. But parents weren't supposed to get sick or go away. They were supposed to be there, to hold you, especially at night when the blackness swallowed the rest of the world up, and your best friend lived ninety miles away.

A longing for earlier, happier times increased tenfold. Sandy was gone, Dad was gone, and Grandma was gone. Growing up wasn't turning out to be such a great adventure after all.

I opened the bedroom closet door and searched among the jumble of board games, shoes, and a few stray stuffed animals on the floor. A few moments later, I resurfaced with Barbie, Skipper, and Midge clutched in my arms.

Debbie watched as I backed out of the closet. "Where are you going with those, Cindy?"

"Aunt Mary and Aunt Martha stopped by. Kimmy is with them. Mom said to give her something to play with." I looked at my favorite dolls worriedly. "Do you think she'll hurt these? She's only five."

"No," Debbie answered with big-sister confidence. "She'll just take their clothes on and off."

I went downstairs and reluctantly handed over those prized possessions to my little cousin. After several minutes of nervous observation, I concluded that Debbie was right. Kimmy was having a great time removing the dolls clothing. No, she wouldn't hurt them.

"Oh! Does Cindy still play with dolls?" I blushed as my eighteen-year-old cousin, Spencer, walked into the room.

"Of course I don't *play* with dolls," I replied indignantly. "In fact, I'm going to give them to Kimmy to keep." *There you see. I'm a big girl now.* Little Kimmy's face lit up, and my heart sank. *Oh!* And I wished I could take back those words. I loved playing Barbie dolls. I didn't *really* want to give them up. But it was too late. Kimmy had already claimed the dolls for her own. Later that evening, my relatives left with a very sleepy but very happy little girl, her new toys clutched firmly in her arms.

It was the right thing to do. I *know* it was the right thing. After all I was thirteen, almost fourteen years old. I was *much* too old to play with dolls. *Wasn't I?*

By September, Dad had improved and was back home. I celebrated my fourteenth birthday, began my first year of high school, and my tomboy role no longer felt acceptable. Changes that had begun a year ago became constant and many. My freshman classes were much larger and filled with unfamiliar faces. And for the first time, I was unsure of my ability to perform well in classes. I was reluctant to raise my hand, unless I was *absolutely* sure that the answer was correct. Only I never was. And I *had* to get A's. A feat that had been achieved easily in grade school, but not so easily in high school. Surely, anything less than perfect meant I wasn't trying hard enough. Or maybe it meant I wasn't good enough?

And the popularity I had achieved at ten . . . eleven . . . twelve years of age felt like nothing at fourteen.

I stared out of the living room window into the cold, gray drizzle of the November day. Laughter floated out from the adjoining dining room. Grandma and Grandpa Chiodo had come for Sunday dinner. Everybody was having a good time. That is, everybody but me. I had cramps from my stupid period, and wanted only to spend the afternoon reading in my room, away from the noise. But I didn't. Instead, I joined the rest of the family for Mom's lasagna dinner and answered, *"Fine,"* when asked about school, friends, and life in general. It was only after Mom had served lemon meringue pie that I could excuse myself to escape outside. I grabbed a jacket from the front hall closet and stepped out into the dampness, which only added to my misery. My head bent downward, against a biting wind, I headed down the road. I reached the end of the street and stepped off the pavement and onto a well-worn, familiar, muddy path that led to an isolated, barren hole deep in the middle of the woods. I stopped in front of a long-ago uprooted tree, hesitated a second, then straddled the broad-based tree and laid face down in hopes of easing the pain in my stomach.

The clearing was where Sandy and I had spent hours, playing horses. The tree beneath my stretched-out body had been an imaginary steed. A similar oak, only a few yards away, had been Sandy's. We had galloped through fields and streams, creating exciting adventures to follow, most times in our minds, but sometimes on foot. I smiled at the pictures in my mind. *Cindy and Sandy.* Dad always said he never knew what mischief the two of us were going to get into next. Our imaginations took us into and out of dangerous missions, always on the brink of excitement— or disaster, depending on who was leading that day's mission.

26

I pressed my face closer against the rough, damp bark and strained to wrap my arms around the tree's giant girth, as I searched for comfort in that cold silent forest. "I guess I'm too old for horses now," I whispered. Alone in the woods, the tears slipped down my cheeks.

The pain in my stomach represented far more than menstrual cramps. I missed my friend.

Chapter 3

Straight Edges and Other Fractions

"*Cindy! Debbie! Jonny!*" Mom called up the stairs. "Time for dinner!"

Up in my bedroom, I set my book down reluctantly. "Hey Cin, haven't you read that book before?" Debbie asked as she primped in front of the dresser mirror. She frowned in concentration, and attempted to tie a ribbon around her shoulder-length hair. "Could you help me with this?"

"Sure." I walked over and looped the red yarn ribbon around her silky mahogany-colored tresses, just the way she liked it. "Yes, I have read it before. I enjoy reading my books over and over again," I replied, though Debbie didn't really expect an answer, and then said nothing more as we headed downstairs for dinner. Was it wrong to re-read my books? But Sandy and I *always* re-read our books. I slid into my seat at the table and mulled over my sister's question.

"Cindy, how did your algebra test go today?" Dad asked, and handed me a steaming casserole of mashed potatoes.

I groaned and took the bowl. "I hate that stupid class!" I muttered under my breath, and scooped out a serving of the potatoes. I held out my glass, and hungrily eyed the veal cutlets. "May I have some more milk, please?" I asked. "Well, the test was kind of hard. I don't like algebra. . . . "

Mom poured milk into my glass, and shook her head. "Cindy! I'm surprised at you. You're a good student. You never had problems with schoolwork before. You *like* school."

I shoveled the potatoes into my mouth. I don't know why math had become so hard all of a sudden. It hadn't been like that in middle school. Maybe it was because I didn't know anybody in this class. Or maybe it was because everybody else seemed to understand what the teacher was saying. "Well, you're right. It probably wasn't that bad. I'm sure I did okay." Maybe if I tried harder, it *would* be okay.

But algebra didn't get easier. And I didn't ask for help, because I *should* have understood why $x = y$, or why the hypotenuse was equal to the sum of the sides of a right triangle. Or was that geometry?

Home, too, felt like the wrong equation. Debbie had paved the way as an older sister, but I was not following. Her idea of success in high school was football games, dances, and dating. Too many times, I assisted Dad in dragging Debbie away from parties that had gotten out of hand, the smell of cigarettes still lingering on her clothes. Poor Debbie, she spent the majority of *her* high school days grounded!

I, on the other hand, vowed to *never* give my parents the same headaches. I worked hard at causing them no further worries, and relished in their approval of my being problem-free. I was learning to ask for nothing. All to which they responded, "We don't have to worry about Cindy. She is such a good girl. She never gives us any trouble. Now Debbie. . . ." And they would laugh, shake their heads, and wonder if they would survive Debbie's teenage years with their sanity intact!

No, I wasn't like Debbie at all.

Yet Debbie was my parents' standard of how teenage girls were supposed to be. While she dressed up, I dressed down. While she went out dancing and partying, I curled up at home with my books. Mom had a difficult time understanding such behavior and questioned why didn't I go to dances or wear those pretty dresses hanging in my closet? And the more those differences were pointed out, the more convinced I was that who I had been as a child, no longer fit the expected criteria of who I should be as a teenager.

Freshman year in high school soon came to an end and with it, so did my excellent academic record. Algebra gave me my first D and Spanish gave me the second one. Fortunately, Mom and Dad were too wrapped up in Debbie's high school graduation plans to notice those failures. That was okay because, next year, I'd try harder.

"You know, Cin," Debbie remarked. "If you push our beds together and put a larger bedspread across the top of them, it will look like only one bed in the room." She folded a blouse and put it in her suitcase.

"I guess." Debbie's graduation, her party, and now her leaving for college in Boston had caused the summer to pass much too quickly. I glanced around the bedroom. *It was so big!* When had it gotten so big? Or so empty? "Deb?"

"Hmmm?" She was busy making sure she hadn't left anything behind in the dresser drawers or her half of the closet. Debbie shut the closet door, and glanced around the room one last time. "Well, Cindy, you are finally going to have your own room. You are so lucky. You always said you wished you had your own room."

Debbie, I don't want you to go away to college. I love you! I don't care about having my own room. Please don't go! "Debbie?" My mouth smiled. "Here, I wrote this for you." I handed her a folded piece of notepaper. "It's a poem. It's just a little something, no big deal." *It's just my feelings, Debbie. I love you and I'm going to miss you.*

Everybody was leaving. Why couldn't things just stay the same?

*   *   *   *   *

"Honey, push your hair out of your eyes. You look like a shaggy dog," Mom admonished, and held out a plate of oatmeal cookies. Two of my aunts had stopped by to visit. I absent-mindedly hooked my long hair behind my ears, said hello, and bit into a warm cookie. I chatted for several minutes, grabbed a couple more cookies, and headed upstairs.

"You know, when Cindy gets older, the guys aren't going to be able to take their hands off of her." I was halfway up the stairs, still within earshot. *Now what could that mean?* I continued up to my room, closed the door, and walked over to the dresser mirror. I munched on cookies and stared into the reflective glass. Round-face, sun-kissed cheeks, shaggy eyebrows that Debbie had *tried* to get me to pluck. I frowned at their clueless meaning. *Why would the guys not be able to keep their hands off me?* I dragged over a desk chair, climbed up on its seat, and evaluated the rest of my anatomy: arms—a bit flabby, could use some firming; stomach—not bad, but not great; legs—chunky, especially the thighs. I pinched an inch of my waist. A little excess skin, but some exercise and dieting should take care of that. Hair—long, thick, flowing, and shiny, just like Penny's on 'Lost in Space,' and obviously, my only redeeming feature. "Hmmm? . . . I wonder? . . ." I climbed back down off the chair, and went into the bathroom where I stripped off my clothes then stepped, stark naked, onto the bathroom scale—*109 pounds.* Too much for my height of five feet? *Maybe I should lose five pounds?* I put my clothes back on and went back to my room and forgot about the earlier comment.

For the next two months, I made a half-hearted attempt to lose five pounds. I consulted some diet books, studied magazine articles, and fashion pictures. Twiggy's big round eyes, hollow cheeks, and boyish body was my ideal. Her hip-hugger jeans draped smoothly across her flat stomach. Her long, lean, willowy legs seemed to extend forever. She looked no older than twelve. I envied her.

I began spending less time reading Trixie Belden mysteries and more time devouring diet manuals. In the process, I gathered an impressive knowledge of How-To-Lose-Weight until it wasn't long that I knew the calorie count of everything I ate. I learned quickly that starches were fattening and were to be avoided. Carbohydrates were the enemy and potatoes and bread were no-nos. A room of my own was giving more than extra closet space. It was affording the privacy to delve more and more into dieting discoveries. Right from the beginning, I vowed to keep this newest adventure to myself. It would be my secret journey.

In quest of a better me, I developed a daily routine. As soon as I arrived home from school, I locked myself in the bathroom, stripped off my clothes, and nervously approached the baby-blue bathroom scale. I held my breath, and stepped onto the small flat square that determined each day's success. Very slowly, I shifted my weight from off my arms (very important!) and watched the dial come to a stop. Whatever the number, it didn't matter. What was more important—that I was less than the day before.

It had been a horrible day at school. Sophomore year was starting as bad as freshman year had ended. I was failing Spanish class. I dropped my schoolbooks onto the kitchen table and headed upstairs to the bathroom. First, I closed and locked the door behind me. Next, I shed my brown A-line skirt, stockings, yellow blouse (I bet it's the same shade as Sandy's room), bra (I had finally conceded to its necessity, though my 32AA size could easily have gone without), and panties. Then, I shivered (the cold seemed to bother me more than it used to), stepped on the scale, and watched the dial stop at—*99 pounds.* "Yes! I did it! I'm below a hundred pounds!" I jumped off the scale, elated! My latest restriction of cutting out lunches at school had worked! *Maybe the numbers were important after all.* I scooped up my clothes and raced back to my bedroom, my poor performance at school fading into oblivion. I pulled on a pair of tan corduroy Levi jeans and an over-sized red-plaid flannel shirt. *Oh, yes! If I worked just a little harder, why . . . I'd be able to lose even more!* Maybe I'd cut down at other meals too. *Let's see . . . if I drink water with dinner instead of milk. That will be another hundred and fifty calories I can cut out.* At that rate, I would be able to lose another four pounds. And if I felt that good at 99, why, I'd feel wonderful at 95!

I glanced at my bedside clock. I had thirty-five minutes until Jonny was due home from school. Just enough time to do the exercises I had added to my dieting regime. Can't lose by cutting food intake alone. Oh yes! I was learning well from my new reading material. I went downstairs and carefully averted my eyes from a plate of chocolate chip cookies that sat temptingly on the kitchen counter. "I will *not* eat one, I am *not* hungry." I ignored the rumbling sounds coming from my stomach. Yes! I was strong and brave! I could . . . I *would* . . . resist temptation! I sat down on the living room floor, my legs straight out in front of me, squeezed my butt muscles tightly, and scooted across the room. Three more times and then, jog in place. I took a deep breath and ran in place for fifteen minutes. Rest for one minute, than fifty deep-knee-bends. I had to work those thigh muscles! My heart pounded in my ears. "One, two, three . . ."

" . . . Forty-seven, forty-eight, forty-nine, fifty. Stop. Now sit-ups. Yesterday I did fifty-three, so that means today I have to do *at least* fifty-four." Back down on the floor, my feet underneath the couch for support, "One, two, three . . ."

Completely unaware of where I was headed, I had started my downward descent.

Ninety-eight, 97, 96, 95 . . . thinner was the winner. And losing never felt so good. The number on the scale became smaller, and I, secretly proud of my emerging bones, vowed to share their birth with no one. I stepped on a merry-go-round ride of, *"just a few more pounds to lose,"* and sophomore year became a blur of passing scenery.

"Cindy, you're failing Spanish. I think we should try a tutor for you, okay?" The school guidance counselor sat back in her chair and waited for an answer.

"Umm, sure," I mumbled. My stomach growled noisily, and I smiled politely at her quizzical look. That morning's allotment of three saltines and one teaspoon of Welch's grape jelly seemed further away than just two hours earlier. *Water. I'll start drinking more water.* Maybe that would help fill me up.

"Have your parents read and sign these papers," she said, and handed me several sheets. "Then," she smiled brightly, "we can start your tutoring sessions."

The water helped, the tutor didn't. I sloshed when I walked; I was barely pulling a D average. My weight dropped three more pounds, and I reached junior year status no longer needing a language elective.

"Cindy, your sister will be coming home in a few days for Thanksgiving vacation. Make sure your bedroom is clean," Mom reminded me for the *hundredth time*. She handed me a pile of clean laundry. "I'm glad I could get this week off from work in order to get everything done by then. Do you know what you're going to wear on Thanksgiving for dinner? You want to look nice for Hank's family, so don't wear pants. Why don't you pull your hair back in a pretty ribbon?"

Debbie had gotten engaged—to Hank. His parents and younger brother had been invited to spend Thanksgiving Day with our family. "I'm not sure what I'm wearing yet," I said, and trudged up the stairs with my loaded arms. *Why did she always have to tell me what to do?*

I dropped the laundry on my bed and walked over to the dresser mirror. I pulled back my hair and tied it with a yellow yarn ribbon. I glared at my image, and yanked the ribbon off, my long hair falling back onto my face. *I'll wear what I want, I swear I will!*

Thanksgiving came and went. I wore a brown, gold, and creme wool-plaid skirt, a gold crepe blouse, and two yellow ribbons in my hair. Debbie got her ring, flashed it all around, the parents oohed and aahed, the little brothers played without fighting, and I weighed 93 pounds.

Sometime during that year of being sixteen, I went on my first date, Sandy's letters became more infrequent, and Mary Jean became the closest friend I had. Though high school had thrown us onto separate paths, I still clung to Mary Jean's familiarity. Each morning and every afternoon, we rode the school bus together. We talked on the phone and—when she wasn't in the throes of a *serious* relationship—we got together after school. What with dieting and exercising starting to take up more of my time, I felt less need and less desire to fill it with too many close friends. Besides, Mary Jean would always be there for me. Of that I was certain.

I sat in the school cafeteria and watched the girls sitting across the table from me eat their lunch. *Look at them stuffing their faces. How disgusting!* I tore off a piece of my tuna fish sandwich and raised it toward my lips, but changed my mind along the way and dropped it into a napkin on my lap. I chewed air, pretended to eat, and took great pleasure in watching others fill their stomachs. But by the time I got home from school later that afternoon, I was starving! Worrying about what and how much to eat—or not eat—made me crazy! I opened my dresser drawer and pulled out a box of Bit O' Honey candy bars I had carefully hidden away. *I'll just chew one little piece. That can't hurt me.* I tore the wrapper off one bar, broke off a section, and popped it into my mouth. *God! It tastes so good!* I chewed and chewed, the piece becoming smaller and smaller in my mouth. *You mustn't swallow it, Cindy. If you don't swallow it, it won't count.*

I didn't swallow it. I only chewed long enough to release the creamy juices and then spat it out. As long as I didn't swallow anything solid, the calories didn't count. A half-hour and twenty-five bars later, I had chewed and spit my way through the entire box of candy. I stood up and swayed, nauseous from the sickening sweetness of too much sugar. I barely made it to the bathroom before emptying my guts into the blue toilet bowl.

I slumped against the bathroom wall, closed my eyes, and stroked my flat stomach. *Why—I don't feel hungry! That's totally amazing! And there's nothing in my stomach!* The overwhelming fear of moments before receded. "Maybe if I should eat too much, I could just throw up, and then I won't have to worry about gaining weight." Relief seeped throughout my body. It was going to be okay. I had discovered another secret to share with no one. Restricting food and exercising now had a third companion—vomiting. Between the three, I had a winning combination. Over the next few months, vomiting became more than an occasional way out—it was also my way in to thin. The pounds melted much quicker from my already lean frame. What people said or did wasn't as important as what the scale told me.

I dropped out of gymnastics, quit the school chorus group, and ignored school-friends attempts to include me in after-school activities and conversations. Exercising, eating, and vomiting had first dibs on my attention and time. I felt so strong, so solid. And with every pound I lost, the stronger I felt. A strength—a wall— that felt so safe, so good! Besides, I had learned from that earlier failure with Janey. If my classmates *really* knew me, they would not like me.

"Cindy? Can I come in?" Dad knocked on my closed bedroom door.

I put down my book. "Sure, come on in."

Dad opened the door and walked over to my bed. "How's it going, Pocahontas?" he asked, and sat down beside my stretched out body, hidden beneath a faded brown, orange and yellow quilted comforter.

"Fine."

"Cindy, I've noticed that you don't call your friends anymore. Can I ask you why?"

Because I'm too fat. And I wish I was thinner. I just want everything to go back and be the way it used to be. Because I miss Sandy. Because I don't know why. "I talk to my friends in school,

Daddy."

Dad was not totally convinced. "Well, why don't you call Diane? She's such a nice girl. Or Mary Jean? I haven't heard you talk with Mary Jean in quite a while."

"I talk to Diane at school, *really* I do. We walk to classes together, and Mary Jean's kind of wrapped up with this guy she's dating, so there's not much to talk about with her."

He studied my face, then smiled. "Okay. So how about you come downstairs and share some of the popcorn I just made?"

Popcorn! I can't eat popcorn! *Yes you can. You can eat it and then throw up. The calories won't even count.*

After that night, Dad stopped questioning my odd behavior. Guess he chalked it up to adolescence. On the other hand, Mom's comments continued. Hair: too long, too plain, and too straight. Clothing: "You're such a pretty girl, Cindy. Why don't you wear that nice dress I bought you instead of those raggedy old jeans?" Friends: "Why don't you get together with Diane, Marge, Mary, Sue, Sharon, Ellen. . . ." I listened politely, and focused on cutting my calorie intake even further. Because losing weight was a marvelous thing. With every pound lost, the better I felt. It's amazing how that worked. I didn't even mind Mom's remarks about my appearance or behavior.

Besides, there were more important topics to talk about. Like the poodle puppies that were making the rounds in many of my relatives' homes. I had been begging Mom and Dad for a dog practically my *entire life!* Now with everyone giggling over the puppies' antics and falling in love with those little white butter-balls, I convinced Jonny to add his pleas to mine. And it worked! Mom and Dad finally consented, and Buttons—because he was cute as a button—tumbled into our home and our hearts.

And my weight fascination deepened its demands. It consumed more and more of who I was, its voice commanding my every step. *What do I eat? When do I eat? How much do I weigh . . . eat . . . say . . . live . . . breathe?* The merry-go-round picked up its pace and only Buttons was allowed to hop on. In a very short time, he became my closest confidant, and the only one I could share this secret adventure with.

Chapter 4

Downhill Times

Thin was in, and I was ahead of the game. By senior year at school, I reached my goal of 90 pounds, and proudly continued a downward quest. The flabby flesh disappeared from my bones, its absence lending weight to feeling confident and good. Confident enough to plan for college and leaving home; good enough to start a relationship with Eddie, a boy from last year's English class. To which another area of life opened up—sex.

Sex. That was a new one. The closest school had come to approaching the topic was a film in a seventh-grade home economics class on bees, pollen, and a woman's menstrual cycle. I was too embarrassed to talk about that subject with Mary Jean, especially since she seemed to not be embarrassed by it at all. I definitely could not talk about sex with my parents. Their viewpoint had been clearly—quite clearly—expressed during Debbie's high school days: *"Only bad girls have sex before marriage. It's wrong."*

As Eddie and I grew closer in our relationship, so did the pressure and the desire to be more intimate. We hesitantly explored our sexual feelings for each other . . . touching, being touched. And my parent's admonishments, along with a Christian upbringing, were caught up in a troubled swirl of adolescent hormones, pleasure, and guilt. When Eddie whispered in my ear, "Cindy, you are so beautiful, you make me crazy!" His hands roamed my thin, firm body. And I couldn't help wondering, was this what that long-ago remark was about?

Debbie and Hank declared a blissful ever-after that October, the parents of bride and groom rejoiced, sister of said-bride threw up at the reception dinner and ended the evening in the Emergency Room of our local hospital.

"Ulcer?" Mom looked blankly at the doctor. "How could Cindy have an ulcer? She's only seventeen years old."

"I'm not certain if it is an ulcer, but all of her symptoms are pointing to that." The young resident smiled at my parents, and patted my shoulder. "Age doesn't have as much to do with it as other factors. Like stress, diet. . . ."

"She doesn't have any stress in her life," Mom interrupted. "She's only seventeen. Her diet is fine. Maybe it was her sister's wedding today. Maybe it had been too much for her."

I cringed under the blanket of the narrow stretcher upon which I laid. Eddie had taken me home after the reception. It had been there, in our family's living room, while we stretched out on the couch, that Eddie's hands had stroked my breasts, and I complained of a pain in my right side, because I wanted Eddie to stop touching the parts that only I had touched. And I wanted to be a seventeen-year-old woman. And my sister was married. And she wouldn't be coming home anymore.

And maybe I had an ulcer. And maybe it would explain everything.

I had an ulcer. They did this test where I drank liquid chalk, and the doctor said it was a "duodenal ulcer." He said I had to change my diet.

"Drink milk and coat your stomach with Mylanta. You need to keep something in your stomach at all times, Cindy. Otherwise, your stomach acid will eat at the ulcer."

Keep food in my stomach always? *Never.* I'd die first. Of an ulcer . . . or groping hands.

Debbie settled into married life, my ulcer healed—surprisingly well—with a steady diet of tiny portions of food and Mylanta. And Dad was in the hospital again. This time, the doctors gave his illness a name: Bipolar Disorder. They told Mom that with the right medicine his condition would stabilize and Dad would get better. But Jonny and I weren't allowed to visit him, because Mom thought it "was best."

While Dad was in the hospital, it was with much reluctance that I prepared for Saturday night dates with Eddie. Dad's illness, uppermost in my mind, left little energy to battle the growing confusion of hormones, and lust of Eddie's ever-present desires. Though it was disturbing, Eddie's attention did provide distraction and a sense of something familiar. I needed familiar.

One Saturday evening we went to the movies and then came back to my home to play Ping-Pong in the basement. It was a strenuous game and when it was over, we curled up together under an afghan on the couch. We kissed, our hands searching . . . fumbling . . . fondling. *No, don't do that!* The words crashed up against an internal wall, unable to climb out. I stiffened, my stomach churned. *Damn! I know I shouldn't have eaten those two hamburgers at Burger King tonight. Maybe I'll make pancakes for breakfast.* As if one had anything to do with the other.

It did . . . didn't it?

The next morning, I stepped on the bathroom scale—94. "Shit! I've gained weight. That means I have to lose more. Maybe nine pounds. Maybe I'll be more comfortable at eighty-five." And instead of eating all the food I wanted, I measured, weighed, and calculated what I would allow.

Over the next few weeks, I skipped classes—by hiding in the garage closet and sneaking back into the house after everyone had left for work and school. I feigned illness—*"Mom, do I have a fever?"* And she put her hand against my hot forehead (courtesy of an electric heating pad) and told me to stay home. When I ran out of excuses, I went to school, but rarely made it to the end of the school day. Instead, I ended up in the nurse's office with a sore throat, stomachache, or some other vague malady. And with Dad unable to rescue me, Hank's mother was called to come take me home.

"Cindy, is everything all right at home?" The school guidance counselor worried over my poor attendance. "You're missing too many days of classroom work. Your teachers are concerned about you. You are going to need tutoring again in order to catch up."

"Well, my dad has been sick and he wants me to stay home with him," I lied. Dad had been in and out of the hospital for the past three months and, once again, was back in the hospital. Not once during that time had he asked me to stay home.

"Cindy, would you like me to talk to your parents?" she asked.

"*Oh, no.* Dad's doing much better now. I'll tell him myself." And I fidgeted on the chair, its hard plastic seat seeming larger than the last time I had been called into the office. My early morning weigh-in had revealed a new triumph—88 pounds.

Despite the extra tutoring and the counselor's concerns, my grades dropped to an all-time low D average. And whenever I heard joking remarks with sexual connotations, my body tensed as I remembered that night in the basement. So I continued my secret adventure. Because striving for thin felt right. Because I knew when I got there, I'd be okay . . . I'd be safe.

Dad, my protector and rescuer, now needed his family to be his strength. Every night after work, Mom went straight to the hospital for four to five hours. Jonny, at twelve years of age, had school, sports, and the understanding that as soon as Dad was well, home would be the same again. I—with both parents unavailable—kept the household running smoothly.

And my obsessions tripled. In the morning, I could eat three saltine cracker squares with a half-teaspoon of grape jelly spread *smoothly* to their edges. Anything less, more, different, and it ended up in the toilet. Going upstairs to my bedroom, I *had* to count the stairs—thirteen. If I forgot or missed a number, I had to go back and start over, until I got it right. And when asked how things were going, I responded, *"Fine."* Because to say differently would cause a shift and possible destruction of the perfect balance I needed to achieve.

I played out this role for over two months. And yet the pressure to keep everything stable, in line, exactly right, wouldn't let up. Until one night, after Jonny had gone to bed, and Mom had not yet come home, I laid in bed and gave in. "God," I cried out bitterly. "I hate Dad for being sick! He's always in that damn hospital. Those doctors are lying. He's supposed to be better by now. Why are you doing this to me?" If God was the good person church taught me, then He would never have allowed life to become so unsettling.

Mom, just home from her nightly hospital visit, knocked on my door and came into the room. "Honey, what's wrong?" She sat down on the edge of the bed and brushed my long, tangled hair away from my face.

"Mom, I don't know what to do!" I whimpered, and she took me in her arms.

She rocked back and forth, and stroked my hair. "Cindy, I know Daddy's sickness is upsetting. It's hard on all of us. But he's doing better. Really he is. It's just taking a little longer than we had hoped, but he is getting better every day." She smiled sadly. "Would it help if you could talk to someone about this? We could ask at Daddy's doctor's office if there is a person you could talk to." I nodded, and she held me safe throughout that night.

A few days later, I visited the bald-headed partner of Daddy's doctor. I shared the confusion of my father's illness and my worry of his being sick. Nothing of anything else, because nothing else was wrong.

The counselor was thoughtful, his forehead wrinkled, as he stroked his chin. "Well, Cindy, what is going on is that you are growing up. You are sitting on the fence of life and trying to decide which side to jump off of. Your father is getting better and will be coming home soon. You don't have to worry about him."

Growing up? Ridiculous! Of course I was growing up! I just needed to understand why!

The counselor stood up and shook my hand. Our session was over. I smiled, and walked out of his office. *What a waste of time.*

Dad got better and returned home. Winter had almost become spring, and I was almost starving. I no longer ate breakfast or lunch and had just a small serving of whatever Mom made for dinner. If I was hungry—and when was I not?—I snacked on a Popsicle.

Eddie and I still dated. He had taught me to ski and I quickly caught on to that new sport. Flying down the slopes, the wind in my face, and the calories burned, was exhilarating! The results on the scale were soon worth it—85 pounds. Every chance I could, I begged to go skiing.

On a cold, snowy evening in March, though Eddie worried over a forecasted storm-front, I cajoled him into another ski trip. We skied several trails, and then decided to call it quits after one more run. The wind and snow had picked up drastically, and the visibility had become quite poor. Eddie stopped on the trail, a few yards ahead, but I waved him on, indicating not to wait. He disappeared around a sharp turn while I, a slower skier, had not yet reached that same turn.

The wind whipped the snow blindly all around, and I fought to keep on course. The trees were a white blur as I reached the bend in the trail and turned—and skied right into a snow fence. I had misjudged the deep bend of the narrow trail. The tips of my skis slammed into the fence's wooden slats and flipped me over to the other side. I landed face down, stunned, unable to catch my breath.

"Cindy! Are you okay?" Eddie had waited at the bottom of the run, but when I didn't appear, he worried that something had happened. He ran now over to my inert body and gently turned me over and brushed the snow from off my face. My face was pale; my eyes were closed. "Cindy, are you okay?" He removed my broken ski goggles. The impact had snapped them in half. "I think she's unconscious!" Eddie yelled, and we were immediately surrounded by a dozen ski patrol members. They carefully strapped me onto a toboggan and towed me to the First Aid station at the base of the mountain. Once inside the tiny bungalow, they summoned an ambulance. I still had not opened my eyes or responded to their voices.

But I wasn't unconscious at all. I was simply afraid of what would occur later, down in Eddie's basement. The accident had happened quickly, unintentionally, and now, it was the perfect way out. If I responded, everyone would assume that I was okay, and we would probably go home. But if I didn't respond, only then would I really be safe.

My eyes still closed, I listened to the worried voices of Eddie and the ski patrol. A wailing siren in the distance became louder as an ambulance pulled up outside the First-Aid Station. I was bundled up and carried into the ambulance; we took off amidst flashing lights, blaring horns, and whiteout conditions. "Cindy, can you open your eyes?" The ambulance medics started an intravenous—IV—and administered oxygen. "Cindy, can you tell us where you hurt?"

No, I can't. My eyes remained firmly closed.

The ambulance pulled into the hospital parking lot where we were immediately surrounded by the hospital trauma team. "Cindy, we're going to help you," somebody whispered into my ear. *Oh, thank you, God!* The doctors and nurses swiftly lifted me onto a stretcher, their moves perfectly orchestrated, and raced into the building. Once inside, they removed my ski boots and clothing faster than Eddie ever had done and hands—*safe hands*—poked and probed every inch of me. "Cindy, can you open your eyes?"

It's okay, Cindy. You're safe now.

I tentatively opened my eyes. A dozen faces hovered anxiously above. "Cindy, can you talk to us?" The attending neuro-surgeon smiled, his hands tenderly manipulated the profuse swelling under my ears. "Do you remember hitting your face?" he asked as he continued to feel for telltale signs of injury. Another IV was started in my right hand and a short stiff board was taped to my right arm to ensure its stability. The doctors wheeled the stretcher down the hall to Radiology, and after several sets of x-rays, I was brought back to the emergency unit.

The neurosurgeon wrinkled his brows and studied the x-rays. "Cindy, can you tell me where you hurt?" he asked.

Oh no! I can't tell you. Can't you see I'm scared, and I don't know what's wrong! Please, help me! I stared pleadingly into his eyes.

He watched me thoughtfully for several minutes. "Cindy, I want to keep you in the hospital for a day or two, okay?"

"Okay," I whispered. He smiled, patted my shoulder, and summoned my parents from the waiting area, where they had arrived just moments ago. The neurosurgeon gathered my parents and Eddie around and gave his verdict: a mild concussion, swollen salivary glands, and a cut on my nose from the broken goggles. None of which explained my initial silent behavior, but enough to warrant a closer look. Three uneventful days later, I was discharged home. I could walk, I could talk, I ate very little, and aside from the unexplained swelling of my salivary glands, I was determined okay.

Back at home, I denied myself even the smallest crumb. Mom and Dad pleaded for me to please eat. "Here, try some pasta . . . meatballs . . . chocolate cake. . . ." they begged. I shook my head and refused the gifts I desperately craved.

"Pocahontas, how about some tomato soup?" Dad sat at my bedside, holding my hand, stroking my face. I had not eaten for several days and had grown very weak.

"I'll have some tea, Daddy." And he hurried to fulfill my request. He held the cup to my lips and I sipped the warm, thin liquid. The number on the scale that morning—81. I had lost twenty-eight pounds in two and a half years.

Eddie felt horrible. He blamed himself for the ski accident, and worried over my slow recovery. He sat by my bedside, held my hand, and took his turn encouraging me to get better. And my bizarre behavior grew worse. I existed on tea and Popsicles and lost three more pounds. Thinning was winning.

Into the second week of not eating, hunger and my parents' distraught faces got the better of me. Their worried, hovering presence weighed heavier than I did. I needed them to be happy again. I needed to please them. I took a few bites of the plain pastina Mom set in front of me and my parents sighed in relief. "May I have some butter to put on my macaroni?" I asked. "And maybe a slice . . . a small slice . . . of Italian bread? Could you put some butter . . . not too much . . . on the bread too? And maybe I'll try a little of that chocolate cake." Mom and Dad smiled, relieved that I was eating. I would be okay.

And the hunger inside grew immense. Its strength was overwhelming. My resistance crumbled. I gave in. Within a week, I regained six pounds, returned to school, and resumed dating Eddie. My external injuries had healed but internally, I was a bloody mess.

"What should I wear?" I pawed through my closet of clothes, and finally decided on a purple crepe blouse and purple velour jeans. It was another Saturday night. "I can't do this," I moaned, and sat down on my bed, the purple blouse half-buttoned.

"Cindy!" Mom yelled up the stairs. "Eddie is here."

"I can't! I can't do this anymore!" I ran to the bedroom closet and crawled inside its dark, cramped space. "Go away! Go away! Leave me alone!"

Silence and then—Mom burst into my room. "Cindy, where are you? Eddie is downstairs waiting!"

I backed out of the closet and stood up. "Mom," I pleaded tearfully. *"Please* . . . tell him I'm sick. Tell him anything. I just don't want to go out tonight!" *I'm scared. He'll want to touch me and do other things, and I don't know how to stop it, Mom. Please don't make me go out.*

"Oh, honestly, Cindy! Why were you in the closet? You're acting ridiculous!" She was annoyed. "I'm not telling him anything! You tell him yourself. What is wrong with you?"

"Mom, please!" I begged softly. "I don't want to go out with him." She left my room in a huff. A few minutes later, Eddie's car pulled out of our driveway.

I curled up on the bed. Mom was angry, and there was nothing I could say that would make her understand. Buttons jumped up onto the bed and planted his furry little body next to mine. His wet tongue lapped my face. I laughed and hugged him fiercely. "Oh, Buttons, I love you so much. You're not mad at me, are you?" He barked and washed away my tears with his wet kisses. I settled back against the bed pillows, Buttons warm body next to mine.

Safe . . . for now.

Chapter 5

Desperate Measures

The winter snow turned to spring rain, and I hit a plateau in my pursuit of thinness. The scale would not budge either side of 84 pounds. Where denial once equated boundless energy, I now found myself dragging to get through each day. It was an effort to get up in the morning, to get dressed, to go to school, to count my calories, to vomit my food, to do my exercises.

Depression. Where had it come from? When had it started? How had it sneaked into my life? My face, still swollen from the ski accident, added further misery to that increasing despair. Our family physician grew frustrated and referred me to an ear, nose, and throat specialist, Dr. Taylor, one of the best in the city. Dr. Taylor puzzled over my very full face and my frightfully thin body. He had no answers, but he questioned that symptomalogy as something gone wrong—*very* wrong.

The depression grew heavier than my body and I, distraught, in my attempts to quiet the taunting voice inside my head. *I want to eat; I'm so hungry. No, you're not! You're fat and ugly. Don't you dare eat anything! You're body will swell to grotesque proportions. You mustn't eat!* Dad, once again, was called upon to play out his rescue role when the voice inside wouldn't leave me alone, and I crawled out onto the garage roof in a desperate attempt to escape the vicious messages of that inner voice. My frantic parents called Aunt Carol, Uncle Pat, and Dr. Taylor, who met us all at the hospital emergency department.

"Cindy, what are you so frightened of?" Dr. Taylor asked, and lifted me up onto the examining table. He touched the still swollen area under my left ear, "is this paining you, Cindy?"

"Please, don't let them hurt me," I mumbled so softly that Dr. Taylor barely caught the words. "Please, don't let them hurt me," I repeated.

"Who, Cindy? Who is hurting you?" I stared blankly at Dr. Taylor. "Okay, Cindy. I'll help you." He admitted me to the hospital's psychiatric floor for observation. After two weeks of therapy sessions with a hospital-assigned resident and tranquilizing medicine, I felt ready to see part of the outside world. Besides, I desperately needed to know some parts of life had not changed.

A few days later, I waited anxiously knowing that when three-thirty arrived so would Mary Jean. With high school graduation only two months away, arrangements had been made for Mary Jean to bring school assignments to the hospital. But when Mary Jean showed up, she was shocked to find me behind locked doors. Nobody had told her a psych floor was where they treated people for depression . . . for being afraid . . . for not knowing how you're supposed to be at seventeen.

Mary Jean nervously handed over my English book, wincing as our hands touched, and turned away from my skinny body. She had no clue of its connection to my fragile, emotional health. And how could she? The closeness we once shared was as children, not as adolescents. I had no reason to verbalize the pain that had grown inside. Besides, how could I explain to another something I could not even explain to myself?

Mary Jean repeated my teachers' instructions and left, without saying a word, without a backward look. She walked out of our friendship—*forever.*

I stared at her diminishing back, my face reddened with shame. *Oh, God. I am such a . . . nobody.* I didn't blame her for not wanting to be around me. I carried the schoolbooks back to my hospital room, alone.

Empty had never felt so heavy.

Four more weeks in the hospital and the only revelation came at a meeting with the therapist, a social worker, and my parents. The social worker said if I didn't get better, the only place left for me was a state institution.

But I'm not a bad person, am I? What am I doing that is so wrong? "Okay," I whispered as everyone craned forward to catch my words. "I'll get better." And they sat back, smiling, and nodding their heads. As if life was a test and I had given the right answer . . . or guessed correctly . . . or lied deliberately. And that little exchange added more bricks to my internal wall, its foundation so strong nothing or nobody could destroy it.

I got out of the hospital in time for final exams. I did poorly, but still graduated. For that summer, weight control, reading, and Buttons were my only companions. At long last, my strange behavior towards Eddie had the desired effect I wanted—he left me alone. We stopped dating and my days settled into a comfortable and acceptable routine of eating, vomiting, and exercising. With both parents working and Jonny preoccupied with his own interests, there was no one to question mine.

Each morning, I waited until everyone was gone before I sat down to eat. Breakfast was an entire box of prepared pancakes or a loaf of French toast, a half-pound side of bacon, and a quart of orange juice. I gorged until my stomach could hold no more, purged, and then began again. After spending two to three hours on breakfast, I planned lunch. When not in the actual act of eating or vomiting, I exercised. With my mind preoccupied by these activities, I had neither time nor energy to worry about anything else. I had one goal: to lose several more pounds before I entered college in the fall.

It was as clear as black and white. A simple equation. If I could control my weight, I could control my life.

Despite my poor attendance the last two years of high school, and faltering grades, I had been accepted at a two-year college an hour away from home. Living arrangements had been made several months earlier. There were to be four of us sharing off-campus housing: Mary Jean, Diane, Nancy (another class-mate), and myself. Other than a polite exchange of words at gradu-ation exercises, Mary Jean and I hadn't spoken since her visit to the hospital. The worry of what she might say to the other girls was a concern, but I chose to focus on the only important issue: "Maybe if I can get my weight a little lower, things will be better." With that thought in mind, I stripped and stepped on the bath-room scale—81 pounds.

I walked back to my bedroom mirror and stared at my image, discouraged. *Why am I not thin yet?* My thighs were *way* too fat and flabby. I don't understand. I had revised my exercise routine from forty-five minutes, twice a day, to exercising *con-stantly* throughout the day. So why did my body continue to de-feat me? Maybe 80 pounds? I opened a dresser drawer, pulled out a seamstress measuring tape and wrapped it around my waist— *22 inches.* I measured my hips—*29 inches.* And my thighs—*13 inches.* No longer were pounds lost enough reassurance. I had to know *inches* lost.

Yes! At 80 pounds, I would be thin enough.

"Cindy! I'm going over to Jimmy's house! We're going bowling, so I won't be home until dinnertime." The screen door slammed, and Jonny disappeared into the bright, July morning sun.

Three-and-a-half hours later, I lay sprawled on the bath-room floor, exhausted from an intense vomiting episode. "Oh, God! I know something is terribly wrong with me! I can't stop this! Why is this happening? What kind of hell have I've gotten myself into?" I pounded the floor with my raw, bloodied knuckles, a result from their constant shove down my throat over and over again. The anger and hatred at what I had become engulfed my entire being. Was there no end to this horrible nightmare of my life? *Oh God!* I had to stop it. "Why can't I eat like everyone else?" I yelled, furious over this lack of self-control. "I hate my body! I can't stand feeling like this anymore!"

I stood up, shaking uncontrollably, and walked over to the upstairs hallway window. Several houses down from ours, neighborhood children noisily played a game of tag, their joyous shrieks intermittently broke the silence of the summer afternoon. It was a pleasant day, a day I was not entitled to—and no hope I ever would be. I pushed up the screen and climbed out onto the garage roof. In a confusing, desperate move, I walked to the edge and jumped off.

I hit the green-carpeted ground feet first. Piercing pain shot through my legs, my back, and then nothing. I laid motionless, beside the garage, afraid to move, afraid to breathe. And I waited for something . . . anything . . . to clear the fog in my head. But the sun continued to shine brightly overhead and the neighborhood buzzed with its afternoon activities. No one had observed my solo flight.

I blinked into the brilliant glare and tentatively grabbed fistfuls of grass. Cautiously, I dragged my suddenly weighted body several feet. No pain reappeared. *I must be okay.* I sat up slowly and then half-stood, the uncertainty over what I had done dictating every move. I straightened up. *I can stand.* Relief flooded my senses. I hesitated, then slid my right foot in front of me and took a step. No pain. *I can walk!* Slowly, one step at a time, I circled the garage and into the house. Buttons yipped and jumped at my legs as the screen door slammed behind me. Searing pain shot up into my back. *Oh shit!* "Buttons. . . ." And I collapsed onto the kitchen floor. As quickly as the pain had disappeared, the faster it returned.

For several minutes, I remained still, the pain, excruciating. I eyed the phone on the wall. *I have to call Dad. Oh, God! He'll be so mad at me!* The fear of his reaction at what I had done, felt far more insurmountable than the phone above my head. Buttons licked my face. "Oh Buttons, help me!" He settled down next to me, his calmness reassuring and hopeful. I looked around and spotted the kitchen broom propped up against a corner wall, less than two feet from where I laid sprawled. I stretched out my arm, my fingertips barely reached the straw bristles. I inched forward, grasped the bristles, and cringed as the broom toppled on top of me. Several more minutes passed before the pain subsided. I looked up at the phone looming far beyond my reach. *"Please, God. Let this work."* I grabbed the broom's wooden handle and lifted it upward. The broom wavered aimlessly for several seconds then banged against the receiver and knocked it free from its cradle.

I caught the phone as it clamored towards the floor and quickly dialed my father's office. I took a deep breath. "Dad, I need you to come home. I fell, and *I-I-*I think I hurt myself."

Fifteen pain-filled moments later, Dad rushed into the house, "Cindy! Where are you?" He hurried into the kitchen. "Oh, dear God! Cindy! What happened? Can you stand up?" He knelt down and moved me into a sitting position.

"Dad, I don't think I can," I whimpered faintly. The pain was horrific.

"Cindy, you have to walk," he said through clenched teeth. "I don't want the neighbors to think anything is wrong." He stood me up. "What the hell did you do?" This rescue made no sense to him.

Oh, God! Dad is so mad at me! I knew he would be mad at me! "I-I was playing w-w-with Buttons. At the top of the stairs. I tripped and I fell." The lie came quickly. Dad's anger was too apparent. Half-dragged and half-supported by him, we walked to the car.

At the hospital, examination proved my injuries to be a

crushed ankle and a compressed vertebrae, a result of the massive force when I hit the ground. When pressed for details of what had happened, I repeated the earlier story of playing with Buttons. The orthopedic surgeon looked skeptical. That explanation did not correlate with the seriousness of the injuries, but he asked no more questions and I was admitted to the hospital. I could not sit up, stand, or walk. While medication numbed the pain, it didn't begin to touch the secret terror of what I had done, or why.

For the first few days, I laid motionless, and wallowed in the guilt of my lie and the shame of my fear. I had no appetite— pain and lack of mobility conveniently forbade any vomiting— and I obsessed over my inactive body. *Oh, God! I know I'm getting fat!* I reached down under the hospital sheet and pinched my flabby thighs. Jumping off the roof had done nothing more than reinforce this helplessness over fat.

After three more days, the swelling in my foot receded enough to allow a plaster cast to be put on my leg, and a metal brace was fitted from my neck to my pelvis. I was discharged home under my parents' care, with orders not to sit or stand without the brace, or to walk without the crutches. I couldn't ride my bike, run with Buttons, do squat thrusts, deep-knee-bends, or get a true weight on the scale. I had become even more of a prisoner in my body than before.

The rest of the summer passed uneventfully. When it was time to leave for college, the cast was still on my leg, the brace still embraced my torso (why were my bones taking so long to heal?), and I weighed 79 pounds. I had figured out how to vomit after all—by removing the brace. My parents packed my belongings, unpacked me at the apartment, and kissed me good-bye.

That first night and day away from home were filled with settling in with the rest of the girls. On the second day of school orientation, I fainted during registration and returned back to the apartment convinced that college life (not poor eating habits) was not working. I was scared (I didn't have the buffer of parents or home), I felt out of control (how did I eat with three other girls sharing mealtimes and one bathroom?), and Mary Jean ignored me. It was only a question of time until the other girls would dislike me also. Of that, I was certain. In less than one week after arrival, I returned home. The friends I had grown up with moved on in their lives, and I remained a lonely prisoner in my own.

Back at home, Mom and Dad remained clueless, and the doctors were just as puzzled. I was in and out of the hospital five separate times, put through blood tests, a liver biopsy, kidney exams, and an endocrinology work-up. All in an effort to rule out every possible medical cause for the unexplained weight loss and vomiting. In the end—there were still no answers.

I had no friends, no future, no life. I hit 77 pounds and kept on going—down.

Chapter 6

Thin—In Name Only

I couldn't fight destiny any longer. I had no other wants, no other needs. Life became a blur as the merry-go-round I had gaily jumped upon whirled faster. I was eighteen and sought only one goal: to be thin. A discovery that continued to elude me. And it wasn't long until the routine that had once energized me, now zapped all my energy. I, who had hiked unknown trails, run through open fields, played with friends, teased my siblings, who *loved life,* suddenly found it an exhausting effort to do anything more than sit. And I couldn't get off the merry-go-round.

Not when there was still a chance at the brass ring.

Not when thin could win.

My weight plummeted to 72 pounds, and I spent the rest of the year in and out of the hospital. The doctors scratched their heads, biopsied my saliva glands to understand their grotesque swelling, and came up with inconclusive findings. I was dying and nobody knew why or how to save me.

I wrapped an afghan around my body and curled up on the couch. It was so cold in the house. Despite my layers of clothing and the thickness of the afghan's multicolored yarns, I still shivered. I snuggled my aching bones into the soft sea of cushions as murmuring voices drifted out from the kitchen. Debbie and Hank had come to visit.

"Debbie, why don't you try to talk to your sister again. Maybe she'll listen to you." Mom's hushed whisper carried to my ears.

"No, Mom. She won't talk to me."

"Go on," Hank urged, too. "Talk to your sister."

Their voices faded, while I rested, safely cocooned, and dozed into oblivion.

"Hi, Cindy," Debbie said. She walked over to the couch and sat down on its edge. "How are things going?" Her voice was hesitant, her hands picked at non-existing lint on the couch.

"Fine," I murmured, and sank further into an internal haziness.

"Is there anything you'd like to talk about?"

"No."

Debbie sat for a few more minutes more, then reached over and hugged me. She stood up and walked back into the kitchen. *Oh, Debbie, please come back! Don't go. I wish I could talk to you, but I can't. I don't know what's wrong. It doesn't make sense to me either.* The unspoken thoughts slid into the dark recesses of my mind, and I remained lost.

Frustrated with his inability to diagnose this senseless condition, my internist admitted defeat and suggested we find another doctor. But Dr. Taylor refused to give up. He worried over my rapidly deteriorating health, and tried to help in any way he could. Unfortunately, his specialty limited what that help could be. Still, his dedication and caring manner kept him searching for answers.

Five months shy of my nineteenth birthday and for the seventh time in as many months, I was hospitalized. In an effort to control the swelling and the facial discomfort it produced, Dr.

Taylor cut the nerves leading to my parotid glands (salivary glands located underneath each ear). After a week in the hospital, I returned home. At a post-operative exam, Dr. Taylor gently examined my swollen face. "Cindy, I want you to tell me how you *feel*. I don't want your parents or anybody else to tell me. I want *you* to tell me what's bothering you. Do you understand it's okay to tell me what's on your mind?"

I lowered my head. "Okay," I responded softly. *But I don't know how I feel.*

"Cindy, I want you to call me any time something is troubling you. You have my phone number. You know you can call me if you should need to talk." I nodded. "And," he continued, "you don't need to *show* me your feelings. You can *say* how you feel and I will hear you."

We walked out to the waiting room and he motioned for my parents to join us. "Cindy, I want to talk to your parents for a moment, okay?" I watched them disappear into his office. Twenty minutes passed before they emerged. It would be many years later before I learned that Dr. Taylor had shared his concerns that something abnormal was going on in my body, and in my mind. He didn't know what it was, but he feared for me. He urged my parents to persist in their efforts to get proper help. "Without it," he announced gravely, "Cindy will surely die."

"Cindy, please, won't you eat something?" Mom pleaded. "I made some pasta fazul. You like that."

"I'm not hungry, Mom." My stomach growled hungrily as the aroma of one of my favorite Italian dishes drifted temptingly out of the kitchen. *God! I wish I could eat. But I can't.* Because if I did, all that fat that I worked so hard to get rid of would come back. My thighs finally looked small. Now when I stood sideways in front of a mirror, I could see that they formed a straight, sturdy line. No curves, no bulges, no soft, pudgy flesh to mar their sharp definition. No. Now that I had finally got my thighs to look good, I couldn't risk eating.

"But honey, you're so thin! You *must* eat something," she worried. "You're turning into a *skinny-mini*. How about some chicken soup? I could put some little noodles in it and maybe just a few carrots. . . ." She was desperate. Surely there was something I would eat.

"No, Mom. I'm not hungry." *I was starving.* All I could think about was food. Mom's pleas had not fallen on deaf ears. I wanted to please her almost as much as I wanted to lose weight. But the tug-of-war between her wants and my own desires was confusing. It was my body . . . wasn't it? Why couldn't people just love me for the way I was, and not for how much I weighed?

Irrational thoughts. The lower my weight, the more irrational the reasoning. My world had become reduced to—food. The more I wanted, the more I could not have. Food was the enemy, and I no longer cared why.

I looked over at the bedside clock—3:35 A.M. I slid my legs out from underneath the warm covers and tiptoed down the hall to the bathroom. I locked the door, shed my pink flannel nightgown and underpants, and stepped onto the scale—70. *Thank God!* The early morning chill sent shivers down my spine, and I put my nightgown back on. I unlocked the door and peeked out into the hallway. The eerie silence assured no witnesses to this secret mission. I quickly returned to my bedroom to finish my nightly ritual—I had to. If I didn't, I couldn't sleep. I yanked my nightgown up over my chest and concentrated on my midriff, oblivious to the rest of my appearance. I ran my fingers down the sides of my torso, and lovingly caressed each rib. Their bold presence confirmed what I needed to know—I was getting closer to thin. My spindly arms and legs—finally shed of their unwanted muscle—were covered with fine, downy hair. The more weight I lost, the more body hair I seemed to produce. Though the hair had seemed strange at first, I had grown accustomed to its thickening growth, and now found it strangely comforting. I walked over to the dresser mirror, my nightgown still hiked up around my shoulders, and leaned in close, my hair falling into my eyes. *My hair.* Once shiny, thick, wavy, and flowing—my crowning glory—it now hung in wispy, fragile strands. I pushed the hair out of my eyes. *My hips are still too wide.* I frowned, knowing I would need to work that area even harder. I put my feet together and studied the space that existed between my thighs. They no longer touched each other. I took a measuring tape and wrapped it around my left thigh—*10 inches.* Relief surged through my body, but only briefly. I couldn't let my guard down. Not yet. Not until I was sure. And I *had* to be sure. Five more pounds and *then* I would be. I went back to bed and snuggled underneath the warmth of three wool blankets.

I was achieving the goal of thinness. I was winning at losing.

One day blended into the next—it was surprising how much time it took to plan what to eat, what to avoid eating, which exercises to add to my already extensive program—until even I could not keep up the pace of such an internal-driven schedule. Exhaustion rendered me unable to walk or talk for long periods of time (though I would not admit to it). I did little more than curl up under the afghan and watch television. My body was shutting down in its own valiant fight to conserve what little strength it had left.

I was starving to death.

My parents were frantic as they watched me disappear into the folds of over-sized flannel shirts and baggy, corduroy Levi jeans. They rushed me from doctor to doctor, in as an elusive search for answers as my own pursuit for thin. Unwilling to accept that nothing could be done they again conferred with Dr. Taylor. This time they decided to take me to Lahey Clinic in Boston. A clinic that twenty years earlier had played a role in saving Grandma Chiodo's life from severe ulcerative colitis. Now it was their last and only hope that the clinic would also save their daughter's life.

*   *   *   *   *

Mom peeked in through my partially closed bedroom door. "Honey, Daddy and I made the plane reservations for Boston. We'll be leaving tomorrow afternoon. We'll pick Grandma and Grandpa up on the way." Dad would remain at home to care for Jonny.

"Ummm." I pulled the bedcovers up to my shoulders and napped while she packed our suitcases. I spent more and more of my waking hours sleeping. The haze and confusion were comforting. It was amazing how good that felt. Why, I didn't even mind being hungry. Maybe the Boston doctors could explain that to me.

Just as long as they didn't ask me to gain weight.

We arrived in Boston and checked in at a beautiful hotel by Fenway Park. If the reason for our trip hadn't been so distressing, it would have made for a lovely vacation. Though I would not admit it, I was secretly glad to have someone else take charge of my life. On the one hand, I *knew* there was nothing wrong with me. On the other hand, I couldn't help wondering—had I gone too far?

On the morning of the clinic appointment, Mom and I met Grandma and Grandpa Chiodo in the hotel's dining room for breakfast. I hated eating in front of other people. Everyone always pretended that they were not watching me eat. But they were. And we all knew it. So I resorted to *fake* eating—whenever they turned their heads—by dropping food into a napkin on my lap, chewing air, cutting my food into minuscule portions, and taking forever to eat three tablespoons.

We exchanged pleasantries and I opened the breakfast menu lying across a china plate set in front of me. *If I eat, will I be able to get to a bathroom without anyone suspecting what I'm doing? And if I can, will I have the energy to vomit? But if I can't throw up, I can't eat. Of course, if I don't eat, then everyone will be upset with me.* I sighed. The mental gymnastics to control food intake and vomiting were too confusing.

My eyes devoured the menu selections as the heavenly smells of *'fresh from the farm eggs'* and *'succulent bacon,'* helped resolve that internal debate. I would eat. When an order of pancakes and sausage were set down in front of me, I attacked them with a vengeance knowing when I was finished, I would get rid of it.

And so I did.

A nurse walked out into the clinic waiting area. "Cindy Nappa," she announced to the crowded room. Mom squeezed my hand reassuringly, and we followed the white-clad figure into a nearby room. She introduced us to the man sitting behind a big oak desk, Dr. Andrews, and left the room.

"Hello." He smiled, and shook our hands. His eyes crinkled kindly. Dr. Andrews looked around my father's age—forty. "It's nice to meet you. *Please . . ."* He gestured toward the two wooden chairs in front of his desk. "Sit down. I want to hear what brings you to Boston."

I sat stiffly and bowed my head. Mom hesitated, and then recited the last two years of events that led to this day's meeting. Dr. Andrews listened intently, and nodded his head every now and then as she described our fruitless search for answers. "We just don't know where to turn anymore. Even though the doctors have performed every kind of medical test, nobody seems to know what is wrong with Cindy. We are desperate for answers. Many years ago, Lahey Clinic was able to diagnose my mother's ulcerative colitis. We . . . my husband and I . . . thought maybe you . . . the clinic . . . might be able to now help our daughter, Cindy." Her eyes filled with tears, and she choked on the words that described our hellish existence. Mom picked up my hand and squeezed it. *"Please,* we don't want to lose her."

Dr. Andrews smiled. "I understand, Mrs. Nappa. I think it would be best if I examine Cindy right now. Maybe you could wait in the next room, and then I will come get you when I have finished."

Suddenly scared, I watched Mom disappear into the hall-way. Dr. Andrews closed the door and walked over and stood in front of me. "Cindy, your mother's explanation was very helpful. Now, I would like to do a short examination. Is that okay with you?" I nodded. "Here, let me help you." Too weak to do it my-self, Dr. Andrews lifted me onto the examining table and placed a stethoscope on my chest. "Tell me, Cindy, how do you feel?"

"Well, I've been losing weight. I don't know what's wrong with me. Sometimes I throw up because the food just won't stay down."

"Cindy, do you still menstruate?"

My eyes widened. What did that have to do with any-thing? I shook my head. "No. It stopped last year."

"Cindy, I want to weigh you. Do you think you can stand on the scale over there?" He pointed at the cold, metal monster lurking in the corner.

I nodded reluctantly, and he helped me off the table and over to the scale. *Oh, please God! Don't let me be fat!* The weights balanced at—60, with my clothes on. A small sigh escaped my mouth. *Thank you, God!*

"Cindy, can you tell me how much you used to weigh be-fore you got sick?"

"One-hundred and nine pounds." I shuddered at the num-ber. *God, I'll never be that fat again.*

Dr. Andrews lifted me back onto the examining table. "Cindy, I would like to have another one of my colleagues, Dr. White, meet you. Is that okay?"

"Sure."

Dr. White was summoned and he, too, patiently listened to my story. At the end, the doctors exchanged a disturbing look. "Cindy," Dr. White said gravely, "you are very sick. We would like to have you admitted to a hospital today." The urgency in his voice surprised me.

"But today is my mom's birthday. We're going out to din-ner tonight." I looked from one doctor to the other. "Can't I wait until tomorrow, *please?*" I just couldn't upset my mom by going into the hospital on her birthday. "It's *really* important. We have reservations at Jimmy's Harborside Inn. *Please,* can't I wait until tomorrow?" The doctors talked quietly amongst the two of them before finally relenting to one more night, but only on one condition: I was to be admitted to the hospital the first thing in the morning.

I sat on the table while the doctors talked to my mother in the next room. Their words were no match for the paper-thin walls. "Mrs. Nappa, if you had not told us the care Cindy had had, or if you had not brought copies of all her medical exams, we would have believed she had been medically neglected. This poor child is terribly sick. We cannot understand why her physical condition has deteriorated to such a critical stage."

I shivered, more from being cold than from the impact of their words. After all, surely they would have been put me in the hospital *immediately* if I was *that* sick.

"It's only a few blocks to the restaurant. And it's such a beautiful spring evening. Let's walk to the restaurant," Grandpa suggested, and he linked his arm through Grandma's.

I pulled my pink wool sweater closer around my shoulders and followed everybody out to the street. Grandma and Grandpa strolled ahead, while Mom slowed her pace to match my own. I struggled to breathe over the pain in my chest, but each step rendered me exhausted. I was unable to walk, not even for one block. I stopped and tugged on my mother's arm. "Mom?" I whispered. "Please, can we take a taxi? I don't think I can make it to the restaurant."

No. I wasn't sick. Just a little tired.

The next morning saw me admitted to the hospital. The doctor in charge of my care wasted no time in ordering an electrocardiogram, blood work, and weighing me. The results were alarming: inverted T-waves; sodium, calcium, and potassium levels—crucial to cardiac function—were dangerously low; and my weight—59 pounds. I breathed a sigh of relief. *Yes! I was still in control. But . . . maybe 58 would be better?*

The doctor wasted no time in inserting intravenous lines into both arms. A heart monitor was hooked up to my chest. "Mrs. Nappa, your daughter's heart . . . her life . . . is hanging by a thread," she told Mom. "I don't understand why she is still alive."

And I laid there, blissful, the goal of 58 pounds my only concern.

Dozens of diagnostic tests were administered over the next week as doctors ruled out every imaginable disease that could possibly cause such devastation upon my young body. "Cindy, we have one last exam scheduled for tomorrow morning in the O.R. It's a colonoscopy," the doctor said as she checked the monitors. A worried look passed over her face and she jotted down numbers on a chart she held in her hand. "Normally, Cindy, we use anesthesia with this procedure. However, your critical condition will not allow us to do so. I'm sorry." She paused, and smiled apologetically. "I know it will be a painful exam but we must do it. Are there any questions you'd like to ask me?"

"Do I have to eat or drink anything?"

"No. You will not be allowed anything after midnight tonight. In fact, we will be giving you an enema later this evening to clean everything out."

Good. As long as I didn't have to ingest calories, I didn't care.

But when the next morning found me stretched out on my side on the cold table, I did care. Several medical personnel held down my arms and legs, while the doctor inched a scope up my rectum. My screams were heard throughout that small community hospital.

A very sick, young girl, the dangerous destruction of denial continued to escape me.

I lifted the cover off my lunch tray and longingly breathed

in its tantalizing smells. *I love tuna fish sandwiches.* There had to be a way to eat it. I had been restricted to bed since the first day of my hospitalization—for reasons I could not understand—and had been allowed supervised bathroom visits only.

A knock came on the hospital room door as I continued to brood over this lunchtime dilemma, and a strange man poked his head into the room. "Hi, can I come in?" he asked, and entered before I could open my mouth.

He walked over and looked down at the tuna-fish sandwich and potato chips on my plate. "When you eat you make yourself throw up, don't you?"

My mouth dropped open.

"Oh, excuse me," he apologized. "My name is Dr. Benson." He extended his right hand, which I ignored. "I'm a psychiatrist. Your doctor asked me to stop by and say hello to you." He sat down in the chair next to my bed. "Do you throw up everything you put into your mouth or just certain foods? When you can't throw up, you can't eat, can you? Why are you so afraid of eating, Cindy? Is it because you're afraid of gaining weight? What is it about gaining weight that frightens you so much?"

I gaped at him. *How dare he say those things to me! How can he know any of this? How can he know about my battle of eating, not eating, bingeing, and vomiting? It is my secret! Nobody knows!*

Dr. Benson leaned forward. "Cindy, did you ever hear of anorexia nervosa?" I shook my head at the strange term.

"Cindy, all the testing so far is leading us to believe that you have anorexia. It's a psychiatric illness. I bet you didn't know that what you're doing to your body has a name. And I bet that you *also* didn't know there are many other young girls, just like yourself, who have this same illness. They, too, are afraid to eat and gain weight."

"I am not afraid!" I yelled, tears streaming down my face. "You're lying! I'm not like those other girls!" *It's my secret. It doesn't belong to anyone but me.* "And I'm not doing those things! I don't have anorexia! I'm not crazy!"

"I didn't say you were crazy. I said you were afraid of eating."

"Get out!" I screamed, hatred spewing out of my every pore. I glared at him. "Get out of my room!"

He smiled and stood up. "Cindy, I will be stopping by to see you while you're here. Maybe we can talk later when you're not feeling so upset with me—or yourself."

Sobbing, I pushed my tray aside. How could I eat after that horrible man had said all those awful things about me! I wasn't like what he said! I wasn't!

A half-hour later, I was still sobbing when Mom came by for our usual afternoon visit. She rushed over to gather me in her arms. "Honey, what's wrong?" Who or what could possibly have upset me so much?

"Mom," I wailed. "I don't want to see that doctor anymore. Please, Mom! I hate him. He was terrible to me. He's wrong! I'm not like he says I am! He is a horrible man! Make him go away, Mommy!"

She rocked me until my sobs lessened. I was her baby girl and no one was going to hurt me if she could help it. If a doctor was responsible for upsetting me, then, of course, I didn't have to see him anymore. Earlier, the doctors had delivered their diagnosis to her. She didn't believe it anymore than I did. Anorexia nervosa sounded like a ridiculous illness. There was no way it could be true.

Even with tubes in both arms, and my body hooked up to machines, anorexia—which I knew I did not have—continued to ravage my mind and my body. The only access to food I had was that which arrived at mealtimes. My critical medical condition and my lack of control over vomiting continued to restrict me to bed and the use of a bedpan. With those limitations, I became even more desperate. I was hungry, but there was no other way to overcome that terrible fear of fat than to rid by body of its insides as quickly as I could.

Mom was successful in preventing Dr. Benson from visiting me again. He remained the consulting psychiatrist, but I didn't have to talk to him anymore. Over the next two weeks, my medical condition slowly improved from its critical status, courtesy of the intravenous lines replacing vital nutrients and minerals. My energy returned and so did my appetite, but then it had never really left. I just liked to believe it had. Never would I admit to the ravenous hunger I felt constantly. Once I was medically stable and it was apparent I would not die, my grandparents returned home. Mom would remain until the doctors determined me well enough to also go home.

"Mom, I think I would like some snacks. Maybe, when you go out to lunch today, you could buy me some cheese twists. Then when I'm hungry, I'll have something to eat and it will help me gain some weight," I said innocently. I reached over and switched on the bedside television monitor. Mom was thrilled that I wanted to eat. She willingly put down her magazine to make a list of what I wanted her to buy.

She returned after lunch, her arms laden with a bag of cheese twists, cashew nuts, and barbecued chicken. It was a glutton's heaven. Mom plumped my pillows, kissed my cheek, and left me alone to nap. But as soon as the door had closed behind her, I ripped open the packages she had brought. I alternately stuffed handfuls of chicken, nuts, and cheese twists into my mouth until my stomach could not hold another morsel. Then, I leaned over the side of my bed and threw up into the wastebasket—a trick I had learned the previous evening when I had eaten too much of my supper. It was only the housekeeping lady who wondered at the heaviness of my trash and its offensive odor when she cleaned my room in the morning.

After two weeks of IV therapy, I was safely out of immediate medical danger. However, due to my prolonged state of starvation, my body retained every ounce of the IV fluids, which resulted in a twenty-seven pound weight gain. The latest morning weigh-in had given a reading of 86 pounds.

"Take the IV out, *please,* take it out!" I pleaded to the

nurse, furious with that morning's weight. Until I had stepped on the scale, I had not realized how much weight I had gained while lying in bed. The nurse smiled and pulled the IV needle out of my arm. My latest lab reports were in the normal range, and the doctors had already given her the order to remove this last IV. They also allowed me to get out of bed. Now, with the last of those restrictions lifted, I begged to go home.

The doctors, however, knew that even though I was medically stable and no longer at risk of dying, I still needed treatment for the anorexia. There were only two hospitals in the country that provided that kind of care: one in California and the other in Pennsylvania. They gave me the option of either.

I chose neither. And Mom supported my wish. After all, the twenty-seven pounds had put rosy color and plumpness back in my face. She could look at me without worrying that I would keel over at any minute. With Mom backing up my demands, the doctors had no choice but to consent to my discharge. They did insist, though, that I be readmitted to our local hospital upon our arrival home. Mom agreed. And I didn't care. I just wanted to go home.

The merry-go-round had slowed its tempo while in Boston, but I wasn't ready to get off. The brass ring was within my reach. Once at home, I was sure to grab it.

Chapter 7

Seems As If This Road Goes On Forever

After another two months in our local hospital, I lost most of the IV fluid weight I had gained, and my weight went back down to 74 pounds. The internist in charge of my care was unskilled in treating anorexia, and completely at a loss in dealing with my demanding, manipulative behavior. I had the advantage and convinced him that my eating was fine. My lab reports cooperated by being within normal ranges. And therefore, there was no reason to not discharge me home. Between the two hospitalizations, I had been gone for a total of four months.

Once I was safely home, I vowed never to let anyone control my eating or my weight again. Thinner was how I needed to be. And, over the next year, we all naively settled into a comfortable denial of this disorder called anorexia. I believed nothing was wrong, and my family believed everything would be fine.

I settled comfortably into a familiar pattern: eating and vomiting from the moment of wakening until early afternoon when Jonny came home from school. No pressures, no responsibilities, and no goals. My entire being was focused on eating and purging. It controlled my thoughts, isolated me from people, and didn't *begin* to satisfy the hunger within.

I sat at the kitchen table, a Trixie Belden book propped open against the salt and pepper shakers, and drizzled syrup over the pancakes and bacon on the plate in front of me. I read of my favorite heroine's adventures while stuffing and re-stuffing my mouth. When my stomach stretched to its limit, I unbuckled my jeans to allow for more. Eating and reading, intermixed with vomiting breaks, went on for hours. The comfort it brought, unbelievably soothing.

After several hours of eating and purging, I stepped onto the bathroom scale—71. I sighed. *Better, but not good enough.* No matter what weight goal I set, once attained, it was no longer thin enough. I opened the bathroom closet door, took out a tape measure from the sewing box and wrapped it around my right thigh—*10 inches.* I frowned. It didn't make sense. If I was losing weight, why weren't my thighs getting any smaller?

A door slammed somewhere downstairs. *Jon's home.* I hurried back to my room, closed the door, and faced myself in the mirror. I stood sideways—I hated looking at my body straight on—and stared at the mirrored image before me. It mockingly insulted every imperfection of my body and my soul. *I'm still fat. A failure.* And that night, I tossed and turned in bed, haunted by my inability to succeed. *Why can't I lose these inches? Am I gaining weight even while sleeping?* I slipped out of bed and stretched out on the cold, hardwood floor. I folded my arms under my head and began doing sit-ups. "One . . . two . . . three . . ."

" . . . Fifty." I stood up and jogged in place, lifting each leg as high as possible. Jumping jacks and deep-knee-bends followed. Two hours later, my heart pounding in my ears, I crawled back into bed, exhausted. Nights had become the newest ritual. No hours were safe anymore.

The hunger no longer let up. Not even for brief moments. And the amount of food required to quench it had grown to astronomical proportions. If I could just figure out how much to eat to please Mom and Dad—to keep their questioning looks and comments at bay—and, at the same time, eat enough to control my out-of-control appetite. Which in reality didn't matter, because no matter how much or how little I ate, I always headed to the bathroom. There, with the faucet running—to cover up any sounds—I purged everything I had just ingested. I stopped only when I brought up bile. That awful, bitter-tasting yellow stuff, the signal that my stomach was totally empty.

My parents rejoiced over my renewed eating, but puzzled over their growing grocery bill. They watched me eat good-sized meals, and shook their heads over my rail-thin body. It made no sense. Why was their daughter still starving? No matter how much food went into my mouth, the number on the scale continued to hover right around 70 pounds—a number I refused to let anyone see. And yet they said nothing, afraid to take the chance that I might go back to eating nothing.

"Cindy, we have to talk about your eating," Dad said, and pushed his dinner plate aside. He and Mom had worried over my ravenous appetite, afraid if they mentioned this concern, I would refuse to eat at all. But my latest attack on the cupboards had left nothing for the next day's breakfast and lunch.

My forkful of spaghetti stopped in midair. *But there's nothing wrong. I'm eating. Isn't this what you want me to do?*

"Cindy, you're eating too much of the food. Your mother and I can't keep replenishing the cupboards every other day. You're not being fair to the rest of the family. This selfishness has to stop. Starting tonight, you will have one shelf in the refrigerator that is yours. The rest is off-limits. The same goes for the cupboards. You are allowed to eat only from the cupboard underneath the silverware drawer. Do you understand?" He waited for my answer.

Selfish? Why is Daddy calling me selfish? "But *Dad*, I'm not eating that much! You're not being fair." I looked pleadingly at my mother and she lowered her head, averting her eyes.

He shook his head firmly, his lips set in a straight line.

"We're sorry, Cindy, but you're the only one being unfair. You're not leaving enough food for your brother to eat." Tears welled up in my eyes, and his voice softened. "Cindy, we are not trying to be mean. We only want to help you. Maybe this will help you control your eating. Please understand that. We don't know what else to do."

I cried softly, my stomach in knots. *It's not fair! Why are they being so mean?*

They weren't being mean. They were only trying to help. If I couldn't control my eating, then they would control the food supply. Made sense in theory, but in reality—it was a total disaster.

Every time I went in or near the kitchen, they hovered in the background . . . watching . . . making sure I ate only what was allowed. I did . . . during the day. At night, while everyone slept, I crept downstairs and foraged through the cupboards, eating as much as I wanted. No restrictions. Afterwards, my hunger abated, I crept silently back upstairs and fell, exhausted, into bed.

Only once was I almost caught. I heard the upstairs floorboards creak, a bedroom door open, and I hurriedly hid the pot of spaghetti I had cooked, in the cereal cupboard. I ran to the little bathroom off the kitchen to scrub the toilet of its telltale evidence. Dad walked into the kitchen a few minutes later and found me sitting at the kitchen table, book in hand, a glass of orange juice in front of me.

"Couldn't sleep, Cindy?" he commented, and walked over to the refrigerator and poured himself a glass of orange juice.

"Uh-uh." My heart jumped into my throat as he leaned against the stove. It was still warm.

He drained his glass and set it in the kitchen sink. "Going to come back to bed?"

"I think I'll read a little longer first."

He came over and planted a kiss on the top of my head. "Okay, Pocahontas. But don't stay up too long. You need your rest," he said, and went back upstairs.

And despite my parents' rules, the food continued to disappear. Policing the situation wasn't working. Their next step: hide the food. But in a very short time, it was clear that approach wasn't working either. No matter how cleverly Dad hid the food, I was much more adept in finding it. I was on a roll and a desperate high. Days, I searched the house for its hidden treasures. Nights, I ate its offerings. I *had* to control my body. Why couldn't anyone understand that?

The road was never-ending. Nothing, or no one, could change the obsessive, destructive direction in which I traveled.

I stood in front of the bathroom mirror, my mouth wide open, and closely inspected my bottom front teeth. Decay littered their gum line. At my last dental visit, Dr. Kenny had voiced his concern over the rapid deterioration of several of my teeth. We had both attributed it to the continuing problem of my swollen salivary glands. I wiggled the teeth with my fingers. They were much looser than a week ago. "Guess I better call and make another appointment."

A few days later, I sat in the dental chair while Dr. Kenny, *again*, drilled my teeth. He set the drill down and stood back, shaking his head in discouragement. "Cindy, I don't know what is going on in your mouth. Your teeth are decaying at an alarming rate. If we don't stop this, you are headed for some major problems." I squirmed uneasily and left the office with fluoride rinses, instructions on flossing, and several more appointments.

The scale that morning had said 70 pounds. The calendar said I would be twenty years old in two months. My head kept saying, *"Don't eat."* Mom and Dad said, *"Eat, but don't eat too much."* I sighed, and pulled my belt a notch tighter. It was on the last hole. Without the belt, my jeans would have nothing to hold on to. I was disappearing into the folds of material. I smiled and walked proudly in my baggy clothing, rotting teeth far from my mind.

It had taken some searching, but my parents finally found

a therapist willing to take me on as a patient. Unfortunately, this doctor was not at all familiar with anorexia. His best advice: *"Don't worry about it. Leave Cindy alone. If it's not focused on, she'll stop."* My family did as suggested, they dropped the topic of my eating and everyone left me alone. Getting permission to ignore the problems had just given me the freedom to let them flourish.

My parents' food restrictions, though, remained enforced. But it didn't matter. I stopped eating *their* food and bought my own. And because the doctor's orders were to leave me alone, no one suspected anorexia's games. The longer I played by its rules, the more proficient I became and the less willing I was to give it up. No one could get in, and I was not interested in getting out.

"Hi, honey, what are you doing?" Mom walked into my room, her arms piled high with folded laundry.

"You know, Mom, I was just reading about journalism in this college catalog. I'm thinking of taking a course at the community college. What do you think?"

"Cindy, you always loved to write. Remember that poem you wrote Debbie when she went away to college?"

"Hmmm." I returned to the catalog.

"Cindy, I was wondering, would you like a new bedroom set? You and Debbie had this one since you were seven. Maybe it's time for some new furniture."

I glanced over at the oak twin beds and matching dresser. *I love this furniture.* "Sure. I guess so, Mom." I hoped she didn't think that having new furniture would encourage me to gain weight. Dad had tried to bribe me the other night by offering me one-hundred dollars if I got my weight back up to 100 pounds. I was tempted, but not for his reasons. Secretively buying my own food had quickly outstripped my ten dollar weekly allowance. But even when that money ran out, it didn't stop me. Now my middle of the night journeys included a tiptoed stop into my parents bedroom. As Mom and Dad lay sleeping, I stole money out of Dad's pant pockets and Mom's purse. I had become a liar, a sneak, and now a thief. I was appalled by my own deceptive acts. Yet as much as I despised taking the money, I needed to be thin more.

The night class was a disaster. I felt completely out of place among the other students. Their easy bantering with the professor and each other was reminiscent of high school. So while the class discussed sentence structure, the use of the English language, and keeping a journal, my thoughts drifted to its comfort zone—*food*. School, writing, and classmates were all but forgotten as I sought solace from the one constant in my life.

The end of each class signaled the beginning of a binge. On my way home, I pulled into the nearest McDonald's drive-through. "Two Big Macs, a fish fillet, two large fries, and two small diet Cokes, please," I ordered into the microphone. I drove to the pick-up window. "My friends always make me go out for the food when we're studying," I complained good-naturedly to the girl who handed me a large paper bag. I drove for one block then stopped and crammed the food into my mouth. Any classroom inadequacies faded into the background as I sank into a satiated fast-food fog.

I reached home, parked my car, and rushed into the house paying no mind to little Button's welcoming barks. My only priority, at that moment, was to get to the bathroom and rid my body of the thousands of calories I had just consumed. Two more hours of secretive eating in my bedroom and purging and only then, could I grant myself a reprieve.

"That's strange, where's Buttons?" Surely he had been in my room this whole time. I dropped on all fours and peeked under my bed, his usual resting spot. He wasn't there. "Buttons, where are you?" I called out angrily, and stormed downstairs. *Buttons, you know I don't like to go to sleep without you!*

I stopped in front of the screen door and noticed that it wasn't shut tight. *Oh, God! Had I not closed the door when I came home?* It wouldn't be the first time in which Buttons had run free. With a sickening feeling in my heart, I racked my brains trying to remember if I had seen Buttons at all that evening and vaguely remembered his earlier welcome. "Please, Buttons! *Please* be in the yard!" But little Buttons was not in our unfenced yard, or any of the nearby neighbors' yards.

Far into that evening and through the following week, Mom, Dad, Jonny, and I searched the streets on foot and by car. But no little white dog answered our frantic calls. We placed an ad in the local newspaper with the hope that someone had seen Buttons and taken him in.

And I kept silent. Not once mentioning the part I may have played in Button's disappearance.

Three more agonizing days passed before the phone call we had been waiting for finally came. "Yes, we lost our dog." Mom motioned to me quickly.

I ran out to the living room. "Dad, Jon!" I jumped up and down excitedly. "Buttons is found!" *Thank you, God! Thank you, thank you, thank you! My dear, dear Buttons was found!*

"Oh dear! Yes . . . yes . . . no. Please . . . just send his collar. Thank you for calling." Mom hung up and slowly walked towards me. "Cindy . . . honey," her eyes teared over, and she sat down beside me on the stairway step. "That was a state trooper. He found Buttons on the side of the road . . . on the thruway. He's dead, honey. I'm sorry."

Oh, God! No! Not Buttons! "Mommy?" I burst into tears and she pulled me into her arms. "M-*m-mommy*, not Buttons!" *Oh, God, please, don't let it be true. I love Buttons! Please, don't let this be true!* I looked over at Jonny and Dad, the tears on their faces more than I could bear. *Oh God! I hurt them. If they know that this is my fault, they'll hate me.* I sobbed deeply into my mother's arms, the horror of this selfish act just one more secret to bury.

The little dog that had loved me, unconditionally, was gone. The only friend I had left in the world was dead. No longer would Buttons be there to comfort me in the middle of the night, when the darkness outside intensified my fears inside. *How could*

I have been so stupid! That stupid, stupid eating!

Hours later, our tears spent, we wearily said good night to each other. Up in my room, I laid down on my bed and drew my legs up against my chest. *Oh God, it hurts so much!* I hugged Button's little sweater . . . the red one . . . the one he always wore when it was cold outside. *Maybe if he had it on that night, the car would have seen him. Maybe if I had done things differently . . . maybe if I hadn't been so selfish . . . if I hadn't been in such a hurry . . . if I hadn't eaten anything. . . .* "God, I'm sorry. I'm so sorry!" I sobbed. "Please, don't let everyone be angry with me." But everyone didn't know. "God, I hate myself! I hate what is happening to me! I hate this *stupid* body! This *stupid, stupid* body!" The hatred dug deep and tore at my heart. Exhausted, I fell asleep. Button's sodden sweater clutched to my chest.

My best friend was dead. And I had only myself to blame.

Button's death became one more parcel of uncomfortable feelings. The following days and nights blurred together as I fell deeper into the secret life I had created. The pressure of trying to keep it all together in a perfect little package had become too much. Something had to give.

School fell apart first. My writing assignments took on death themes—short stories full of families dying in tragic ways. A required journal included entries documenting my best friend's death in a car accident with myself in the driver's seat. The writings came back with the professor expressing her sympathies and praising my style.

Less than two months into the class, I quit. But on Tuesday evenings I still pretended to leave for school. Only instead of sitting in a classroom, I sought solace from grocery stores and fast-food chains. Later, far into the night, lying on my new bed, book in hand, I devoured potato chips, cheese twists, and cookies.

I put down my book and walked over to the bedroom mirror. I winced at the sight of my swollen cheeks and monstrous thighs. "These stupid, *stupid* thighs! Why can't they just go away! I slapped them viciously. They were so disgusting.

I headed to the bathroom and stripped off my black corduroy jeans, a gray sweatshirt, white cotton turtleneck, wool socks, bra, and panties. Naked, I stepped on the scale. *"Seventy-seven!* Shit! How could I have gained *five* pounds! That's it, I'm *never* eating again!"

I put my clothes back on, opened the bathroom door, and ran into Jon as he bounded up the stairs. "Jonny, do you want to ride your bike to the store for me?" I looked out the upstairs hallway window into the white madness of the swirling February snow. Earlier storm warnings were proving to be accurate. "Would you go and buy me a box of Popsicles?"

Jonny glared, his disgust evident. "No, Cindy. I won't go to the store! Go yourself!" he spat out angrily. At fourteen, he had little tolerance for my strange eating.

I grabbed Jon's arm as he brushed past me. "Jonny, *please* go to the store! I'll play Scrabble with you when you come back. *Please!" Jonny, you have to go to the store! Popsicles are the only safe thing I can eat and not throw up.* He shook his head, and yanked his arm from my grip. Furious, I shoved him.

"Huh?" Startled, Jon lost his balance, and tumbled down the flight of stairs—all thirteen of them—and landed in a heap at the bottom.

Oh, shit! What have I done?" I raced down the stairs. "Jonny, are you all right? I'm sorry! *Please* . . . are you okay" I fell to my knees and helped him sit up. He appeared more shaken than hurt. "Jonny, I didn't mean it. You don't have to go to the store. It's okay. I'm really, *really* sorry." *Damn eating! It keeps hurting the things I love most.*

Jon stared at me, but said nothing as I babbled on, apologizing incessantly. He shook his head, as if trying to clear the confusion of what I was saying . . . of what I was doing. "Okay, Cindy," he said resignedly. "I'll go to the store for you." He stood up slowly.

"Jon, *I* . . . *I*. . . ." But he ignored me and put on his ski jacket. "God, *please* don't let Jonny hate me," I pleaded silently. "I didn't mean to hurt him. I love my brother. I would never *ever* do *anything* to hurt him." I hung my head, ashamed of who I was becoming, and my inability to stop it.

An hour later, Jon returned and handed me the offensive package of Popsicles. "Thanks, Jon," I whispered, and waited until he went up to his room before tearing the box open. I bit into the cold, sugared confection and immediately felt better.

I stopped midway on the stairwell, and listened to Debbie and Hank visiting with Mom in the kitchen. *I wonder how long they've been here?* I sat down and leaned against the wrought iron spindles.

"Where's Dad?" Debbie asked.

"He went to the IGA."

They all laughed at Mom's reply. Dad's nightly excursions to the grocery store had become a family joke. But his trips were not because of my ravenous appetite. My secret food shopping excursions had deleted that problem. No, Dad had his own reasons for going out at night. His restless personality, along with the cyclic nature of his illness had created tense times between my parents. Rather than confront the increasing breakdown in their communication, Dad chose to leave, saying that he was going to the grocery store. Hours later, after Mom and Jonny had gone to bed, Dad returned home. I was up in my room, still awake, as bingeing and purging kept me up for most of the night. I didn't say anything to Dad, because as long as I didn't question his behavior, he didn't question mine.

"Mom, what's wrong with Cindy?" I leaned in closer against the railing. "It's been over two years, and we *still* don't understand what's wrong with her." *Will Mom tell Debbie and Hank I have anorexia?*

"Debbie, your sister has a blood condition," Mom answered. *Mom's ashamed of me.* And I couldn't blame her. Anorexia *was* a shameful disease.

I walked down the stairs and into the kitchen. "Hi, Debbie . . . Hank," I said softly, and joined them at the table. Debbie smiled and said hello. Hank neither looked my way nor acknowledged my greeting.

"Hi, Hank," I repeated, my voice a bit louder this time. But the words fell on deaf ears. His only acknowledgment—to glance at the wall behind me.

My face reddened, and I slid into a chair at the end of the table, pretending not to notice—or care—that I was being ignored. After all, it wasn't the first time. Hank had stopped speaking to me several months earlier. Like Jonny, he could make no sense of this strange illness. Obviously—he believed—I was only doing it for attention. After all, why else would I be playing such stupid games with food? Maybe—he believed—if he didn't show me attention, or accept me, I would then stop.

As if stopping the caring would open my eyes.

I pulled my navy blue cardigan sweater closer around my neck, missing a hurt look cross Mom's face and an embarrassed one redden Debbie's. Huddled there, I listened as their conversation went on without me. As if I were invisible. As if I had stopped being a person and become a *condition* . . . to be tolerated. To be put up with. As if I was ignored long enough, I'd go away . . . like a bad dream.

So I left. Because I wanted so badly to stay . . . to belong. And no one called me back or asked where I was going. And I didn't blame them. Because it wasn't their fault that they could make no sense of this senseless thing. They saw only that I was starving, and that I wasn't listening.

I went up to my room and stood in front of the dresser mirror. Skin and bones everyone said, yet I saw only fat. *"I hate you, Cindy! You are so stupid! You can't do anything right! You are a nobody! A nothing!"* I pounded my stomach and threw myself across the bed, my head buried in my arms. *I hate my body! God! I hate my body! If people would just leave me alone, I know I could get thin enough, and then everything will be better.*

But it wasn't getting better. After several more months of constant battling with Mom and Dad as they tried to reason, plead, and even threaten me into eating *normally*, it was decided that I would have to move into a halfway house—a group home. The arguments over food, their mounting frustrations as I locked myself into the bathroom, the constant purging of needed nutrition from my body, endless begging to please stop, and the attention and time being deprived from my brother had finally forced them to make that decision. They wanted only to help me get better without destroying the rest of our family in the process.

"You don't want me?" I looked from one parent to the other in disbelief. They didn't know what else to do. It had been my therapist's suggestion and they reluctantly agreed. Yet even as they rushed to reassure me of their continued love and support, I was convinced only that I had let them down—again. I moved out.

It didn't help. My voracious eating and purging grew even more erratic as the inexperienced house counselors had not a clue to anorexia's guise. I weighed no more than 70 pounds, and looked more like a ten-year-old child than the nineteen-year-old young woman I really was.

Dr. Roberts—the white-haired therapist, who had given my parents the advice to ignore the strange eating behavior, and that I should move out of their home—sat behind his big desk, papers piled high in front of him. "Yes, Cindy. What is on your mind today?"

Oh, he is such a busy man. Maybe too busy for me? I gulped nervously, and stared down into my folded hands for several minutes. Not nearly enough time to gather the amount of courage I needed to speak. "Dr. Roberts, I'm scared," my voice barely broke a whisper, and I focused on my fingers. "I don't know what to do. I've lived at the halfway house for a year and a half. But things are getting worse. I'm sneaking food out of the kitchen at night, *and . . . and* I've started s-t-stealing money from the other people so that I can buy even more food." *Oh, God! How can I say this! Dr. Roberts will think that I'm a horrible person.* "I-I don't understand what's going on. I'm . . . I'm . . . a *terrible* person, and I know what I'm doing is wrong, but I can't stop. Please. . . . I need someone to help me." I closed my eyes and held my breath. Silence. *Gosh, he must think I'm so horrible he doesn't even want to talk to me.* I raised my head. The good doctor was leaning back in his chair, his eyes closed, and softly snoring.

Mortified, I slipped out of his office. *It just isn't safe to share these feelings.*

"Cindy, your Mom called and asked me if I would like to go to New York City with the two of you." I sat at the kitchen table with Mrs. Parker, the group home manager. A warm, motherly person in her fifties, Mrs. Parker and I had developed a close relationship. During many of my mother's visits to the group home, she, too, had developed a fondness for Mrs. Parker.

I bit my lip, nervously. The trip to New York City was the latest of Mom's ideas for bringing some fun into my life. She had this notion that if she could buy me things, or take me to places I had never been, I would be happier and, therefore, I would eat and get better. So far, it wasn't working. As much as I wanted to go the Big Apple, eating in front of other people was a big problem—purging required privacy, *lots* of privacy. It would be almost impossible to keep it hidden while in New York. Everything I did, and everywhere I went had to be planned around having the ability to purge. It was the only way I could eat. If I couldn't purge, I couldn't go to New York. Unaware of this dilemma, Mom and Mrs. Parker determined a trip to New York was a wonderful idea. They set our departure date for two months down the road. I had until then to get my act together.

I didn't. Instead, I continued to unravel. The pressure of trying to keep up the pretense of everything being okay was too much. The midnight raids on the refrigerator and the stealing were resulting in a lot of finger pointing throughout the home. I was not suspect, but time was not on my side. Sooner or later, it would all blow up in my face.

A week before our trip, it did.

There was only one pay phone at the halfway house. I waited until the hallway was cleared before dialing my parents' number. "Dad, could you pick me up? I want to talk with you and Mom."

An hour later, I faced the two of them in their living room. I took a deep breath. This was not going to be easy. "Mom? Dad? It's . . . I'm . . . not getting any better. In fact, it's . . . I'm . . . getting worse. I've been stealing money from the people I live with," I admitted, and looked away from their horrified expressions. Rumors had been circulating at the house. I needed to confess before I was confronted.

"Oh, Cindy!" Mom shook her head, disappointment written all over her face. Her good little girl, who caused no problems for anyone, was a *liar* and a *thief*.

"Mom, *please* . . . don't." And the knot in my stomach intensified. "Remember that doctor in Boston . . . Dr. Benson? Could you call him and ask about that hospital in Philadelphia? Maybe I can still go there. Maybe the doctors in Philadelphia can help me."

"But Cindy! How can you still be sick? I bought you that beautiful bedroom set!" My shoulders slumped. Mom just didn't get it. And Dad said nothing. He didn't have to. His lips set in a straight line, said it all.

Defeated, I went upstairs to my room. The room I had begrudgingly moved out of, in the hopes of returning to *all better*. As if material things would make me better. As if promises would not be broken. As if I really wanted to be fat.

Phone calls were put through and within a short time, arrangements were made for hospitalization. The next day, Dad made restitution with the halfway house. It was agreed by all that I would return home to live until it was time to leave for Philadelphia.

Very sick, very depressed, and very scared, I, once again, would fly to another state for help with anorexia.

Chapter 8

If Hope Has Wings, Then So Do I

I entered the Philadelphia hospital weighing 70 pounds and severely depressed, hopelessly so. If the hospital couldn't help me, then death would be my only reprieve. Treatment for anorexia would have to wait as stabilizing my mood became the doctors first priority. They started me on an anti-depressant—Sinequan—and the black cloud that had surrounded me for six years lifted slightly. *Maybe I'll be able to live after all.*

Next, I was given a piece of paper to read. "It's a contract," the medical team said. It spelled out the terms of my treatment plan: gain a half-pound each day and I was free to participate in all hospital activities. If I *chose* not to gain a half-pound (as if I had a choice?), or if I *lost* weight, I would be required to wear short sleeve blouses and short pants, denied phone calls and mail.

The rules were simple—just like my life. Yes or no. Black or white. Gain weight or be punished. Live or die. I swallowed hard, signed the contract, and worried about the body-baring clothes I might have to wear. The medical team picked my weight goal: 95 pounds. I shuddered and regretted my signature. There was no way I could gain to that much weight—and live.

The contract went into effect immediately. That first morning, I weighed in at 69 pounds and bought myself an extra day. Better to start out less then more. Nobody talked to me about weight, and I went to ceramics and baking classes.

Meal times were the worst. I was allowed to choose my own menus, but I agonized over food choices and serving sizes. If I could just figure out how much to eat, or how much to throw up? How did I balance the scales to make us all happy?

By the third week, I had gained according to the plan and the staff was pleased by my efforts. All was safe, because my waist still measured 19 inches, and my thighs still measured 10 inches. But when my weight reached 75 pounds, I no longer believed the tape measurements. My thighs had started to thicken. *Can't they understand? I despise having pure fat on my body!*

The first morning of the fourth week, I stepped on the scale and watched the night nurse slide the weight slowly across the metal bar, stopping at—74. She shook her head. "I'm sorry, Cindy. You didn't make your weight. You lost one pound. You should be seventy-five and a half pounds this morning." I walked back to my room, not at all disturbed. I put on the new pair of powder blue cotton bib shorts Mom had bought me shortly before I had come into the hospital, and its matching blue and white-striped short-sleeve blouse.

"Cindy, that's such a cute outfit," Kathy, a fellow anorexic patient, complimented as we passed in the corridor. And I walked a little taller, a little prouder. Maybe revealing my body wasn't so bad after all. Besides, Kathy, at thirty years of age, was so old to have anorexia. Why, when *I* reached thirty, I was going to be all better.

Three more days and three more lost pounds. My mind preoccupied only with coordinating cute outfits. The team of therapists put their heads together and added more specs to my contract: gain the required half pound or spend the next twenty-four hours in my room with the door shut. No visitors. No contact with hospital staff—including my doctor—and bathroom privileges only. "Sign the contract or be discharged, immediately," they said. I signed the contract.

Again, my weight climbed to 75 pounds and I could not continue. The nurse balanced the scale. "Uh, uh, uh," she admonished, and I returned to my room. The day staff piled books, clothes, stuffed animal—*"please,* may he stay?" I asked, reaching for my little stuffed tiger. But they shook their heads and wheeled everything out of the room, closing the door *tightly* behind them. The sudden quietness—more disturbing then the frenzy of moments before—and I paced the floor, not quite sure what else to do. I alternated sleeping with pacing and the day passed quicker than I thought possible. The next morning I stepped on the scale, *positive* that the previous day's forced inactivity had added *tons* of fat on my body.

The nurse slid the weights and I held my breath. The bar quivered, I trembled, and closed my eyes. "Seventy-three, Cindy. You lost two pounds." *Phew!* And I went back to my room.

The second day on bed rest (isolation, elsewhere) proved more difficult than the first, but my determination strengthened. I scraped my meals into the trashcan and did relays around the bed. The morning of day three brought no weight loss, but also no weight gain. I dragged my feet, a bit more unwillingly this time, and returned to the room that was beginning to feel more like a barren prison cell. Loneliness took on a whole new meaning as anorexia's number game became more complicated. This solo victory had produced no glory. The staff wanted more; I wanted less. To please and obey would be to give up and give in. The more they tried to take anorexia away; the more I hung onto it.

The days slipped by, and the staff struggled to break the cycle of my destruction. They furrowed their brows and added more conditions to the contract: bed rest only, no walking around the room, no running in place. I scribbled my name on the dotted line and planned my next moves. *Lying around was not good for my thighs. I wonder. . . .* And I stood up in bed, jumped cautiously,

91

and the bed coils squeaked. I jumped again, higher this time, and reached for the ceiling. Fifty times. "Now sit-ups, Cindy." I got out of bed and stretched out on the floor. One hundred sit-ups spurred on by the challenge of getting caught. I stood up and bent my knees—fifty times. Exhausted, breathing rapidly, I climbed back into bed where *finally,* I could rest.

I was winning the weight game.

But I was losing in the people department. I had been on bed rest for a week. The only human contact was at meal times, when a tray was brought to my room. *Why can't they just help me without making me gain weight? Don't they realize that I will never let fat win?* I pulled the bedcovers up to my chin. *I miss the nurses talking to me about something other than how much I weigh. I miss Mom, Dad, Jonny, and the rest of my life. Maybe I'll never leave this room. Maybe I'll just die in this room and nobody will even care. Oh, dear God! I don't think I can stand being this alone.* I hugged my frail, bony body. Surely, this fight will be worth it someday.

One of the evening staff nurses knocked on my door and entered with a dinner tray. Wordlessly, she set it down on the bed and turned to leave. I grabbed her arm. *"Please,* Haley," I cried out, my sobs catching in my throat. *"Please,* talk to me!"

Haley, stopped by my desperate grip, turned towards me, her copper-brown face emotionless. She reached down and gave me a hug. Then she gently unwrapped my clinging body from her's and walked out of the room. I huddled under the layers of blankets and howled. Like a wounded animal, left to die. "God, why are you doing this to me?" I screamed. "What did I do that was so wrong? I can't take this anymore! Don't you hear me? I can't take it anymore!" I picked up the dinner tray and flung it at the closed door. It smacked against the door. Tomato sauce splattered into the air and strands of spaghetti slid down the door and adjoining wall. Its oregano smell mingled with the smell of vomit that permeated from the small wash basin in the corner of my room. I was cracking.

The conditions of the contract were stronger than my courage, though no match for my fears. The total isolation broke my spirit and I gave in. I started gaining weight. I did it for the staff. I did it for their approval. I did it so that they would like me again. I *needed* for them to like me. Besides, I knew, almost instinctively, how to please other people. It was my responsibility. My role. My nature. Make everyone happy. I *had* to keep everyone happy. I had learned it early, as a child. So in order to regain acceptance, I regained weight. I did it because I had no choice.

My starved body grabbed and held onto every morsel fed into it. The pounds came on quickly and the cute outfits no longer fit. I swallowed panic as my body grew against my will. Mom mailed larger-sized clothing, but still, I felt like a pork sausage too big for its casing. My straight lines lost their harshness, and my skin became more pink than gray. Gaining weight restored my lost privileges and resumed my family visits as well.

Five weeks after they had said good-bye, Mom and Dad returned. I threw myself into their arms as they emerged from the elevator. Laughing and crying simultaneously, I hugged them both.

Dad squeezed my shoulders. "Pocahontas, you've got some meat on you, just like before." I smiled nervously. At 85 pounds, had I undone the past six years of trying to free myself of fat?

I introduced my parents to the staff who beamed and said how hard I was working. I showed them the ceramic mug I had sculpted, and offered the chocolate-chip cookies I had baked. They munched on cookies, I had a glass of orange juice, and we went back to my room to visit privately.

Back in my room, Mom held out a portable tape recorder. "Honey, your brother wrote you a song. We taped it so you could listen to it."

A song for me? Why? I sat down on the bed, and balanced the tape player on my lap. I pushed the play button and Jonny's sweet tenor voice filled the room. *"It seems so many years. It seems so many tears. . . ."* And we listened to the words that had come from his heart, from his pain. *". . . Success is in our view. And if you're not healed today. Then tomorrow will be the day for you."*

"Mom?"

She gathered me into her arms. "Because, honey, Jonny loves you. This is his way of letting you know that." The tears slid down my face. Anorexia had not been mine alone. It had confused, saddened, and angered my entire family. We had all suffered.

The search for Cindy had begun. Ten more pounds and I would be all better. Isn't that what everyone promised?

I stood in front of the opened refrigerator door and eyed the selection of juices and fruit. *Do I want a glass of apple juice or an apple?* Which had more calories?

"Hi, Cindy. Getting yourself a snack?" I jumped as Rob, one of the staff nurses, strolled into the galley-sized kitchen.

"Yes," I mumbled, and grabbed the apple juice carton. *Shit! Why is someone always around when I want to eat something?* I poured a glass of juice and tried to slip past him. There was no way I could eat now. Not while someone was watching.

Rob stepped in front of me, his six-foot height blocked any chance of escape. "Gotcha!" he kidded. "Guess you have to talk to me now."

"I . . . I . . . guess," I said, and my face blushed bright red. Rob was right. I did go out of my way to avoid talking to him. Not that I had any reason to. I would love to talk to him. He was *so-o-o* cute! His sandy brown locks; his muscular arms. I really did want him to notice me.

But only from a distance. Because that was the safest. Because then I didn't have to worry about saying something stupid, or try to impress him. Or wonder why I was so nervous, or so scared.

Rob sensed my uneasiness and stepped aside. "Okay, I'll catch you next time," he teased. I left my juice on the counter, untouched, and escaped.

Over the next month, I spent many more days in isolation. I had given in, but I resisted all the way. At times, the lone-

94

liness was preferable to gaining weight. And as the pounds piled on, I fought to hang onto the identity I had come to know so well. Anorexia had become my symbol of person-hood. Without its presence, there would be no meaning to what and who I was.

Despite my shying away, Rob remained determined to be a friend. Gently, patiently—never threatening—he was the one to answer my call button when the weight gain became too terrifying and I, badly in need of reassurance. In group therapy sessions, when the team of doctors tried to reach inside of me and pull out my feelings, I ran out of the room. And it was Rob who came running after me. He promised that it would be okay. That *I* would be okay. And some of the fears I had pushed deep inside came out. Like Eddie. Like, I thought I loved him and didn't know if, maybe, he still cared.

And Rob was there to offer comfort and supportive words. "Gain the weight, Cindy. You need to get on with your life," he encouraged. "If you still care about Eddie, and know why you pushed him away, call him when you get back home. Let him know how you feel. You may be surprised. I bet he still cares about you, and has no idea what you're feeling."

Good advice. Face my fear. Risk rejection. Anyway, I'd think about it.

Two more months passed before I had finally met the conditions of my treatment contract. I weighed 95 pounds. I waddled when I walked. I had grown completely out of my clothes. I didn't feel cold all the time. My hair had grown thicker, bouncier. I was healthy.

I was terrified. It was time to go home and start anew.

On the last day of hospitalization, I packed my things and looked around the little room I had gotten to know so well. "Cindy?" Rob knocked on my opened door. "Almost ready?"

"Almost." I beckoned him in, placed my stuffed tiger on top of the folded clothes and snapped the suitcase shut.

Rob sat down on the hospital bed. "Now remember, Cindy. Write and let me know how things are going for you. Keep that weight on because I don't want to see you end up back here in the hospital." He gave me a big hug. "Hey, you did great! Just keep on going in this direction and you're going to make it."

Would I? Were the worst of anorexia's battles behind me? If gaining weight was supposed to make me better, then why didn't I *feel* better . . . safer? Other than talking about Eddie to Rob, I had kept the majority of my feelings under wraps throughout the entire hospital stay. And no one knew of the vomiting. Not once had it been questioned of me. And I never admitted to its existence. I was leaving the hospital with the same worries and twenty-five additional pounds to compound them.

And I was leaving behind the only people who seemed to understand why I was there in the first place.

I flew back home and was met with open arms. "Oh, look at Cindy!" my family rejoiced. And their hands squeezed my fleshy arms, pinched my rosy cheeks. They were ecstatic and I, cautiously optimistic. This new body of mine was uncomfortable to walk around in, to breathe in, to live in, and I was not entirely confident of my ability to sustain it.

I peeked out of my bedroom door. No one was in sight. The coast was clear. I ran down the hall to the bathroom, stripped off my clothes, and stepped onto the scale—90 pounds. *Thank God!* I would just lose a few more pounds and then I'd stop. I put my shorts and T-shirt back on and walked out to the hallway.

"Everything okay, Cindy?" Mom smiled as she came up the stairs.

"Sure, Mom. I'm just going to read in my room for a while." My heart pounded, and I lowered my eyes. *Oh, God! Please let her believe I'm okay.* I needed for her to believe I was okay. I needed for her to be happy. If she was happy, I was happy. If I was happy, the family was happy. It was my role—keep everyone happy. Status quo. I had to balance the scales. I had to lose just a little more weight.

*   *   *   *   *

On Rob's advice, I phoned Eddie. I would show him I was better, that I was okay. That I was woman.

"You want to start dating again? Sure, okay," Eddie, at first surprised, quickly agreed. Saturday night . . . dinner . . . a movie . . . his house.

Saturday night? Dinner? His house? Maybe I wasn't quite ready.

On Saturday, I smiled a lot and ate none of the prime rib dinner, half of the baked potato—sans sour cream and butter—and all of my salad, dressing on the side. The movie didn't last long enough and the television in Eddie's basement remained off. The lights were on low, Eddie's hands . . . *Oh God! Maybe I'm not better . . .* and I pushed him away.

"Cindy, being physically close is important in a relationship." Eddie said bluntly. "If we are going to date, you have to understand that."

I straightened my blouse. "I'm sorry Eddie. *I-I* can't." *Damn body! I know I shouldn't have gained all that weight.* "I would like to date you, but I can't go to bed with you." *Shit! What's wrong with me?*

Eddie shrugged his shoulders and reached for his keys. His message was clear: this relationship was over.

In seven more days, I dropped several more pounds, wanting only to be thinner. Within a month, I was back down to 83 pounds. In spite of the medication, in spite of my good intentions, in spite of Rob's promise of better, the depression returned. One step forward?

"I'm sorry, but I don't seem to be able to help Cindy." The young female therapist apologized to my parents. "She has been losing weight and it is my recommendation that she be re-admitted to the Philadelphia hospital. I wish I could help, but Cindy doesn't seem to want it."

I squirmed in my seat. *That's unfair. Of course I want her help. I just don't understand why I have to weigh 95 pounds in order to get it.*

Mom and Dad exchanged a tired look. The young doctor had come highly recommended. If she couldn't help, there was no choice but to send me back to Philadelphia.

Anorexia was seven years strong and its end was nowhere in sight.

Back to Philadelphia, back on the contract, back up to 95 pounds, and back home, again. Anorexia continued to lurk in the background, and I vomited *only* a few times a day. The next question: What did I do with my life now?

Since my earlier attempts at college had failed, the next logical step was to find a job. I signed up with an employment agency and accepted a full-time office position in a mid-sized grocery chain. It was definitely a step in the right direction.

"Hi Mom, I'm home." I checked the day's mail laying on the kitchen table hoping for a letter from Rob, but found only bills and a magazine. Nothing from Rob. *Hmm, he hadn't answered the last couple of letters. Could he be mad at me?* I had written to Rob about my job, that disastrous date with Eddie, Mom and Dad's troubled relationship, and the new car I had bought. *Maybe Rob wasn't interested anymore?* After all, he did have a very busy schedule, what with working, college, and a girlfriend—fiancée, actually. "I guess he just lost interest," I concluded, and went upstairs to change out of work clothes.

After dinner, I phoned Debbie. Our relationship had become less strained since I had gained weight. We chitchatted for several minutes before I plunged into the reason for my call. "Deb, I'm trying to figure out why Rob hasn't answered my last four letters. Do you think maybe he's mad at me or something?" I asked. "I don't know if I should keep writing or not."

"Well, why don't you write and invite him to visit you. He'll probably acknowledge the invitation, even if only to turn it down."

"But he has a girlfriend. They're engaged."

"Yeah? Well, from the way you always talk about Rob I think you kind of like him. You never know, Cin. Rob could have broken up with his girlfriend. Look, all you can do is extend an invitation. It's up to Rob if he accepts it or not."

Great! Another risk for rejection. I was nuts to think he'd travel six hours just to see me. Besides, maybe he was married by now. But Debbie's idea was attractive. The next morning, I mailed an invitation for him to come down Fourth of July weekend. A week later, Rob responded. Not only did he tell me his reasons for not having answered previous letters—he *had* broken off his engagement—but he accepted my invitation.

Oh, my God! He was coming to see me! "Mom! Rob is coming to visit us!" I ran into the kitchen and threw my arms around her waist. "I can't believe it! He's really going to come!" My eyes sparkled, and I danced around her in circles. Rob was coming! And he was coming to visit *me!*

The following four weeks were hectic as I planned what we would do, what I would say, and how I would eat. I managed an uneasy compromise: I wouldn't eat breakfast, I would vomit my lunch at work, I would eat a small dinner, and I would binge—secretly—in my bedroom at night. As long as I did not seem to be losing weight, and appeared to be eating okay, no one would question me. Convincing my okay-ness to my family had been easy. Convincing Rob would be a whole different matter.

The day of Rob's arrival dawned bright and sunny. I was up early making sure there were clean sheets on the twin bed in Jonny's room, the mushrooms for that night's dinner were marinating, the oatmeal cookies I had baked were neatly arranged on a platter, and the house was in *perfect* order. At noon, I drove to the bus station to anxiously await his soon-to-be-there bus. I wore my new navy blue denim shorts, a white cotton blouse, sandals, and a big smile. Last year's shag haircut had grown out nicely; my hair now reached to my shoulders.

The Greyhound bus pulled in and it was a few minutes more before Rob appeared in the doorway, head and shoulders above the crowd of jostling people. "Rob!" I called out. "Over here!" His blue eyes lit up, and he pushed his way over to my side.

"Hey, you're still as short as I remember you," he teased, and swooped me up in a giant hug.

"I see that you haven't lost any inches," I joked back, as Rob set me back down and we made our way out to the parking lot.

"You look good, Cindy."

"So do you, Rob."

We drove back to the house talking about everything. There was so much to catch up on. Rob shared the circumstances surrounding his broken engagement, and I relayed the relief of anorexia's dormant demands. We had two solid days of talking and enjoying each other's company. By the end of his stay, I invited him to my cousin's wedding in two months. He accepted, and I floated on clouds for the next several weeks.

The second visit went even better. The wedding was beautiful. And its romantic setting, a perfect prelude to what happened next: Rob and I fell in love. We planned to marry the following summer.

Gaining weight had been the first step off anorexia's merry-go-round. Marrying Rob would most certainly take me even further away from that mesmerizing music.

Rob and I dumped piles of wedding literature onto the kitchen table. "I don't know about you guys, but I don't even know *where* to begin!" I bemoaned good-naturedly. Debbie and Mom sorted through the massive amount of information we had collected. I sat back while Rob and my family bantered back and forth over guest lists, reception locations, and dinner menus. In the two months since our announcement, Rob had visited every other weekend to help with wedding plans.

"I don't know, Cin," Debbie remarked. "I think you should have the reception where cousin Ronny had his. That's still my favorite."

"What do you think about this menu," Mom interjected as she read through the list of entrees she had jotted down. "Roast beef, mashed potatoes, green beans, baked ziti, meatballs. . . ."

"Pierogies. You got to have Pierogies," Rob insisted. "My parents would be thrilled if we included a Polish dish." Mom happily obliged, and added Pierogies to her list.

It was surprising the way Rob fit so easily into our family. Mom and Dad said he was wonderful, and looked forward to his weekend visits. Jonny, Debbie, and Hank all gave Rob the thumbs up. It felt good to know that I had finally done *something* right. Still, I found myself uncomfortable with Rob's sudden ease into our family. He didn't even have to work at getting their approval— they just instantly adored him. With my family's quick admiration and eagerness to be a part of wedding planning, Rob and I had few moments alone. As a result, our long-distance engagement had little opportunity to develop the intimacy that had so threatened my relationship with Eddie. And with so much to do in regard to the wedding, that area and the issue of anorexia were willingly swept aside.

Or under the rug. I was supposedly cured. I was getting married. Yes, Rob was going to be a wonderful asset to our family.

And yet as our wedding day drew closer, the happiness and excitement that usually accompanied this wondrous event eluded me. Instead, I slipped back into the familiar nightly bingeing and vomiting routine that had never really stopped. My earlier compromise no longer worked. The closer the wedding, the more I panicked. *Oh, God, maybe I'm making a mistake. Maybe I'm not ready.*

The merry-go-round stepped up its pace. Its familiar tune displaced any troubled thoughts and comforted me in the way I knew best: I ate, vomited, and worried about my weight.

*   *   *   *   *

"Cindy, Rob is on the phone!" Mom called through my closed bedroom door.

"Huh?" I glanced groggily at the alarm clock—11:00 P.M. *Oh, shit! I had forgotten it was Rob's turn to call tonight.* We took turns calling each other the weekends he did not come to Syracuse. I rolled out of bed and stumbled out to the hallway phone.

"Hi, Honey." Rob's exuberant voice bounded across the phone lines. "God, I miss you. I've been trying to figure out how I can see you more often and I had a great idea. . . . Why don't you come visit me? My class schedule is really crazy right now. What with final exams and all. Besides, I *really* miss you. If you come here, we could spend time by ourselves. You know . . . without so many people around. I thought you could fly down after you get out of work next Thursday, and then fly back home on Monday. What do you think?"

"I . . . I miss you too. But I'm not sure Mom and Dad will let me come," I stalled. We had never spent a weekend together . . . alone. In fact, we had hardly spent *any* time alone.

"Ask them," Rob insisted. "I'm sure they won't mind. Honey, I love you. I *need* you."

"Okay. I'll ask them in the morning." I hung up and went back to bed, not at all happy about his idea. The next morning I approached Mom and Dad, confident that they would disapprove. After all, they had preached long and hard about sleeping with a man before I was married. Surely they knew that spending a weekend away did not mean separate beds.

"Cindy, that's a wonderful idea! This will give you and Rob a chance to spend some time alone." Mom approved.

I stared at her in disbelief. *Mom, don't you know what that means? Rob will want me to sleep with him! Mom, I can't do that! Please say I can't go!*

"You won't have to worry about having all your family around, bugging the two of you." She and Dad smiled knowingly at each other. "Now, what do you think about this band for the reception. . . ." And she handed a brochure to Dad, my weekend trip decided and dismissed. They had given their blessing. In one week, I would be on my own with Rob.

A week later, I stepped off the plane and into Rob's arms. It was just a short drive to his apartment. "I'm going to put your suitcase in the bedroom," Rob said, and headed in that direction. I followed him down a long corridor and into his bedroom. He set the suitcase down and gave me a long, hard hug. "You know, Cin, I'm glad you're here. I've really missed you." Rob ran his fingers down my spine. "It's pretty late and I know you must be tired," he whispered huskily. "Why don't we go to bed now?"

I smiled uneasily. "Sure, honey, whatever you say."

Rob released me and stepped back. "Hey, it's okay," he said gently. "I can sleep on the couch if you want me to." He put his arms around my shoulders. "It's just that I've missed you so much."

Oh, Cindy! Don't push him away! "Its okay, Rob . . . *really.* You don't have to sleep on the couch. I . . . I *want* to be with you." I smiled, and led him over to the bed. We both undressed and slipped beneath the sheets. Rob reached over and pulled me close. He nuzzled his face close to mine, and kissed me gently on the lips. Throughout that night, our behavior remained chaste, but guilt filled my body and soul anyway. *How could Mom and Dad do this to me?*

The next morning, Rob left for his classes and I found the nearest grocery store. I filled my arms full of dry pasta, a pound of butter, and a package of cherry Kool-Aid. I brought the groceries back to the apartment, and spent the next three hours eating spaghetti and vomiting.

I leaned over the toilet one last time and puked my stomach empty. Shaking, I wiped the remnants of my afternoon activity from the toilet rim. The sound of a turning key in the front door told me I was just in time. "Hi, honey. How was your day?" Rob came into the kitchen and kissed me hello. I smiled nonchalantly, though my heart pounded frantically against my chest. "I couldn't wait to come home to you," he said, and pressed his body up against mine.

I felt his desires and let him lead me to the bedroom. His kisses, his hands, all of him, confused my longings with repulsion. His naked body, next to mine and he was no longer Rob. He was Eddie. He looked like Eddie. He acted like Eddie. He smelled like Eddie.

The rest of the weekend passed in a blur. On Monday, Rob reluctantly brought me back to the airport. We hugged, we kissed, and then it was over. I took my seat by the window, and peered down at the disappearing lights of Philadelphia. We were two young people in love, yet I had been repulsed whenever Rob had touched me. There were no words or reasons to explain it. All I knew was that once I said, *"I do,"* I would never be able to say, *"Don't."*

In May, three months before the wedding, Rob graduated, moved to Syracuse, and into my family's home. He would stay with us until July, when the apartment we had rented would be ready.

Being close just got scarier.

I stepped on the bathroom scale; the dial stopped at—83. I opened the bathroom door slowly. An eerie silence assured me that I had not awakened the sleeping household. I tiptoed past closed doors and crept softly back to my room.

Bingeing and purging were not enough to comfort my growing uneasiness. I resisted Rob's loving touches, and pushed him away. That puzzled Rob. So he sat me down over and over, in the hopes I would open up and share what was bothering me. "Please, Cindy! What is wrong with you? You make me feel like you don't want to be with me." Rob's worried eyes looked anxiously into my own.

"I'm sorry," I mumbled.

"Cindy, *please* let me help you," Rob pleaded, and he put

his arms around my frail body and hugged me.

My defenses melted slightly. "Rob? I . . . I'm . . . I'm losing weight. I'm having trouble eating again, and I don't know what to do." It was my body that was the enemy. And Rob immediately slipped into his familiar role of nurse. Anorexia was something we could talk about. Once I admitted to anorexia's reoccurrence, I obsessed more openly. Rob's immediate concern further reinforced that behavior. I had his attention and affection without the intimacy. Anorexia and bulimia reared their ugly heads once again, though, in essence, they had never really gone away.

Still not understanding the troubled direction I was headed in, Rob tried to fix what he thought was broken. We sought couples counseling in the hopes of opening the fast closing lines of communication between us. The therapist talked of the importance of sharing feelings in a relationship, and I talked about food and my weight.

The merry-go-round spun faster. We canceled my bridal shower and called a halt to wedding plans. The brass ring slipped out of my hand. The wedding would have to wait until I was better.

Chapter 9

Cindra-rella Lost Her Slipper, and the Prince Can't Wake Her Up

"You're calling the wedding off?" Mom's voice shook as she looked from Rob to me. "But the shower is in less than *three days!* All those people I invited!"

"Joyce, we're only *postponing* the shower and wedding." Rob's arm went around my shoulder. "We both feel this is the best thing to do right now." He turned toward my father who had been sitting silent, just listening. "John?"

My father shook his head and sighed.

Enough said. I had failed again.

Rob hugged me. "Hey, it'll be okay, honey," he whispered in my ear and gave me a quick kiss. Rob left for his evening shift at the hospital, and I went up to my room. Without Rob's strong arms and supportive words, I had no defense against my parents' disappointment.

"Cindy, can I talk to you?" Mom walked in and sat down on my bed. "What is wrong with you?" she spat out angrily. "Most people who love each other *want* to be together. I don't understand! All those people I invited! You have really embarrassed me this time. What is everyone going to think?"

I cringed under her onslaught of words. *Mommy, please don't be mad.* "I'm sorry, Mom," I apologized. But she had already left my room, still as confused and as upset as I was.

Two weeks later, Rob moved out of our home and into the apartment. I would join him as soon as we were married. For now, I helped him pack his clothes. "Cindy, we can start spending our time at the apartment instead of at your parents. It will be better, you'll see," Rob reassured me. We loaded several suitcases into his car. "Now that I'm back working days, we can have our nights together. In fact, let's celebrate tonight with a steak dinner. Did I ever make you my famous garlic bread?"

"No." *Don't make me eat. I hate eating.* And worrying about how to eat in front of him. *Don't do this to me!*

"I'll come back and pick you up at six. Tell your mother that we're having dinner together."

"Okay." *I can throw up the steak. It'll be okay.* I waved goodbye to Rob, the voice in my head finally quieted.

"Cindy, I'm afraid your back molar will have to be pulled." Dr. Kenny shook his head, frustrated. "The root canal isn't helping. I just don't understand why your teeth are so bad." He numbed my mouth with Novocain and extracted the tooth.

I left his office and drove to my grandmother's nearby home. I needed to talk to someone. Gram would listen; she always did. And when Grandma opened her door, she welcomed me into her home, not at all surprised by my midweek visit.

"Gram?" We sat down at her kitchen table. "Nobody believes I really love Rob. But Grandma, I *do* love him. We just can't get married right now."

She leaned over and patted my hand reassuringly. "Cindra," Grandma soothed, using the pet name she had given me as a child. "I know that you love Rob. Don't worry about what everybody else believes. It's what's in *your* heart that is important."

"I don't think so, Gram. It seems like whatever I do or say, is wrong. No matter what, I'm just not good enough. I know I want to get married. I mean, I think I want to get married . . . someday . . . I think. Does that make sense to you?"

"Yes, Cindra, it does."

"Gram, I . . . I. . . ." My voice quavered. "Do you think I'll *ever* get married?" And I braced myself for her answer—the answer. Because I was asking for more than just an answer. I was asking for validation—validation of me. And Grandma didn't let me down. She never did.

"Yes, you will get married some day. If that is what you want, *and* when it is right for *you*. Cindy, only you can determine when that will happen. And only you should. Don't worry so much about what everybody else thinks. Sometimes, we must do things that we believe in even if other people don't approve of our decision. It doesn't mean it's right or wrong. It's about you deciding what is right for you. No one else has to live in your shoes. So if this is your decision then it is the right decision. Remember, first and foremost, you must be true to yourself."

I sighed. Gram was right. Listen to myself. The hell with everyone else. If I didn't want to get married, I didn't have to. If I didn't want to go to bed with Rob or Eddie, I didn't have to. If I didn't want to be fat, I didn't have to.

For the next month, an unhappy truce was called between my parents and me. No one talked about the canceled wedding. Things weren't going as well at work either. My job, that had so far been unaffected by my struggle with eating and weight, was becoming increasingly difficult. The numbers on the bathroom scale every morning were more important than the numbers on the price reports I was in charge of. One morning, I stopped to chat with several of my co-workers before proceeding on to my desk, and the next thing I remembered was waking up in the hospital emergency department, lying on a stretcher, with Rob by my side.

"You passed out at work, Cin. This doctor," he nodded

toward the man who stood on my other side, "is a neurologist. He thinks you had a seizure." Rob picked up my cold, clammy hand, squeezed it tightly, and turned to the doctor. "Do you know why Cindy fainted?" he asked.

"No, I don't. From the reports by Cindy's co-workers and the ambulance people, and by looking at these initial blood reports," the doctor held up some papers in his hand, "I believe she may have suffered a seizure. Cindy's lab values are not good. Her potassium, calcium, and sodium levels are dangerously low. This electrolyte imbalance could have caused the seizure, but I'm not certain. I would like to do a complete neurological work-up on her. Cindy," he turned to me, "I would like to admit you to the hospital, okay?"

"Uh-huh." *Sure, go ahead. Maybe there is something really wrong with me. Maybe it's not anorexia at all.*

Seven days later, the neurologist stopped by on morning rounds. So far, all the exams had proved inconclusive. "Cindy, there is another avenue that I believe we need to check out. I would like for you to see a colleague of mine, Dr. Kane. He's a psychiatrist. Rob and your parents tell me that you have been under a lot of stress lately. And that your anorexia is acting up again. It might be helpful for you to talk with Dr. Kane."

A psychiatrist? I'm having seizures and he wants me to see a psychiatrist? He thinks it's all in my head! The irony of the thought escaped me.

"In the meantime, I would like to perform one more test. This test is called a pneumoencephlagram. It's a way to take x-rays of your head, but it's a bit more involved, and, unfortunately, quite painful. But you will be sedated," he reassured me. "Once you are sedated, I'll be inserting a needle into a space here," and he placed his finger on an area at the base of my spine. "And I'll withdraw some spinal fluid. I'll then inject some helium . . . that's a gas . . . into your spine and take pictures of your head. Afterwards, you will need to lay flat for about a day or so. You will have a pretty significant headache. Believe me, you won't want to sit up. Sitting will only make the pain worse."

I'd be asleep. I've had headaches before. No big deal.

Early the next morning, I was given an injection and wheeled down to the radiology department. I was pretty groggy by the time the technician strapped me onto the table. More medicine was injected into my IV line and I fell asleep. Some time later, I awakened to find the table I laid upon tilted, and myself spinning, as a large machine whirled around me. The pain was excruciating. The pressure in my head was immense. I screamed, and fell in and out of consciousness. The time passed in a blur, and the forewarned headache was a thousand times worse than expected. The accompanying nausea wiped out any worry of how I was going to be able to eat and vomit while lying down.

The test results were negative. After ten days in the hospital, I was discharged home with a prescription for Dilantin, an anti-convulsant medication. I went to see Dr. Kane the following week. He appeared to be a pleasant man, and he didn't fall asleep on me. But then, he offered no answers either.

"Cindy, what about going back to Philadelphia?" Rob asked. He buttered a slice of bread and took a bite.

I paused, my fork in midair, and considered his words. "I don't know, Rob," I replied slowly. "Mom and Dad will be awfully mad if I go back into the hospital again. Mom already hates me for not getting married."

"Cindy, your mom doesn't hate you. Come on, I'll help you tell your parents. They'll understand. Believe me, they just want you to be well." He leaned over and planted a kiss on my lips. "So do I. I want you to be better. It will be okay. Trust me. Just go and get this behind you. We can talk to your parents after dinner."

"I need to brush my teeth," I said, and carried my plate into the kitchen. Dinners with Rob had worked out well after all. He cooked fabulous meals and never once suspected my frequent bathroom trips.

Later, my parents' reaction was as I predicted. Dad gave me a hug and said nothing. Mom was horrified. "I refuse to pay for your airfare to Philadelphia. If you go, you'll have to make your own arrangements. I want nothing to do with this," she stated brusquely.

I cringed against Rob and looked to my father for reassurance, but he had already left the room. Only Mom and her anger remained. "I'm going and I'll pay for it myself," I replied quietly. *No matter what I did, it was always wrong.*

Once again, for the third time in less than two years, I returned to Philadelphia in an attempt to gain control over anorexia. Lonely, sad, and confused, I faced a merciless foe. The hospital staff reinstated the behavior contract that had worked so well before. Only this time they added one more condition: on those days I did not make my weight, I would also be denied use of bathroom facilities. No shower was bad enough, using a bedpan was even worse.

Three days of no weight gain and solitude took on a bleaker meaning. It was Fourth of July and I was not allowed Rob's phone call. Alone in my hospital room, I pushed the bed up against the wall. I climbed on top of the pillow and leaned my head against the small, grill-covered window on the wall above the bed. I watched exploding fireworks fill the sky outside. Independence Day in Philadelphia and our nation's bicentennial. Everyone was celebrating being alive, being American, and being free. Everyone but me. I was locked in my room. A prisoner of my own demands.

"I don't know why they won't let me see my mom," I pouted. Mom had come to Philadelphia in the hopes of a weekend visit with me. In spite of her anger, in spite of her disappointment, she loved me and just wanted me well. I knew that. "I don't know what *they* want from me. I just want to see my mom," I whimpered. I could have seen her if I had gained the expected weight for this day. But it would have been giving in. It would have been letting them win. It would have meant giving control of myself to other people. But I couldn't. Because this was the only thing in life that was truly mine. The only thing I could say no to. The staff could take away my privileges, they could take away my clothes, my books, my furniture, my family. But they couldn't take away control of my body. It was all I had left.

Someone knocked on the door and I scrambled down from my perch. One of the evening nurses came in with my dinner tray. She set it on the bedside table and left the room. I stared at its steaming contents in dismay: fried chicken, potato salad, corn, and apple pie. *I can't eat this food! It's too fattening! Don't those people down in the kitchen know that you don't serve this kind of food to a person with anorexia?*

But it was my responsibility to fill out my menus. And I had chosen the meal in front of me. It was a binge meal. I had planned it that way. Only I hadn't planned to be in my room.

My stomach growled hungrily. I picked up the fork and poked the chicken breast, which released its succulent juices. *Oh, God! I'm so hungry. Maybe I can eat just a little.* I peeled off the offensive crunchy skin. *Way too many calories.* I set it aside. The white meat underneath was permissible. I pulled off a sliver of the chicken and chewed slowly, savoring the luscious shred of life. I debated the corn. *Maybe just a little bit.* I scooped up a spoonful of the steaming vegetable. Its sweetness mingled with the mild flavor of the chicken. My hunger grew larger. I eyed the golden-brown skin that I had so carefully discarded to the side of the plate. I cut off a tiny corner and nibbled at it. The delectable skin crunched in my mouth, releasing flavor and memory of old picnics gone by. I cut off another piece of the skin . . . and then another . . . and another . . . until I had eaten it all. Next, I attacked the chicken breast. This time tearing off hunks of moist meat and stuffing them into my mouth. I dragged my fingers through the potato salad and shoveled the creamy mixture into my mouth. *God, I'm so hungry!* I wolfed down the entire meal and picked up the plate, licking it unashamedly clean. I needed every crumb it held.

I crumbled my napkin and laid contentedly back on the pillow, my swollen, lead-filled tummy loomed huge in front of me. *Oh, dear God! What did I do? I shouldn't have eaten so much! Cindy, you're just a fat pig! All those calories. How could you have been so stupid?* "Oh, shit!" I jumped out of bed and ran over to the tiny basin sink in the corner of the room. I placed both hands against my stomach and pushed—hard. My stomach heaved, I gagged, and my gut emptied, vomit filled the sink. I pushed and heaved, until it was all out. Until there was nothing left inside. I sprawled on the floor, exhausted. *Safe, and still in control.*

Several more weeks passed, and many more days in my room, before I regained fifteen pounds, all the way up to 95 pounds. It was time to go home. I said as much to the resident doctor in charge of my care. "Dr. Saunders, I've gained my weight and I would like to be discharged tomorrow. My fiancé is here visiting and I want to go home with him." Rob had come for the weekend.

"Cindy," Dr. Saunders said, "it's not going to be easy when you go back home. You made your weight, but I'm not quite convinced that you are ready to be discharged. Philadelphia is a long way to keep coming for help with your anorexia."

"Oh, but I am, Dr. Saunders! My contract states that when I reach my weight goal and maintain it for five days, then I can be discharged. Well, today is the fifth day."

Dr. Saunders studied my face. He had only been assigned to me for the last few weeks. Barely enough time to delve behind my carefully constructed walls and into the hidden issues that he suspected. "Tell you what, I'm going to give you the name and number of a friend of mine, a doctor, who has a practice in Rochester. It would be better if you could get help closer to your home. If you promise to give him a call, I'll agree to your discharge." He scribbled a name down on a piece of paper and handed it to me.

I took it and glanced at the name, *Dr. Stevens.* I stuffed it in my pocket. "Thank you for all your help, Dr. Saunders." I shook his hand and left the room.

I had gained weight. I was going back home. I would be getting married. On the long ride back to Syracuse, Rob and I decided on a November wedding. It was only three months away.

"Are you going up to your room to eat, Cindy?" Mom asked angrily. My shoulders slumped in response to her words. The tension between the two of us hadn't decreased in the weeks following my return home from the hospital.

"No, Mom, I'm not," I said, and walked past her. She reached out and grabbed my blouse as I walked past her. "How dare you do this to me! *How dare you have anorexia! How can you do this to me?*" she shouted, unable to control her anger any longer.

"Leave me alone! Just leave me alone," I cried, and yanked my blouse out of her grip. "I'm not doing anything to you!"

"I will never believe that you love Rob! I know he loves you, but you don't love him. I will always believe him over you. You are so selfish! All you think about is yourself and food! You'll never get married. What is wrong with you? Are you queer or something? Why can't you be like other girls?"

"You love Rob more than you love me!" I spat out angrily. "If you love him so much, then why don't *you* marry him!" I ran to my bedroom and threw myself on my bed, weeping uncontrollably. *She hates me. Mom hates me because I'm not getting married. If everyone would just leave us alone, Rob and I would be fine.*

But would we? It was proving very difficult, almost impossible, for me to carry on a healthy, intimate relationship with another person. To do that required giving of myself. And people were already asking too much of me. They wanted me to give up anorexia. And I couldn't. It was the structure . . . the power . . . that was holding my life together.

So I lost ten pounds. And the wall that anorexia had built grew higher and stronger. Its boundaries worked to shield me from hurtful words and disapproving glances. *Why did everyone only see my weight? Why couldn't I be like everyone else? Why was I so scared to let anyone get close to me?* All I had succeeded in doing so far was to push away those I loved the most. *Maybe I didn't deserved to be loved? Maybe I wasn't good enough to love . . . to live?* And I remembered the piece of paper given to me by Dr. Saunders. What had I done with it? I rummaged through closets and dresser drawers before I finally found the crumbled up piece of paper. I smoothed it open. *Dr. Stevens.* I'd give him a call. Maybe he could help me. Maybe he could help me be good enough.

Chapter 10

Thin Perceptions

"Hi, Cindy. This is Dr. Stevens. I'm returning your call. How may I help you?"

I explained my need for help, and how I had received his name in the first place. Dr. Stevens thought it might be better if I could get a therapist in my hometown and provided me with several names. I was to call him back if those sources proved unsuccessful.

Over the next week, I tried every name on the list and then some. As soon as I mentioned anorexia to the receptionists, I got no further. That reaction reinforced my own belief that having anorexia was shameful and *bad*. I placed another call to Rochester. "I'm sorry to keep bothering you, Dr. Stevens, but nobody wants to help me!"

"Cindy, I'm sorry that you are having no luck. I'm not certain that I can help from this distance. But I'll tell you what . . . why don't we schedule an appointment so that I can meet with you and your family."

"That's fine . . . and thanks, Dr. Stevens." I hung up the phone. No guarantees and no promises. But at least Dr. Stevens hadn't said no.

Mom and Dad were very supportive of our going to Rochester, ninety miles away. Even though they still felt badly over my fragile situation with Rob, they wanted me to be healthy and happy. A week after my call to Dr. Stevens, we traveled to the large medical center in which his office was located. Mom, Dad, Jonny, and I sat in the waiting area. Would Dr. Stevens be able to help me? Would he *want* to help me? Several minutes later, a very tall, smiling, friendly-looking gentleman walked towards us. *"Oh!"* I grabbed Mom's arm. "I think that's him!" He stopped in front of us. It *was* Dr. Stevens.

"Hi, you must be Cindy," Dr. Stevens said, and held out his hand. Nervously, I rose and shook his outstretched hand as introductions were made all around.

Mom, Dad, Jonny, and I followed Dr. Stevens to his office. "I thought that the best way to get started would be to have you share how it has been over the last several years," he said as we settled into a circle of chairs. "Cindy? Would you like to start?" I shook my head.

Mom smiled nervously and cleared her throat. "Dr. Stevens, I think I'd like to start. You see, when Cindy was just a little girl, she was the best little girl a mother could ask for. She enjoyed playing by herself, but she also played very well with other children. She was easily pleased, and she never asked for much or demanded anything. *Why,* I could put a dish of candy on the table, and as much as little Cindy might have wanted it, she wouldn't touch it. Not like her sister, Debbie. Debbie would have eaten the entire thing!

"Though Cindy *was* somewhat shy, she was such a healthy, happy little girl. We didn't have to worry about Cindy. Of course, it always took her a while to adjust to new surroundings. We realized that when we moved into our home when Cindy was nine years old. *Oh dear!* She had the worst time adjusting to that new house. She broke out in hives and it was just terrible for her. But she still made friends easily. Everybody liked Cindy. And she liked them. Though she *did* seem unusually close to her father and I. I guess she was insecure back then and we just didn't see it. *Oh,* and she never liked to stay overnight at anybody's house." Mom smiled, and her face lit up as she shared my early years. "One time, when she was around seven, I went to New York City with my older daughter for a few days. Cindy and Jonny stayed at their grandma's house. John," she nodded in my father's direction, "was working, and wasn't able to watch them. But Cindy," and Mom laughed at the memory. "She made her father come and pick her up *every* night so that she could sleep in her own bed. I guess she hated not being in her own bed. She hated anything that upset her sense of normal." Mom paused and took a deep breath. "We are not sure when Cindy started losing weight. She never complained or told her father . . . or myself . . . that anything was bothering her. It wasn't until she developed all sorts of physical problems that we realized something was wrong. After many months of Cindy being dreadfully ill, one of her doctors in Syracuse urged us to find more help for Cindy. He was certain that she would die. It was at that point that we took her to Boston. It was there that the doctors told us what Cindy had. I was just devastated when they said it was anorexia nervosa. We had never even heard of it. The doctors in Boston wanted Cindy to go to another hospital, but I guess none of us were ready to admit that she had this horrible condition. And when she finally did go to Philadelphia, I thought she would get better. It's a terrible disease and I don't understand it."

"She told everyone that I have a blood disorder." All heads turned and stared as my quiet voice cut in. "Well, she did!" I defended myself.

Mom's face turned beet red. "I just didn't want others to know. Yes, I do admit that I'm ashamed of Cindy having anorexia, but Cindy's personality *has* changed. She's become very withdrawn from *everyone*," she emphasized. And then she went straight to the reason for our visit. "Cindy lies and she's very manipulative. I know she thinks she's covering up what she's doing, but when food disappears overnight, we all know that Cindy is responsible. And she thinks by wearing baggy clothing, we won't be able to see how much weight she's losing, or how skinny she really is." Tears welled up in my mother's eyes and she struggled to remain composed. "I feel defeated. I blame myself, and I wonder where I failed. No matter what I do or say, Cindy doesn't listen to me. I love her very much and want what's best for her, but I can't seem to help my daughter. I wish I could take this illness from her rather than watch what she is doing to herself—physically and emotionally." Mom smiled weakly at Dr. Stevens. "I cry a lot. I know I have to be strong for Cindy, but I have a husband and two other children. All I can do is pray and ask God to protect her from harm."

Shamefaced, I slid down in the chair. There was no way Dr. Stevens would help me now! Not after all those horrible things Mom was telling him.

Dr. Stevens turned to my father. "Mr. Nappa, what are your thoughts on all of this?"

Dad smiled sadly at me. "Well, everything my wife says is true, but I would like to add that we *both* love Cindy very much. Anorexia nervosa is so new to us. We had never heard of it until the doctors told us Cindy had it. But the Cindy sitting here today is not the same person she used to be. I've tried on many occasions to try and get her to open up and talk to me, but she just won't. We were always very close. But she's pulled away from all of us, her friends as well. We keep telling her to call them, but she won't. Sometimes, I find notes that Cindy has written lying around the house. She writes that maybe she'd be better off dead. I think . . ." And Dad stopped abruptly. The ensuing silence, deafening. He grabbed my mother's hand and held it tightly. The strain of anorexia's power was clearly etched across their faces. "Like my wife, I just don't understand how to help Cindy."

I slid a bit further down in the chair.

Dr. Stevens turned to my brother. "Jon, I know Cindy's illness must be difficult for you. She has been getting a lot of attention from your parents and doctors. How do you feel about it?"

Eighteen-year-old Jon smiled a bit self-consciously. He had recently entered his first year of college at Rochester Institute of Technology. I had been ill for half of his life. "Yeah. It has not been easy. I love my sister, Dr. Stevens. But she keeps eating all the food and then throws it up. I don't know why she does that. She used to be so pretty and now she's just so skinny. And I don't know why she canceled her wedding to Rob. I know he loves Cindy. He's a really nice guy."

"I didn't cancel my wedding!" I protested. "I only postponed it! Rob and I are *still* going to get married."

Jon avoided my eyes. "All Cindy does is eat. She thinks that by running the water in the bathroom we don't know that she's really throwing up."

I lowered my head, hiding behind my long brown hair that fell across my face. Jon's words embarrassed me. As much as I wanted to deny them, I could not.

"Cindy, I know it must be hard for you to sit here and listen to what your family is saying," Dr. Stevens said. "I'd like to talk with you now. I'm going to ask them to leave the room so that you and I can chat for a little bit. They can wait out in the waiting room." My family got up and filed out of the room. Dr. Stevens closed the door and turned to me with a compassion I had not expected. "Cindy, from what your family is saying, it sounds like you have been having quite a struggle. I know Rochester is some distance away, but I would like to help you. I believe it would be beneficial for all of you if we scheduled some family therapy sessions. You and I can meet after the family meeting. How does that sound? Do you think your parents would be able to make the drive that often?"

He was going to help me? Dr. Stevens was going to help me? Thank you, God. Thank you, thank you, thank you! Tears threatened to spill out, but I remained dry-eyed. Besides, I was strong. I *never* cried anymore. I smiled at Dr. Stevens. He had thrown me a lifeline. With or without my family, I would get to Rochester.

Mom and Dad were agreeable to family therapy, and we began bi-weekly meetings. Even Rob attended several sessions. The therapy helped in the beginning, or at least while we were in Dr. Stevens' office. But back at home, nothing really changed. Old roles and old patterns were hard to break. What worked in theory in the doctor's office could not seem to carry over to our home environment. Anorexia had provided a convenient scapegoat for other family issues, like Mom and Dad's troubled relationship. No. It was much easier for everyone to focus on Cindy and her illness than to face those other as serious problems.

In just under three months, my family stopped going to Rochester altogether. What had looked promising in the beginning was no longer true. Ingrained behaviors were hard to break for everyone, not just for me. Besides, my family still viewed the situation as my problem and I was the only one who needed fixing.

On my own, I continued weekly sessions with Dr. Stevens. His soft-spoken demeanor and gentle approach were not put off by my guarded behavior. He did most of the talking during our sessions and he asked me often, how was I feeling? But I remained cautious. Not yet sure of this new doctor.

"Oh . . . Dr. Stevens? I almost forgot to tell you, but I have to cancel next week's appointment. I'm having surgery to remove my left parotid gland." I lightly touched the swollen area underneath my left ear. "My doctor said it's called a parotidectomy."

"Why are you having the gland removed?" Dr. Stevens' voice was concerned. In the few months since we had begun meeting, this was the first time I had ever mentioned a problem with my gland.

I frowned. "It's because of that *stupid* swelling in my face! It won't go away! Even though the biopsy that was done on the gland was benign, now it's more swollen than *ever!*" My face brightened. "At least I won't look like a chipmunk anymore." The telltale sign of chronic vomiting—chipmunk cheeks—was always present.

"Well, I'll keep you on my schedule for the following week, but you call me if you need to before then," he said. Only a handful of all my doctors had ever been as thoughtful and as concerned about me as Dr. Stevens was. I left his office and walked out into the bright, sunny afternoon, feeling unusually hopeful.

The surgery went well. After a week in the hospital, I returned home bandaged, sore, and minus one salivary gland. The surgeon told my parents that, someday, I might want to have the right gland removed, even though its swelling had not been as pronounced as the now absent left gland.

For the third time in less than five months, I was placed on work disability. So far, I had stopped menstruating, I had come close to cardiac arrest and death in Boston, I had screwed up my electrolytes, suffered seizures, lost several teeth and one gland.

But—I was thin.

The surgery offered only a small reprieve. After two weeks of recuperation, I went back to work *and* . . . bingeing and purging. And though Rob and I had done no further planning, we still insisted a November wedding—only weeks away—would still take place.

"Cindy," Rob said, "I added you to my insurance policy at work today. It'll become effective once we are married." He took a handful of popcorn and pushed the bowl closer to me. "Here, have some." We were stretched out on the living room floor of his apartment, enjoying old movies on television.

My heart pounded. Was it because of the popcorn, or the fact that Rob had put me on his policy? Either one terrified me: the popcorn because I'd have to figure out how to throw up without his suspecting; the insurance policy because it meant we were *really* going to get married.

Rob chattered on, unaware of the fear his words had evoked. He turned off the television. "Come on, Honey. Let's go in the bedroom." I smiled nervously, and followed him into the bedroom. *I don't want to, Rob. Please! I don't want you to touch my body.* Rob turned towards me and unbuttoned my cotton blouse, slipping it from around my shoulders. He unzipped my blue jeans and helped me step out of them. "Mmmm . . . you feel good," he murmured, and laid down on the bed, pulling me on top of him. His hands caressed my bare breasts. I laid rigid in his arms, my thoughts frantic before they settled on the handful of popcorn I had just eaten, and the food I would later consume.

Rob hugged me tightly. "No matter how thin you are," he whispered into my ear, "you will always be sexy to me."

My stomach turned somersaults. *Damn body! Would I never be safe? Oh, dear God! I can't marry him. I can't do this!* And my body betrayed me as it responded to his touches. *If I hadn't eaten the popcorn, this wouldn't have happened.* An hour later, while Rob dressed for his night shift at the hospital, I purged the cursed popcorn from my soul.

I kept to myself over the next few days. Mom and Dad were caught up in their increasingly troubled marriage, Jonny was very busy being a college freshman, Debbie and Hank prepared for their upcoming move to Florida, Rob worked double shifts to save money, and I was disappearing. No matter what Rob said, I *would* get thin enough.

I laid quietly in bed and listened to the sounds of my parents getting ready for work. The rain beat harshly on the roof above. The dark, dreary early morning downpour further intensified my already gloomy mood. *Oh, Buttons, I wish you were here! I don't know what to do!* Waves of sadness engulfed me, and I burrowed deeper beneath my cocoon of blankets. At that moment, all I wanted was for somebody, *anybody,* to put his or her arms around me and tell me that it would be okay. "Dr. Stevens. Maybe I should call Dr. Stevens." I got up and went into the bathroom, stripped off my pajamas, grasped the towel bar, and stepped onto the scale. The numbers spun slowly and came to rest—76. *Safe?*

No. Rob's words the other night had proved otherwise. I slipped back into my pajamas and placed the call to Dr. Stevens.

Dr. Stevens' secretary heard the urgency in my voice and, within seconds, I heard his familiar voice. "Hi, Cindy. What's up?" he asked.

I made my plea. "Dr. Stevens, I think I'm losing weight again. I've lost ten pounds."

The message came across loud and clear. "Cindy, our agreement is that below 86 pounds, you are at medical risk. It was our deal that you would have to come into the hospital if you went below that number. I have no choice, but to hospitalize you. Do you understand what that means?" He meant another behavior program.

"I think so," I answered. I did know and I didn't care. The hospital was quickly becoming an escape from what I could not understand at home or inside of me. I hung up with instructions to come to Rochester that afternoon. How could I tell my family, including Rob, that I was going back into the hospital?

I didn't. I took the easy way out. With everyone at work, I decided to leave a note on the kitchen table explaining where I had gone. Sneaking away was all I could handle. I hurriedly packed and lugged my heavy suitcase down the stairs in the hopes of a clean get-away. I opened the kitchen door and my father walked into the room. I hadn't heard his car pull into the driveway.

Dad's eyes traveled from me to the packed suitcase. "You're going into the hospital, aren't you, Cindy?" It was more of a fact than a question. After several years, he still could not understand my problems. His shoulders slumped and all of a sudden, my dad looked old. I lowered my head and nodded shamefully.

"I guess you have to do what you think is best for yourself," he said quietly, his lips set in a firm, but straight, line. My heart sank. I hated when he did that with his mouth. It meant he was angry . . . or upset . . . or disappointed. At that moment, I was sure he felt all three.

"I only hope you know what you're doing. Don't worry

about Mom. I'll let her know." Dad hugged me tightly, and we clung together for several minutes.

More than anything, I wished I could be his little girl and start over again. I desperately wanted to reassure him I would be okay, but I couldn't. Maybe someday we would both understand what went wrong. For now, this was the best that I could do.

I pulled away and Dad kissed the tip of my nose. "Let Dr. Stevens help you, Pocahontas. We'll be here if you need us." He picked up my suitcase and carried it out to my car.

I drove off and spent the next five weeks on another behavior program. Not quite as rigid as the one in the Philadelphia hospital. Nonetheless, it was still scary and uncomfortable. Rob wrote often during that time and visited once. I did not write at all. Even in the safe environment of the hospital, I was scared, and focused only on my weight.

"Hi, can I come in?" Dr. Stevens knocked on my hospital room door. I looked up from the book I was reading. "Cindy, Rob called. He asked if the three of us could meet together when he comes to visit you on Friday. I told him only if it was okay with you."

Rob hadn't said anything to me about wanting to meet with Dr. Stevens. "Okay," I approved, a bit hesitantly. Maybe Rob wanted to set a wedding date.

On Friday, I hovered anxiously near the elevator. When the doors opened and Rob stepped out, I ran over and embraced him. He kissed me uneasily. My first warning that the reason for his visit may not be as I had thought.

Dr. Stevens arrived shortly thereafter. "Hello, Rob . . . Cindy. We're meeting in this room over here." We followed Dr. Stevens down the hall. I looked questionably at Rob, who refused to meet my eyes. *Something's wrong. I know something is wrong.*

Dr. Stevens waited for us to sit down "Cindy, Rob asked for this meeting today. He has something he wants to say, so I'm going to turn this over to him."

Rob cleared his throat, nervously. "Cindy, I asked Dr. Stevens for this meeting because I know what I have to say is going to be very painful for you to hear. I've given this a lot of thought, and I've come to a decision concerning us and our future."

Our future? So, it was about our wedding. My stomach muscles tightened.

Rob swallowed hard. "I don't know how long it's going to take for you to get better and, well, I need to get on with my life. I believe it is best if we broke our engagement."

Break up? I looked from Rob to Dr. Stevens. One lowered his head, the other watched me sympathetically. *Oh, Rob! I know I'm not ready to get married, but I'm not ready to end our engagement either. I love you. I just need more time!* I clenched my hands and looked down at my lap. "I guess you want the ring back," I said softly, and I slid the diamond off my finger and handed it over to Rob. *But if you love me, how can you leave me?* Rob hesitated, then took the ring.

I kept my eyes on my fingers—my bare fingers, and I did not see the pain cross Rob's face as awkward silence filled the room. He didn't share how difficult it had been for him over the past few months as he agonized over how best to help himself and me. When I had shut him out, he was left to come to his own conclusions of the distance between us. I had successfully pushed Rob away. For him, I was the one who had left.

Dr. Stevens and Rob talked, but I did not join in. I sat ramrod straight, too numb to think . . . to hear . . . to feel. At that moment, all I felt was empty. The meeting was over and we all knew it. Dr. Stevens shook Rob's hand and gave mine a squeeze. "Cindy, I'll be up to talk to you later this evening." He worried of the impact of Rob's decision on my shaky emotional state.

I squared my shoulders and smiled bravely, as if my 80-pound, twelve-year-old-size body could shield me from the pain of my world.

Rob walked me back to my hospital room and waited awkwardly at its threshold, not knowing if he should enter or say good-bye. But he had already done that earlier with his announcement back in the therapy room. I looked at the floor and said nothing. After several minutes of silence, Rob said good-bye and walked out of my life.

I sat alone on the edge of my hospital bed, the earlier thought echoing over and over. *If you love me, how could you leave me?*

My heart was breaking, but the girl who had no tears did not cry.

Chapter 11

Shattered Dreams

"What do you mean I have to move out of my home?"

Dr. Stevens had suggested to my parents and myself that living on my own would be the best next step. It was agreed all around, though I more reluctantly, that maybe an apartment would help me achieve needed independence.

Two months had passed since Rob had broken our engagement, and I was still in the hospital. My weight had slowly inched its way up to 86 pounds and stabilized. The reasoning behind the lower weight goal was that it might be a more realistic weight for me to maintain.

Back in Syracuse, my parents looked at numerous apartments, most of which they found horribly depressing. My grandfather, who owned several multiple-family dwellings, had a recent apartment vacancy and offered it to me. It was a one-bedroom apartment in an older section of the city and only ten minutes away from my family. "Perfect," everyone thought.

"Well, maybe," I agreed, begrudgingly. After a total of four months in the hospital, I was discharged to this new home. For the second time since anorexia had entered into my life, I would not be living with my family.

I sat down on my new plaid couch, a gift from my grandparents, its stiff fabric unyielding to my 86 pounds. The silence hurt my ears and my soul. There was no mother, no father, and no brother to fill the empty air with noises. There was nobody to break bread with, nobody to be lonely with.

I sighed and turned on the television. *Nobody* had told me that being independent meant being all alone! Having no family around to talk to meant having no family to watch my every move. I was free to binge, purge, starve, and exercise whenever and however I wanted. But my resolve to *be better* was strong. I had made a promise I intended to keep. No more anorexia. No throwing up in my new home with its linoleum floors, garbage disposal, and newly renovated bathroom. Along with childhood, those problems were to be finally left behind.

Unfortunately, as sincere as I was with that promise, the war inside raged on. *How much should I eat? Do I vomit? Do my thighs touch? Am I scared? How much do I weigh this morning . . . this afternoon . . . this evening? Maybe if I vomit only once a day, I can get through the rest of the day.* Let's see, if I had to be at work by eight, that meant I had to get up at five. Would that give me enough time to make breakfast (four eggs, a quarter pound of bacon, eight slices of toast, three glasses of orange juice), throw up, take a shower, dry my hair (when had it become so thin?), get dressed, and drive to work? No. It was barely enough time. I set my alarm for four-thirty. Vomiting only once a day went out the window.

Maybe living alone wouldn't be so bad after all.

But it was.

I dragged wearily through each day. All I could think about was food. No one, not even Dr. Stevens, was aware of the months, the weeks, the days, the hours, the minutes, the *seconds* I spent thinking of how to stop bingeing and vomiting, even as I binged and vomited. I didn't know how to *not*.

Anorexia was not a diagnosis; it was my life.

After six months on my own, I ended up back in the hospital. Depression and suicidal thoughts were the reasons. It was much easier to be angry with myself than with others. Besides, it *was* all my fault. If I was so unhappy, I *should* be able to just stop it. Just like I *should* have married Rob. Just like I *should* have been a better daughter, a better friend, a better person.

After three months as an inpatient, I returned to life as I had left it. My boss at work, though happy to see me back, laid me off. I didn't blame him. I was not dependable. If I wasn't in the hospital, I was forever going to doctor appointments. I also left work often, in the middle of the day, feigning illness or an appointment, just so that I could go home to eat and vomit. When I did manage to work my scheduled hours, I spent that time thinking about food and how to control the hunger. I no longer functioned (had I ever?) at work. I was a nice person, but work couldn't count on me to do the job.

It didn't matter. The eating was fully out of control, and I no longer could deal with the intensity of its cravings. I couldn't work. I couldn't live with my family. I couldn't get married. I couldn't go to school. I couldn't give up vomiting. I couldn't let anyone know.

If I did, the feelings inside would kill me.

If I didn't, the vomiting would kill me.

I went on unemployment, and my weight, which had been holding its own at 85 pounds, began another slow decline. There was no longer any question of my ability to work. As soon as the unemployment checks ran out, social security disability kicked in. I was twenty-five years old and declared permanently disabled.

My days became just more of the same. I was awake by seven and ate breakfast (which never remained in my stomach, no matter how small the amount) by eight. I showered by nine, then I was off to the grocery store (where I bought two, sometimes three, bags of groceries) by ten, and then I was back home by eleven, at which point I binged and vomited, nonstop, until seven at night. Only then, could I put my pajamas on and curl up on the couch to wind down. But the cookies in my cupboard, the spaghetti in the refrigerator . . . the pizza . . . the potato chips . . . the turkey salad . . . still teased me to eat. More often than not, I gave in and ate and vomited for another two hours. Finally, exhausted, the demon voices inside would be quieted and I could go to bed. And then I ended the day with the same prayer: *"God, tomorrow . . . I promise . . . I'll stop eating and vomiting."* And each following morning, I broke that promise.

After yet another daylong eating and vomiting marathon, I huddled wearily on the couch, feeling utterly dejected. The feeling wrapped its ugly claws around my heart, squeezing tightly, its pain filling my entire insides. The intensity of it made no sense. *What's wrong with me? Why can't I just be like other people?* "Oh, Dr. Stevens," I prayed silently. "Please, you have to help me!" In spite of our now twice-weekly meetings, I had yet to say those words out loud. I was positive the depth of this despair and the ugliness of the inner pain would make him turn away in horror. I just couldn't take that risk.

My eyes darted around the living room and settled on three old plastic model horses displayed on my fireplace mantle—the ones Sandy and I had played with so many years ago. Memories of what used to be and were no more. Would I ever laugh again? Would I always have to fight this sadness? I missed me, and I didn't even know where I had gone. How would I ever get me back?

I ran my fingers across my stomach, and received little comfort from the jutting sharpness of my hipbones and the sunken contours of my abdomen. "I have no life. I only exist. Maybe I'll just die." But I was as afraid of dying as I was of living. I didn't fit in anywhere. "Maybe I'll write Dr. Stevens a letter." If I couldn't speak my thoughts, maybe I could write them on paper. Somehow I had to let him know.

Dear Dr. Stevens, I'm so sad, it's spilling out of me. I need

132

your help so badly. Please, don't go away. Please stay and help me. I want to live! Let's not let me die. Please help me get past this wall of fear so that I can be alive. The eating and vomiting are so awful, yet I know it's helping me stay together while I'm alone.

I do care about people. I do care about me. But I'm crying. Can you hear me?

I'm so tired! I don't mean to run away. I don't know what to do. Everything feels out of my control, so confusing. I am scared. Terrified, actually. This damn anorexia keeps me all alone. Maybe I'll always have anorexia, and I'll forever be alone!

I don't think I'm crazy! I just can't figure out this eating part of life. I use to know how to do it, but something has gone wrong. And I just can't figure it out. I want to be okay. I want to live! But my strength is weakening, and I'm losing hope.

I've tried so hard to be good. Yet I can't stop eating and vomiting. I want to die! I want to close my eyes and go to sleep. I'm not sure how long I can keep up this pace. I feel so hopeless, so helpless.

I feel guilty for being sick and having these problems, like I shouldn't feel this way. I must pretend who I am, because if people knew the real me, they wouldn't like me. Are you getting fed up with me? Please don't. I'm really not a bad person.

Debbie and Hank left. I miss them so much. I want to be as important to them as they are to me. I want to be missed also. I am trying to stay in control, but I hate who I am. So much pain and I can't bear to see it. I have to write this while I have enough courage to put it on paper. I did love Rob and Eddie very much, but I can't separate them in my head. I lost Rob because of that, and I know I may never be able to love.

Dr. S., we must work very hard to keep me alive because I'm right on the edge of falling off. Can you help take the terror away? Please, tell me that I'll be okay, that I will live through this! Because I'm finding it hard to believe that I will.

This is my life and I'm very frightened of it.

I crumbled the paper. I couldn't send it. Even on paper, those feelings were too threatening.

And my life didn't change. I traveled to Rochester to see Dr. Stevens and starved, binged, vomited, exercised on the days I didn't. Anorexia remained the focus and the roadblock in our therapy sessions while my weight hovered around 80 pounds. Because I was so skinny, it was too easy to convince others that anorexia was the only problem. I could not—and would not—admit to Dr. Stevens that bingeing and purging were as much of a problem as refusing to eat. And yet it was the vomiting that was the most destructive to my physical and emotional health.

My monthly disability checks of three hundred dollars, plus thirty dollars in food stamps, could not keep pace with the amount of food required for food binges. I spent an average of ten to fifteen dollars *per day!* When money and food ran out by the second week of each month, I resorted to bouncing checks, shoplifting, and stealing money. I didn't think I was doing anything wrong but then again, I wasn't thinking clearly about anything.

It was a cold, wintry day and the bus stop offered little protection from the fierce, bitter wind. I stomped my feet and blew inside my cupped hands to keep warm. The approaching bus seemed to take forever. In an effort to hurry it along, I yanked my mitten off and sent two quarters flying into a snowbank. I dug through the snow trying to find those quarters. It was fruitless. I waved the bus on by and walked downtown.

Two months later, I stood in front of an opened cupboard. Two packages of French's brown gravy mixes, a bottle of Hunt's ketchup, and a jar of unopened dill pickle spears. Two and a half weeks to go until the first of the month and I was out of food. How was I going to get through until my next disability check arrived? I searched through every pocket of every coat I owned in hopes of finding some loose change. *Wait a minute! My bus fare!* Those dropped quarters of two months earlier. I ran to the living room window and peered out at the March sunshine. Could they possibly still be there? I threw my jacket around my shoulders and dashed up to the street corner. I fell to my hands and knees, and crawled along the street. And I'll be damned, *my quarters were lying alongside the curb!* I snatched them up in my hand, closed my eyes, and breathed a sigh of relief. I wasn't stealing— these were *my* quarters! Yes, there was a God! "Thank you, thank you, *thank you,* God," I whispered. Oh, yes! I was the luckiest girl! Fifty cents would buy a pound of pasta and a package of Kool-Aid. It would be enough to get me through a couple of hours.

Could the true meaning of desperation be any clearer?

"Cindy, do you want to come over to my house and visit?" Mary Jean asked. *Mary Jean!* My heart leaped with joy as she waited for my answer.

"I drove my car to school, so we can ride home together." Mary Jean started walking towards her car and I eagerly followed. *Oh, Mary Jean! I knew you would come back and be my friend . . .* Abruptly, I sat up in bed and the dream faded. In the dusky light of early morning, I laid back down. *Damn dreams!* I glanced at the bedside clock—4:30 A.M., time to get up. Dad would be by to pick me up in two hours to take me to the Greyhound bus station. Losing my job had forced me to sell my new car; I now traveled to Rochester by bus.

Five hours later, I walked into Dr. Stevens's office and settled into my favorite chair: an old, corduroy-soft, gold-shaded, easy chair. "I had one of those dreams again, Dr. Stevens." When I had first started seeing Dr. Stevens, I often sat the entire session without saying more than two words. In a short time, though, I had begun to look forward to our weekly sessions. It was there, surrounded by medical textbooks, his sons' drawings hanging on the wall, and the worn carpet under my feet that I, encouraged by the gentle nature of my caring doctor, felt safe enough to share who I was. I liked the fact that Dr. Stevens didn't take notes or fall asleep He didn't push or probe for information. Instead, he gently encouraged me to talk about whatever was bothering me or whatever I felt most comfortable sharing. Many times, I sat silently as Dr. Stevens tried to verbalize the pain I struggled to share.

"And which dream is that, Cindy?" he asked now.

"Mary Jean came back and wanted to be my friend again." I stared at the carpet. "I woke up feeling so sad . . . it *hurt,* Dr. Stevens," I said in such a small, quiet voice that he strained forward to catch my words.

"Cindy, feelings can't hurt you."

My head snapped up. "Oh yes they can!" I declared firmly. "Feelings *can* hurt you! *My feelings hurt me!*" Why didn't he believe me? Nobody ever believed me! "Dr. Stevens, my feelings make me feel *sad.* And that *hurts!*"

Dr. Stevens sat for several minutes, his face thoughtful. "Cindy, I had never thought of it like that before. I think I understand what you mean. What you are telling me is that you are very, very sad and it's those sad feelings that are so painful for you."

I nodded my head vigorously. *Oh, he did understand!* "Dr. Stevens, the sadness feels like it's going to choke me . . . and kill me."

"Cindy, I hear you and I believe you." He smiled gently. "So, have you ever tried to get in touch with Mary Jean again?"

I shook my head. "I couldn't do that."

Dr. Stevens furrowed his brows, puzzled. After all, I had been dreaming about my old friends coming back for quite a while. This had not been the first time I mentioned dreaming of them. "Why not, Cindy? What are you afraid of?"

I watched him wearily, and huddled deeper into the large, overstuffed chair. "I'm not afraid. You don't understand. When I am thin, I'll be okay."

"I see. Well, maybe you would feel more comfortable calling Sandy? Or what about Diane, your old college roommate?" Dr. Stevens persisted. "I know you had invited her to your wedding."

I glanced out the window. "I have to get better *first*. When

I'm better, *then* I'll call my friends." Anorexia had sent people away. When it was gone, they would come back. Out of the corner of my eye, I watched a concerned look cross his face and knew that my message had come across loud and clear. "You know, Dr. Stevens," I said, as I stared out the window, "someday I'm going to be somebody. And I'm going to have *tons* of friends."

Dr. Stevens swallowed hard, the reflection of my pain in his eyes. "Oh, I see. But Cindy," he continued gently, "you *are* somebody right now. You are a *good person*. You are someone who has so much to offer to people. Do you understand that? The way you are right now is okay. Even if you are to always stay exactly this way, you will *still* be okay. You don't have to get better just so people will like you. Don't you see that you are not responsible for the way people behave or think. I want you to know that if you were never to get better, and I don't believe that you *won't,* I will always be your friend. Do you hear me?"

A *friend. Dr. Stevens would always be a friend.*

"Cindy, what else makes you sad?" he asked.

"Dr. Stevens, sometimes *I . . . I . . . really* miss my dog." My bottom lip quivered. "I wish *so* much that he were still alive."

"Cindy, tell me about your dog."

"He was my best friend, and I killed him," I admitted. I looked down at the muted threads of the carpet. "And I never told anyone that it was my fault Buttons died," I added quietly. *Oh, God! Dr. Stevens must think I'm a terrible* person *for killing my dog.* Afraid of his judgment, I raised my head and met his tear-filled eyes. "Why are *you* crying?" I demanded angrily. "He was *my* dog, not yours!" His emotions confused me. Buttons' death was my pain, not his!

Dr. Stevens looked at my skinny, little body sitting defensively in its favorite soft cushioned chair. "I'm sorry if I upset you, but that is a sad story, Cindy. Tears are an expression of my feelings. Don't you cry when you are sad?"

I gripped the chair's armrests and shook my head from side to side. "Never. I don't cry," I answered crisply.

Dr. Stevens was puzzled. "What do you mean, you don't cry?"

"I don't have any tears . . . so I don't cry." I replied matter-of-factly. With those words, I rose from my chair and headed towards the door. I could not have made it any clearer—the discussion was over. Dr. Stevens called out to my departing back, reminding me that he had to reschedule our next session.

At home, later that evening, I whipped up a batch of chocolate-chip cookies—32 of them—and devoured each one. I leaned over the toilet, my hands firmly pressed against my abdomen, and vomited up the chocolate gooey lump in my stomach. I rinsed the bitter taste out of my mouth and met my gaunt, pasty reflection in the bathroom mirror. *Somebody, someday, somehow.*

Chapter 12

Perceptions of Reality

Anorexia was my parents' focus as long as I had remained their sick child at home. Moving out on my own removed that convenient distraction, and forced them to confront their crumbling relationship. No longer could they deny what anorexia had helped them ignore for several years—their marriage was in trouble. In a last-ditch effort to save their marriage, they decided that selling our family home would provide a new environment and possibly, a different perspective. Sort of the same reason I moved into an apartment. Guess we all believed our problems would be left behind.

The house sold in a matter of weeks, and Mom and Dad and Jonny moved from our big white colonial family home to a tiny two-bedroom apartment. The smaller place meant less room for storage, and as a result, most of my childhood dolls and toys were given or thrown away. No one even thought to ask if it was what I wanted.

While Mom and Dad packed up the house, and fought their battles, I continued to fight anorexia. But I wasn't winning. Depression and eating disorders went hand-in-hand. If one didn't land me in the hospital, the other one did. After one year in the apartment and for the eighth year in a row, I was hospitalized. Anger turned inward. That is what is said about depression. In the protective environment of the hospital, and with a broken piece of hand mirror, I slashed out at the one person I could be mad at: myself. After all, anger at others was not acceptable. *"Why, Cindy,"* Dad would say. *"I'm not going to talk to you if you are angry. You have to calm down first, then talk like an adult."* I was eight years old, too young to be an adult. But I had learned well. To be angry was to be wrong. Straightjacket, restraints, full-sheet, Thorazine. Dr. Stevens and the hospital staff worked around the clock to keep me safe from me. Three months later, they had.

It was a tough fight. Battle-scarred, but determined, I was discharged home. I returned to find our big white house sold, and Mom and Dad headed for divorce court. Jonny had already gone. He had moved down south to concentrate on his filming career. As soon as the divorce was final, Dad followed him.

And I stayed to pick up the pieces—a devastated Mom. I temporarily moved out of my apartment and in with her. She needed me. It was a role I willingly accepted. I gave her the love and reassurance she needed as she grieved the loss of thirty-two years of marriage, her home, and the family life she had loved. For six months, I poured my strength into her, furious with Dad for leaving us both.

In April, almost eight months after the divorce, Mom and I flew to Florida to visit Debbie and Hank. When we disembarked from the plane and stepped into the sunny, tropical air, I took a deep breath, and knew we had made the right decision. Here, in the land of blue skies, white-sand beaches, palm trees, and constant sunshine, *surely* everything would be better.

Debbie and Hank were wonderful hosts. And we thoroughly enjoyed our first visit in over two years. Mom, Debbie, and I laughed and talked for hours, went sightseeing, and shopping. "I can't believe that you came to Florida without a bathing suit, Cindy!" Debbie joked. "Anyway, you came to the right place to buy one. Every store here carries them."

We walked into a department store and headed toward the racks of bathing suits. Laughing, we loaded our arms and searched for the dressing rooms. Debbie and I entered a small cubicle and closed its curtains. Debbie stripped off her clothes and stepped into one of the many suits she had carried in. "This is fun. I know I don't really need a suit but . . . as long as you're trying some on, I think I will too."

I removed my shorts and cotton T-shirt a bit more apprehensively. It had been many years since Debbie had been exposed to my body. I slipped on a pretty, dark-blue tank suit. *"Ohh* . . . I like this one, Deb. What do you think? Is blue my color?" I preened in front of the full-length mirror.

Debbie's eyes widened as I unconsciously displayed my cadaverous body. "Cindy, that's a pretty suit. Why don't you try on some others. I'll be right back." She turned and ran out of the room.

I opened the curtain and peeked out. "Mom, she looks terrible!" Debbie sobbed into my mother's arms. "She's skin and bones. She's deteriorating right in front of us! All I see are ribs! I can count her vertebrae! She looks like one of those starving children I see on television commercials, but this is worse—*she's my sister!"*

"Debbie, your sister is very ill. We have taken her to every specialist we could think of. All we can do now is let her know that we love her. Maybe, honey, you might try talking to her about how you feel."

"She doesn't listen to me, Mom! I've tried . . . for years! Why Mom? Why is Cindy doing this to herself? What if she dies?"

"Honey, I don't know what to do anymore. I don't understand either. I guess the best we can do is just to keep hoping . . . and praying . . . that God will keep her safe . . . and alive," Mom answered sadly.

Debbie's sobs lessened, but her tears continued to fall. "Mom, I'd rather see Cindy be a *whore* than live her life like this!"

"Deborah Lee! How can you say such a terrible thing?" Mom was horrified.

"Because a whore is the lowest life I believe there is. Cindy's life is even lower than that! Her life is just hospitals and doctors. She's just existing, Mom!"

I closed the curtain and stood in front of the mirror. *What did Debbie mean?* No dangling skin on my arms or legs. My thighs were solid, my stomach flat, my breasts were tiny buds of firmness. *Why, I looked pretty good!*

I bought the blue bathing suit. It was definitely my color.

After two weeks with Debbie and Hank, it was time to head on to Ft. Lauderdale to visit Jonny, where he was living and attending college. With much reluctance and many tears, we bid farewell and proceeded on to the next part of our vacation. We were to stay at Jon's one-bedroom bungalow not far from Ft. Lauderdale beach. It might not have been too bad if Jon didn't also have a roommate—Dad. It was too soon to be together again. The divorce was still fresh in all our minds, and none of us had yet adjusted to our new family status.

Four people in one cramped, tiny living space proved to be tough. What was tougher—watching Mom and Dad flirt with each other. In a town where all their problems seemed to have happened in another time, it was too easy for them to escape the reality of our broken family.

I watched miserably as they walked the beach hand-in-hand, acting as if the last several months hadn't happened at all. Nobody acknowledged the problems or pain we had all endured. As if we were still connected—just one, big happy family on vacation.

But we weren't.

And I couldn't pretend any longer. Not after all those earlier years of explaining to Mom why Dad went out at night, or why he thought she should be able to work all day and wax the kitchen floor at night. Or that Dad's nightly outings were because of his illness, and not because of mine. While at the same time, Dad made me his confidant in an attempt to justify his own uncomfortable feelings. And I, especially, couldn't forget the past several months that I had comforted Mom, and he had not. It was a role I had played silently, though willingly, and it had come with a price. And I paid dearly. Watching them act now as if nothing had ever gone wrong, all I could feel was—betrayed.

The anger started deep, in the pit of my stomach, and it grew larger and larger, like a burning fire, out of control, until it nearly smothered me. And I *had* to visit every restaurant, every fast-food place, and every deli around Ft. Lauderdale. It was the only way I could survive the boiling rage inside. I ordered huge quantities of food, ate everything on my plate, and then vomited it all out in the privacy of the restaurant restrooms. Over and over again. For hours. Exhausted, I returned to the bungalow shortly before Mom, Dad, and Jonny got back from the beach. Nobody asked about my afternoon activity but instead, discussed what movie we should see. It was our last evening before Mom and I flew back home in the morning.

I changed into a pair of jeans and a long sleeve blouse. In spite of the warm Florida temperature, I was cold. "Cindy? Can Dad and I ask you something?" Mom knocked on the bathroom door. She and Dad both approached me—almost apologetically—with the proposal that the three of us drive back to Syracuse—together.

"Mom, you can drive back with him if that is what you want to do, but I'm flying home as planned," I spat out disgustedly. For the first time, I said no and I didn't care who hated me.

In the end, Dad drove back, alone, and we took our scheduled flight, which was delayed on take-off, causing us to miss our connection in Philadelphia. We had a nine hour wait before the next available flight would leave. Mom, still miffed at our not driving back with Dad, found the delay even more aggravating. In her eyes, it was all my fault.

Tired and hungry, we walked toward the airport coffee shop. I dragged my weary body alongside Mom. The last several days had totally drained me. Mom looked at me, and shook her head, disgusted at what she saw—a skinny, sickly-looking person, responsible for her being stuck in this strange city. She stopped in mid-stride. "You look terrible!" she yelled. "You are so selfish! You only think of yourself! I don't know why you're going to bother to eat, you are only going to puke it up anyway!"

My face reddened, and passersby stared at us. Embarrassed, I attempted to walk in the opposite direction but exhaustion from the visit, the delay, lugging a very heavy suitcase, and my poor physical condition, prevented any success. And Mom stood there screaming, informing the world of my lazy, stupid, and selfish ways.

But mostly, she accused me of being sick.

I reeled under her torrid stream of words. *Dr. Stevens. I have to call Dr. Stevens.* I headed for the nearest row of telephones.

"Go ahead!" she yelled after me. "Call Dr. Stevens. *You can't even think for yourself.* Go ahead! Tell him, see if I care!"

My fingers shook, barely able to dial the number I knew by heart. "Dr. Stevens!" I blurted out when his secretary put my call through. "I'm never coming home! I hate her so much! I didn't do anything wrong. She won't leave me alone!"

Dr. Stevens listened while I relayed the events. "Don't listen to what she is saying," he said calmly. "Your mother is very angry and is taking it out on you. Cindy, you're okay. You don't deserve to be treated like that. You are not doing anything wrong. I'm sorry that I am so far away, as there is not much I can do from here. I do want you to come and see me when you're back home. Okay?"

"Okay. I'll be there." *I hadn't done anything wrong.* I hung up the phone and walked back to Mom, who sat in the coffee shop. I approached her cautiously, not sure if she would lash out again.

Her anger spent, Mom sat quietly in a chair. "Honey, I'm sorry," she apologized sheepishly, a cup of coffee cooling in front of her. I slid into the seat across from her. "I shouldn't have said those things to you. That was wrong of me to do that. You know I love you. Let's forget what happened, okay?" She got up and came over to put her arms around me, and gave me a long, hard hug.

My anger dissolved. I needed her love, her acceptance. This time, with our arms around each other, we walked back out into the terminal, and stopped at the airport gift shop. I browsed through a rack of T-shirts and found the perfect souvenir for our trip. I paid for the shirt and slipped it on over the one I wore. Grinning broadly, I walked out into the terminal. Scrawled across the front of my chest was the message—*"I'm Madder Than Hell and I'm Not Going To Take It Anymore!"*

Chapter 13

Obsession Lesson

The vacation had taken a toll on my health. Over the following weeks, I experienced a new set of puzzling symptoms: a tremendous pressure in the middle of my chest, a strange clenching around my heart, and sharp pains that shot down my left arm. Worse—my lips would go numb. The symptoms came with a frightening regularity and I did what came naturally—I ignored them, and worried only about the number on the scale each morning.

My parents, their relationship now re-established, made plans to re-marry. During my sessions with Dr. Stevens, he explained that their actions and their feelings were their own. He said it wasn't my responsibility, or my role, to keep everyone happy.

"Dr. Stevens, I understand what you're saying, but I still feel so guilty that everyone except me is happy over my mom and dad getting married. I know I should be happy to be a family again, but it just doesn't *feel* right to me!" Exhausted, I sank back in the gold chair, my frail body gratefully cushioned by the thickly padded seat and back. With the fading of my Florida tan, the sick yellow pallor of my skin was much more obvious.

"I *do* want to be happy for them, but . . . I don't *feel* happy. I just feel so . . . so . . . *confused!*" I worried. "You'd think that I would *want* my parents together, and for us to be a family."

Dr. Stevens studied my face and carefully chose his words. "Cindy, I know that you love your family very much. But you need to trust your feelings. You doubt yourself so much, and you always question your feelings . . . as if the way you *feel* couldn't possibly be right. But, Cindy, you *are* a person who feels, and your feelings are giving you a message. Sometimes that message is a happy one and sometimes it's not. A feeling doesn't have to just be a *good* one in order to be right. Feeling sad is as okay as feeling happy. Do you understand that *all* feelings are acceptable? If this situation feels uncomfortable for you, it probably is. There is nothing wrong with wanting what is best for your parents. But it is their life and their decision as to what they will do. Whether they are making a mistake or not, it is up to them to decide . . . not you. Maybe this will be the best decision for them, or maybe it will be the worst mistake of their lives. But *you* don't need to decide that. You need to focus on what is right for you. You can't change others, but you *can* change the way you react or respond to them." He smiled gently. "After all, if your parents could make *you* get better, don't you think they would have by now?"

I sighed heavily. "Dr. Stevens, I love my mom and dad *very much*. It's just that I . . . I . . . *hate* them too . . . sometimes. Dr. Stevens?" I searched his face for reassurance. "Does it make me a bad person to say that I hate my parents? I mean, they have sacrificed so much of their lives for me. I *do* love them. And I know they have tried to do *everything* in their power to help me. It's just that I get so . . . so . . . *mad.* . . ."

"Cindy," Dr. Stevens interrupted gently. "It is said that there is a very fine line between love and hate. You can love people, and yet hate what they say or do. Your angry feelings don't mean that you don't love them. You can have both those feelings at the same time. It is perfectly normal—*and appropriate*—for you, or anyone else, to feel this way. That's because *all* feelings are okay.

As much as you'd like to believe otherwise, we don't live in a black and white world. Life is not *either or.*"

My chest clenched, and dull pains traveled down my left arm. I rubbed my arm and licked my numb lips.

"Are you feeling okay?" Dr. Stevens watched as I tried to make myself more comfortable.

"I'm a little cold, that's all," I hastened to reassure him. "Could you turn off the air-conditioner?"

"Cindy, it's only April. The air-conditioning is not on." Dr. Stevens was worried. "I am very concerned about you. You do not look well. My friend, you look like you have lost more weight to me."

"I didn't lose any more weight. I'm fine! *Really . . . I am!*" I sat up straight and gripped the arms of the chair. "I'll be okay. I'm just worried about my parents' wedding, that's all."

But over the next few days, the pressure in my chest, and the pain in my left arm did not go away. If anything, they came more often and more intensely. *Maybe something is wrong?* But I dismissed that disturbing thought and dressed for dinner. It was Mother's Day, and we were going out to a restaurant for dinner with some of my aunts and uncles. I zipped up the side of my skirt and it slid down below my hips. *Shit! Why don't my clothes fit me anymore?* I tried on several more outfits before settling on a nice pair of slacks, size 10, *girls* size 10. Nothing else fit. I stepped over the pile of clothes, and rubbed my chest. The pressure slowly subsided.

At the restaurant, I sat next to Dad and nibbled on the salad in front of me. *Do I just eat all of it, and then vomit? Or should I only eat a little?* My chest tightened, and I rubbed the area between my breasts, hoping no one would notice. The pressure deepened and I struggled to breathe. "Dad," I nudged my father's side. "Something's wrong," I whispered. "I think I'm . . . I'm going to pass out or something." The room started to spin. I blinked my eyes, and tried to focus.

Dad quickly put his arm around me. "Here, drink some of

my tomato juice, and take some deep breaths," he whispered back, not wanting to alarm the others.

I did. It didn't help.

"Do you want to go outside and get some fresh air? Do you want to go home?" Dad asked, not sure what else to do.

"No. I'll be okay. I'll just sit here until it passes." Dad kept his arm around me. Several moments later, the dizziness receded, and the heaviness in my chest let up. "Okay, I'm better now." He smiled, and returned his attention to the family dinner. And I decided to eat nothing.

The next morning I awakened early, having slept fitfully from being unable to get comfortable all night. I called Dr. Stevens' office and canceled that day's appointment. I moved listlessly around my apartment, unable to get comfortable all day either. *Why am I so tired? I don't even feel like eating. Is something wrong? Could these feelings be telling me something is wrong? Dr. Stevens says I have to learn to trust my feelings.* I called his office back. He answered his phone. "Dr. Stevens, I think something's not right. I don't feel very well. I'm just so . . . so . . . tired," my voice faded.

"Cindy, I think we better get you back into the hospital, *today,*" Dr. Stevens decided immediately, alarmed by my lethargic tone.

I called my dad and he agreed to drive me to Rochester. These hospitalizations had become a familiar pattern. I would probably gain some weight, be discharged, come home, lose more weight, and somewhere down the road be re-admitted again. The cycle of anorexia was predictable and never-ending.

Upon admission to the hospital psychiatric unit, I was given a physical exam and an electrocardiogram. The results were not good. I hadn't even had a chance to settle into my room before one of the unit nurses informed me that I was being transferred to the Cardiac Critical Care Unit. She immediately ushered me into a wheelchair. For the first time since calling Dr. Stevens, I felt utterly alone—and scared. Dad had already left for home.

"Jenny, why do I have to go to another floor?" I asked as she rushed me through the hospital corridors. This didn't make any sense. For the past four years, Dr. Stevens had always admitted me to the same unit and staff.

"Cindy, you are *very, very* sick. Your test results were not good. We can't give you the medical care you need right now. Hopefully, you won't have to be in ICU more than a few days. You will come back to our unit when you are better."

Very sick? I frowned. What did that mean? Why did everyone keep saying I was very sick? It didn't make any sense. I was just tired, that was all.

Or maybe I had been sick so long, that I no longer knew what it meant to be well.

Jenny wheeled me into one of the spacious ICU cubicles and stood aside. The ICU nurses helped me out of the wheelchair, out of my clothes, and into a hospital gown. Intravenous lines were inserted into my right arm and heart monitor electrodes were taped to my chest. Only then, could Jenny lean over to hug me through the tangle of lines. "I promise to see you soon, Cindy." In minutes she was gone. I grabbed my little stuffed tiger, Whiskers, as the nurses gathered up my belongings to be sent downstairs to storage. "Please," I asked, my voice small, "may I keep him with me?" Grandma had given him to me when I was only seven years old. He had been by my side for every hospitalization. At twenty-six—*almost* twenty-seven—years of age, I clung to him as fiercely as I had as a young child. The nurses left with my clothes, and I, with Whiskers safely in my arms, settled back in bed and closed my eyes.

I opened my sleep-laden eyes slowly and struggled to focus on the figure by my bedside. It was Dr. Stevens.

"Hi, my friend," he said softly. "How are you doing?"

"Dr. Stevens?" I asked drowsily. "Am I going to die?" Maybe it was because I was half-asleep. Or maybe it was because I couldn't find the energy to open my eyes all the way. Or maybe it was be-

151

cause, for the first time since taken ill, the thought of dying from anorexia crossed my mind. After all, anorexia had always been my strength, not my weakness. Even in Boston, when the doctors said I was close to death, I didn't believe them. Even when Mom and Dad pleaded with me to eat, terrified by my deteriorating body, I never believed I would die. Even when anorexia robbed my energy, my stamina, and my health, I never believed it.

Maybe because, for the first time, it had finally occurred to me, I *could* die.

Dr. Stevens took my hand, squeezed it, and looked firmly into my frightened eyes. "Cindy, we're going to try and not *let* you die." I smiled, and closed my eyes, reassured. Dr. Stevens wasn't going to let me die.

Sadly, I did not realize that Dr. Stevens had to choose his words carefully. He did not want to scare me more than I already was. For the first time in the four years he had been treating me, it looked like I was about to lose my battle with anorexia. The EKG had shown a disturbing pattern of angina—I was not getting enough blood to my heart muscle. My lab workup had shown a potassium level of 1.9. The ICU doctors could not understand why I had not gone into cardiac arrest. The nature of my symptoms said heart attack. And the status of my vital signs said I should already be dead. Yet there I was, still alive, but in critical condition.

My eyes flew back open. "Dr. Stevens? Are my parents coming to see me?"

Dr. Stevens shook his head. "I called to let them know that you are in the ICU. They wanted to come right up, but I told them it was better if they waited. Right now, you need rest. They said to tell you that they love you, and that they will come up when you're back on the other unit." What he didn't explain was the critical importance of keeping me calm. Angina is worsened by physical and emotional stress. My parents' tumultuous relationship was clearly one of the most stressful events going on in my life, and, therefore, not worth the risk of getting me upset. He remained in constant phone contact with them, and, if things took a turn for the worse, he would never keep them from my side. My parents had come to respect Dr. Stevens' advice, and they agreed to wait. If staying away was best, then that was what they would do.

The staff worked hard to stabilize my medical condition, and I worried about how to eat without vomiting. Even though my earlier question to Dr. Stevens indicated I knew I could die, I was more fearful of not being able to purge. Sadly, I no longer knew how to eat any other way.

"Cindy, would you like to try some dinner?" The unit nurse set the tray down and propped me up amidst all the wires. I lifted the cover off the dinner plate and sniffed its teasing aromas. My stomach growled. *God, I'm so hungry! Maybe I can have just a little taste.* I unwrapped a fork and poked at the meatloaf. The fragrant smell of hot-cooked beef permeated the air. My resistance crumbled. I shoveled the meatloaf, mashed potatoes and gravy, green beans, dinner roll with two pats of butter, milk, and the chocolate pudding into my mouth until every morsel, every crumb was gone.

Stuffed, I laid down the fork and relaxed against my pillow. *Oh my God! What did I just do?* The calories were adding pounds, as I lay imprisoned in bed! My body was hideously spreading as of that moment. I could feel it! How could I have eaten all that food? I had to get rid of it! My eyes darted frantically around the little cubicle and lit upon a blue plastic basin. I grabbed it and threw up into the bedpan. The wrenching movements set off my heart monitor alarms, and within seconds, the medical staff came running from all directions. They slowed down when they spotted my small body hunched over the plastic basin. There was no question in anyone's mind as to what had happened. Pale and shaking, I looked up at them. "It wouldn't stay down," I announced in a soft, squeaky voice. "It just wouldn't stay down."

After that vomiting episode, I was allowed nothing heavier than liquids. The vomiting had further stressed my heart and depleted more potassium from my body. Removing food had just solved my problem of how to eat. If I couldn't eat, I couldn't vomit. The doctors added another IV line to my left arm. They needed to administer more potassium and other life-saving fluids. Time was not on my side.

Two more days passed before my potassium rose to a normal level, the electrical imbalances of my heartbeat had converted to a normal rhythm, and blood, once again, was being efficiently pumped through my heart muscles. The medical crisis was over. The IVs and heart monitor were removed and my clothes were returned. I was ready to be transferred back to the other unit.

I gratefully exchanged the hospital gown for my jeans and struggled to pull the denim material over my hips. *Why can't I get my jeans on?* I stood up and inadvertently glanced into the little mirror above the cubicle sink as I tugged, unsuccessfully, on my jeans. A bloated, swollen face stared back. What happened? *Why is my face so fat? I hadn't eaten anything!* But it had nothing to do with eating. It had everything to do with my long struggle with anorexia. Malnutrition and heart problems were not the only side effects of that battle. Anorexia had interfered with normal kidney functions. With my heart unable to properly circulate the IV fluids, my kidneys became ineffective in ridding those fluids from my body. As a result, the retained fluid added another medical complication: edema. And the edema added another dilemma to the anorexia: twenty pounds of fluid weight.

Bloated and uncomfortable, I returned to the psychiatric unit to recover from this latest brush with death. Even though Dr. Stevens and the nursing staff explained the weight would disappear as my body stabilized, I was convinced only that my body had failed me, I was fat. The fluid caused daily fluctuations of my weight, which made it impossible to deal with anorexia in a behavioral way. I was thrilled to not have to worry about a weight program, but it wasn't as joyous as I would have preferred. My legs were so painfully swollen and large, I was forced to rely on a wheelchair to move around. I suffered short-term memory difficulties, due to the retained fluid in my brain, and struggled to remember things that were being said or done. I cried constantly over the littlest things, and Dr. Stevens explained that the edema was responsible for this lack of control over emotions. But the confusion was the worst. My brain felt swathed in layers of cotton. Each day, I struggled in vain to see through the cotton fibers, and tried to make sense of what was going on. Frustrated, crying, unable to walk, I was out of danger as far as dying, but I had a long way to go before treatment could even begin for anorexia.

Five long weeks passed before my body settled at a weight of 68 pounds. Once again, I was placed on a behavior program. Four months later, I reached a goal weight of 86 pounds.

The latest crisis faded into the background, as Mom and Dad went ahead with their re-marriage plans. I still had reservations about the success of their union, but I did not butt in. Dr. Stevens had worked hard to get me to accept that they were in charge of their life, and that I was in charge of mine.

It was a lesson that was taking me a long time to learn.

Chapter 14

Beautiful Butterfly, Fly Away Free

I stood in front of the frozen food case of the local supermarket, looked to my left and then to my right. Nobody was in the aisle. Quickly, I slipped a couple of frozen macaroni and cheese dinners into a green plastic shopping bag that I had placed in the kiddy seat of a shopping cart. I pushed the cart over to the bread aisle, and added a loaf of whole-wheat bread to the box of dry pasta, a box of Rice Krispies, a half-gallon of 2% milk, a box of Oreo cookies, and a bag of barbecue potato chips that were already in the cart. I made my way over to the checkout counter and unloaded the groceries, but held onto the green shopping bag. The cashier rang-up the items, and wished me a nice day. I wrote out a check, smiled a bit nervously, picked up the two grocery bags, and walked out of the store. I stuffed the bags in the front basket of my bike and headed back home, the green bag still clutched firmly in my hand. "I'm not a bad person, I'm not a bad person, I'm not a bad person," I repeated over and over, and looked over my shoulder as I peddled home.

Once at home, I emptied the bags and immediately plunged into cooking up my usual large quantities of food. Several hours later, I had successfully emptied my stomach, my just-stocked cupboard, and all my thoughts.

The following morning, Dad picked me up at seven o'clock and took me to the Greyhound Bus station. I was silent as we drove the short distance from my apartment. It was a gray day, and when Dad pulled up in front of the station, I reached for my umbrella.

"Pocahontas? Can I kiss the tip of your nose?" Dad asked, smiling. Though he and Mom had remarried shortly before Christmas, a month later, they had divorced again. Unlike their previous breakup, I was trying hard to heed Dr. Stevens' advice and stay far away from their issues.

I leaned forward to receive Dad's affectionate good-bye, and then scrambled out of the car and waved as his car disappeared into the early morning traffic. A half-hour later, I boarded the Greyhound bus and settled myself in the front seat.

"Would it be okay if my daughter, Annie, sits with you?" I looked up to find a strange woman smiling down at me, a young girl held tightly onto her hand. "She's meeting her father in Rochester, and I would feel more comfortable if she didn't have to ride alone."

"Sure, that's okay," I replied. I moved my jacket out of her way and went back to staring out the window.

"Hi. My name is Annie. I'm ten years old. How old are you?"

Startled out of my reverie, I looked over at my bus companion. She was a stranger. I'd never see her again. And with a current weight of 75 pounds, I probably weighed less than she. "Twelve," I lied. We chatted the entire trip to Rochester. I told her I lived in a big white house with my sister, my brother, *both* parents, and my dog, Buttons. We parted ways upon arriving at the Rochester bus terminal and I, reluctantly, went back to being twenty-seven. I boarded a local bus for the rest of my trip and arrived at Dr. Stevens' office ten minutes before our scheduled appointment. I waved hello to Julie, and wandered over to the children's play area, and sat down at the small wooden table in the middle of the room to color in one of the coloring books.

"Cindy, Dr. Stevens said to go on down to his office," Julie called out.

I walked down to his office. "Hi, Dr. Stevens," I greeted him pleasantly, and headed for my usual seat, but stopped abruptly—*the gold chair was gone!* "Dr. Stevens! What happened to my chair?"

"Cindy, that chair was pretty old. One of its legs has been unsteady for quite some time now. I can't take the chance of one of my patients getting hurt. There are plenty of other chairs here that you can sit on."

I reluctantly sat down on the hard, wooden, straight-backed chair he offered. "But it was so soft, and I liked it!" I protested. Even though the chair had played an inanimate role in our sessions, I had become used to curling up into its deep cushions. Whenever our sessions headed toward a scary subject, I felt safer talking from within the protective arms of that gold chair. Its absence now was just one more reminder that life was unpredictable. That you couldn't count on *anything*. "I suppose you get rid of your patients when they get old too!" I sulked.

Dr. Stevens burst out laughing. *"My* . . . you are not happy with me today, are you?"

"I don't know why you had to get rid of *my* chair!" I shifted uneasily and folded my left leg up underneath me in an effort to cushion my tailbone. With no fat to protect that bony protrusion, sitting had become a very real and painful problem. The layers of clothes I wore were more successful at hiding my thinness than they were at padding it.

The threatening sky outside let loose and rain pounded against the office windowpanes. The day's dreariness matched my mood. "Dr. Stevens, sometimes I get so tired of fighting and . . . I'm scared that it's . . . *this* . . . is never going to end." I declared mournfully. "I . . . I don't know how to describe it. I guess it's kind of like . . . like . . . an *undercurrent* of sadness. Yes, that's what it feels like." I struggled to sit comfortably, but the wooden chair was not as forgiving as its predecessor was. "It never ends, Dr. Stevens. It just constantly flows—right through my body." I paused, and listened to the words inside my head. "Even though I've been taking Sinequan since I was twenty years old, the sadness just doesn't go away . . . except when Rob and I were first engaged. I was happy then." I looked at Dr. Stevens. "Do you think I'll ever be free of anorexia?"

Dr. Stevens sat back thoughtfully. It wasn't often that I shared my feelings so easily, so freely. "Cindy," he answered, "you are like a caterpillar in a cocoon. Your anorexia has wrapped itself around your feelings and hidden who you are. But, yes, someday, you *will* be free. Just like a caterpillar. You will break free from this anorexic cocoon and become a beautiful butterfly to soar among the clouds."

"Dr. Stevens?" My lips trembled. "I wish I could be like that right now. Be beautiful. And I wish I could have just a *little* of what other people have." I smiled sadly. "Friends . . . a home. I don't think you . . . or anyone . . . *really* know how awful . . . how lonely . . . anorexia is. I think people believe I *want* to be like this. But I don't." If he could just understand that the captivating music of thin was so hard to resist, so hard to walk away from.

Dr. Stevens nodded, and leaned forward in his chair. "Cindy, I believe I *do* understand how awful it is because you tell me. There is so much more to you than the anorexia you struggle with—I know that, but I'm not sure if *you* know it. Sometimes, no matter how much we try, we can't force things to happen. When you are ready to see you, to look at those scary feelings, I will be here to listen. Lucky for you," he added teasingly, "I'm a patient man."

The room grew dark as the rain beat against the windows. I watched Dr. Stevens out of the corner of my eye, his face, warm and compassionate. His eyes, behind his brown wire-rimmed glasses, were caring and sincere. I took a deep breath. "Dr. Stevens? Sometimes I don't believe anybody could *ever* love me forever."

There, I had admitted it. I was unlovable.

Dr. Stevens smiled. "Oh? And what makes you believe that, Cindy? Because I know a lot of people who do love you. Your family, the nurses, and the other staff here at the hospital. We all care about you. *Why* . . . people are always stopping me in the corridors and asking how you are doing. I've never had anyone do that about a patient of mine before."

I sighed impatiently. "I know my family loves me, Dr. Stevens. And I know that the nursing staff likes me. That's not what I mean." I took a deep breath and tried again. "I'm talking about *love*. I don't think *anyone* could *ever* love me *forever!*"

"But, why do you believe that?"

"Because nobody has," I answered bluntly. "I'm all alone. I'm twenty-seven years old. I can't work. I can't go to school. I can't do *anything!* I'm just a . . . *nobody!* Besides, look at all the people who've left me," I argued. "Look at my parents. They were married thirty-two years and they didn't last forever!"

"Cindy, do you realize that you started out this session being angry at me, then you started talking about your sadness, and ended up talking about your parent's divorce?" I nodded. He smiled gently. "Don't you see that you are truly angry at your parents *and* at all those people who have left you. Do you see the connection between your feelings and what has happened to you?"

I shook my head. "But Dr. Stevens, I *hate* my *body!*"

It was Dr. Stevens' turn to sigh. Our sessions always ended, inevitably, back on my weight. Yet one small, tiny step at a time, I attempted to share my feelings and the issues behind them. Though I wouldn't admit it, Dr. Stevens' words did make sense. I *did* feel angry with all those people. I just wasn't sure what to do about it.

I wasn't ready to fly away but, *maybe,* I was starting to emerge.

Over the next six months, Dr. Stevens continued to patiently encourage these budding feelings and I, to tentatively acknowledge them. Still, anorexia's obsessive grip did not lessen.

Once again, dealing with the feelings behind anorexia sent my weight plummeting. And, once again, I backslid into trouble as the familiar twinges in my chest returned. At 72 pounds, I remained trapped in the deceptive web of anorexia. Blinded by the success of its ability to deaden thoughts and feelings, I also remained blind to its ability to destroy health.

A flu-bug knocked me off my feet for several days. My woozy stomach became unable to tolerate little more than tea and ginger ale. One evening, Dad stopped by to visit and brought with him, a quart of ice cream. I curled up on the couch, my legs wrapped in an afghan, and swallowed a spoonful of the frozen dessert, its cold consistency soothed my raw throat. For the first time in over eight years, I allowed myself to eat without thinking about when, and how, to throw it up. "Fudge ripple, my favorite," I rasped. "I loved this when I was little, remember?"

Dad chuckled and sat down beside me, his own bowl of ice cream in his hands. "Pocahontas, you were the sweetest little girl. Sometimes when you were sick, you'd look at me with those big brown eyes and my heart would just melt. You'd look at me as if to say, 'Daddy, I hurt. Make me better.' And I'd do anything to make you better. Do you remember that one time . . . I think you were around seven . . . you were quite ill with a terrible flu. . . ."

"Like now?" I interrupted.

"Like now. And you wanted some grape juice late at night? We didn't have any. But I found a store that was open and bought some for you."

"And you came into my room a short time after I had asked for the juice and gave it to me," I continued. "I remember thinking, 'It's the middle of the night and stores are closed, yet my daddy got me the juice I wanted.' You were a hero to me that night, Dad." I savored the picture our words resurrected. "Do you remember how I used to love to stay home when I was sick, and I couldn't go to school? As soon as everyone left, I would get out my dolls and play." I grinned slyly. "Or maybe you didn't *know* that I was playing when I was supposed to be in bed resting." We laughed together at that childhood innocence and my mischievous ways.

"Oh, Cindy!" he groaned. "You were always getting into some predicament. If you weren't roughhousing with your sister and brother, you were climbing fences, or trees. It was so hard for me to be mad at you. Even when you'd do something naughty, I had a hard time disciplining you." Dad was thoughtful for a moment. "There was always something special about you. You had such a unique quality about you. Your mom and I had more people say to us, *'There's something special about Cindy.'*" He smiled. "And there still is. I've always believed that."

The silence between us was comfortable. I ate another spoonful of ice cream. "Dad . . . do you think I'll ever get better?"

The question caught him off-guard. He hesitated, then reached over and wrapped his strong, protective arms around my frail frame. "Yes, Pocahontas," he answered huskily, "you *are* going to get better."

"But *when*, Daddy? When is it going to get better? Because, sometimes, I'm so scared that I'm going to die before I even have a chance to live!" Anorexia's battle was twelve years long. I needed my daddy to make everything okay, just as he had done when I was a little girl. But my daddy couldn't. This disorder was bigger than both of us. "Daddy . . . why is God doing this to me?"

His hazel eyes saddened. "Pocahontas, God doesn't work like that. He isn't *doing* this to you. God loves you as much as he loves all of us. I don't know, sweetheart, why you are suffering so much. But maybe God has a very special plan for you, and we just don't know what it is yet. Do you know that your mother, your brother, your sister, and I pray for you every night? We all want for you to be well. We want it more than anything else in our lives. Someday, I believe that this will all be behind you, and your life will be a healthy and happy one again."

But it wasn't going to happen any time soon. I had a hard time recovering from the flu. Even my appointments with Dr.

Stevens had to be put on hold, as I was no longer strong enough to travel to Rochester. A public health nurse visited daily, and brought hot chicken soup and baked chicken breasts, her efforts to get nutrients into my weakened body. After another week of no improvement, she and Dr. Stevens both agreed that another hospital admission was necessary. Once again, Dad drove the all-too-familiar route to Rochester. I was not admitted to the intensive care unit, but my health was, nonetheless, extremely poor. The chest twinges were constant reminders that I *could* die if I did not change my ways.

After another three months, my health stabilized. This time, it was Mom and her new boyfriend, Dick, of six months who brought me home. It was on our way back to Syracuse, that she shared their decision to marry, and informed me of Jonny's upcoming move to New York City.

I sat in the back seat and mulled over the latest developments in our family—or rather, what was left of our family. Dad was building his own life as a single man, Mom was getting married to a stranger, and Jonny was taking off for another city.

In just one week after leaving the hospital, I was back at Dr. Stevens', this time with a packed suitcase. I dragged it into his office, deposited it next to my chair, and sat down. "I'm going to Florida," I announced.

Dr. Stevens' eyes traveled from the suitcase, to my folded arms across my chest, to the determined line of my mouth. Though it was quite obvious, he teased, "are you running away from home?"

"I'm going to Florida," I repeated sternly, "and I came to say good-bye." Dr. Stevens' twinkling eyes exasperated me. I was desperate! Couldn't he see that?

"I see. Does this mean you aren't going to come see me anymore?"

Oh! He infuriated me! I clenched the handle of my suitcase tighter. He was not taking me seriously. I was *terribly upset* over the recent scattering of my family. Everyone was involved in their own lives, and they didn't care about me. In the few days I had been home, I had binged and vomited nonstop. Dr. Stevens *had* to know me well enough to see that something was *horribly* wrong.

Dr. Stevens sat back, and his chair creaked slightly. He studied my face. "Cindy, I can't let you go."

My grip loosened. "I'm going to go to Florida to . . . to live with my sister," I insisted weakly.

"Does your sister know that you are coming?"

"N-*n*-no."

"Cindy, I think that you must be feeling pretty scared right now. I know how much you love your family. There are a lot of changes going on, more than you're able to cope with. And that's okay. However, I can't let you go to Florida, but I do think you should come back into the hospital."

Within an hour, I was admitted back into the hospital. I weighed in at 76 pounds. In the one week I had been home, I had lost ten pounds. Dr. Stevens and I both agreed that the anorexia would need to be furthered addressed. But over the next few months, I fought him, the staff, and refused to let go of that control. As much as I wanted to give up anorexia, I was more terrified to be rid of it. It kept me strong. It helped me get through. It was who I was. Without it, I would have nothing . . . do nothing . . . be nothing.

In November, Mom and Dick were married—without me. I was still in the hospital. On the morning of their wedding day, I awakened early. "God, I don't want Mom to get married. *Please,* don't let her get married." I hugged my little stuffed tiger, and huddled under the white hospital blankets. A knock came on the door, and one of the night nurses stuck her head into the room. "Cindy, time to get weighed," she announced cheerfully.

I grumbled and reluctantly climbed out of bed. I hated morning weigh-ins. The worst part of the behavior program was trying to figure out how much to eat and how much to vomit. It had become purely a guessing game. I usually ended up devouring huge quantities of food and then vomiting. The weight that showed up on the scale was courtesy of paper-wrapped rolls of pennies tied around my waist.

After all, there was just no way I could *really* gain weight.

I walked into the examination room and stepped onto the scale. I watched nervously while the nurse balanced the weights. "Sorry, Cindy. You are just under where you need to be today," she apologized.

"Shit!" I cursed under my breath. That meant no phone calls, no mail, no activities off the floor, and getting my door locked for one hour after meals. During my last admission, the staff had finally figured out it was more stressful for me to be locked *out* of my room than in it. That was because, unbeknownst to them, I secretly binged and vomited while in my room (each room had its own bathroom). Even in the hospital, while on a program to change my eating behavior, and being watched constantly (room checks every half-hour), anorexia flourished.

After breakfast, my door was locked and I innocently wandered down the hall. In as nonchalant of a manner that I could muster, I approached a pay phone located at the end of the long hallway. I glanced up and down the corridor, and then quickly dialed my mother's house. "Mom," I whispered hoarsely, when she answered at the other end. "Please, don't get married! Please, please don't get married, Mom." A nurse, Jenny, hurried towards me. *"Mom,"* I wailed, *"please, don't get married!"* With one eye on Jenny, I screamed into the phone, *"they won't let me talk to you, Mom! Mommy! I love you, Mom!"* I hung up as Jenny reached me. "My mom is getting married today! I had to talk to her!" I yelled, and burst into tears.

Jenny led me back to my room. We sat down on the bed and she hugged me, giving me the comfort I longed for from my own mother. "Cindy," she said soothingly, "I was going to let you talk to your mother. It was okay. We know that she's getting married today. We would have let you talk to her." And the tears I had courageously hidden for so long, flowed freely. The little girl, who believed she had no tears, had them once more.

In spite of my pleas, Mom married and moved into Dick's house, Jonny moved to New York City, Dad moved somewhere, and I moved into the hospital. I spent not only my twenty-eighth birthday there, but also Thanksgiving, Christmas, and Easter. Was everyone's life but mine, moving forward?

The constant caring and acceptance from the nursing staff helped to fill some of the emptiness left by my scattered family. Was it enough to help me lick anorexia? *No.* But fighting everyone had proved exhausting. I gave in and allowed myself to gain weight. Letting go did more than put flesh on my bones, it also marked the return of my menstrual cycle, a true sign of returning health. Its telltale sign was like a banner proclaiming: *I am woman.* I had fooled nobody but me.

"Cindy?" Dr. Stevens knocked on my door. "We need to talk before I leave on vacation." He entered my hospital room and shut the door. "I know you are having a hard time adjusting to the weight you've been gaining. Does it help if I tell you that you are still thin?"

I squirmed uneasily, and put down the book I had been reading. I didn't want to talk about my body. "I guess so," I mumbled unconvincingly. A lot he knew about how uncomfortable I felt! I *hated* the way I looked!

"Cindy, what size are those overalls you are wearing?" Dr. Stevens asked.

I looked down at my corduroy Levi's. "These? Size twelve, why?"

"Cindy, my *twelve-year-old son* wears the same size you do. Doesn't that tell you something?"

Puzzled, I shook my head. Just what was Dr. Stevens trying to tell me?

"Cindy, you are a *twenty-eight-year-old woman,* you should not be wearing the same size as a little boy."

"But, Dr. Stevens, I'm *exactly* the right size for my weight."

Dr. Stevens laughed wryly at that logic. "You're absolutely

right. You *are* the right size for weighing 88 pounds." He cleared his throat. "Cindy, there is something that you and I need to talk about. I believe it's time that you start thinking about moving to Rochester. Wait," he held up his hand as I started to protest, "hear me out. You and I have been trying to work together, long-distance, for seven years now, but it's not working. We—you and I—work very hard to stabilize you here in the hospital, then you return home to the same environment, the same behaviors, the same situations, and you still end up back here in the hospital. This is not working. I feel that I really can't give you the help you need *unless* you are living here. I want you to think about moving to Rochester while I'm away next week, and then I would like you to make a decision by the time I get back."

"But . . . but. . . ." I stammered. "Dr. Stevens. . . ."

"Cindy, we've talked about this once before. You convinced me then that your living long distance would not be a problem. But we're not getting very far. I've been thinking about this for a while now. If our therapy together is to work, it would be best for you to live here." My mind reeled. How in the world would I ever be able to leave my home and my family?

He stood up. "Cindy, if you decide you can't move here, it's okay, I understand. But I have to be honest and tell you that I won't be able to keep treating you. If you decide you cannot move here, I will help you find a doctor in Syracuse—I promise."

His ultimatum sent me into a panic, and I spent the next week trying to decide what to do. One of the staff nurses, Aggie, whom I had grown quite close to, worked hard to convince me that moving ninety miles away from what was left of my family was the right thing to do.

"But, Aggie, I don't know *anybody* in Rochester! I'll be all alone! Where will I live? I don't have a car. How will I get around? How will I get groceries?" I came up with a thousand and one reasons why I shouldn't move to Rochester, and Aggie came up with a thousand and one reasons why I should.

There was one question though that I was afraid to ask,

and it was one of the main reasons I was afraid to make the move. I asked it of the doctor covering for Dr. Stevens while he was on vacation. "Dr. Conners, what if I move here and Dr. Stevens goes away?" Just like the other people I had cared about.

Dr. Conners smiled. "I understand your concerns, Cindy. I believe I can honestly say that Dr. Stevens has settled in Rochester and is here to stay. He has a nice home here, he's involved with the community, and his kids are in a great school. I don't think you have to worry. Dr. Stevens plans on being in Rochester for a long time."

Later, Aggie promised that she, too, would be here to help me. If I moved to Rochester, she said I would be able to visit her and her family on weekends. She would take me grocery shopping. She promised I wouldn't be alone.

I made the decision to stay.

When Dr. Stevens returned, I gave him my answer. His acknowledgement of how hard it was for me to come to that decision didn't make it any less scary. And for the next three months, I struggled not only with continued weight gain, but also with the realization that life was about to change for me, again.

The hospital's social worker found a subsidized apartment that I could afford, and Mom and Dick emptied the Syracuse apartment that was supposed to have made me independent. After thirteen months of hospitalization, I was ready to be discharged to my new home. On my last night in the hospital, I climbed into bed, hugged Whiskers, and turned off the bedside light. "Please," I prayed in the darkness, "please let it be different this time." Surely, a new home, in a new city, would be enough to put anorexia out of my life—forever.

A new city? A new home? A new life? The move to Rochester was a step forward and many steps backward. Anorexia could not be stopped by geography. The loneliness, the sadness, and the pain had become who I was. I longed to shed its weight. Instead, I shed the pounds. The previous year's struggle to gain weight was all for naught. Dr. Stevens increased my therapy to daily sessions. I lived from one day to the next, and survived on the knowledge that he was still there.

Just as she had promised, Aggie and her family invited me into their home. Even though hospital policy strongly encouraged staff to *not* get involved with their patients, Aggie recognized my need for a friend and risked her job anyway. With a hearty approval from Dr. Stevens, she, her husband, Jack, and her two sons became my *other* family.

For the next year, I spent almost every weekend at their home. The hurt over the loss of my own family was soothed by the affection I received from Aggie's. Fifteen-year-old Michael teased and treated me like an older sister; twenty-one-year-old Don was friendly and kind. I basked in the normalcy of their family life. But what I loved most was that, to them, I was just a regular person. Nobody questioned my eating habits, nobody talked about how skinny I was, and nobody asked me to change. Their love, their encouragement, and their hugs sent the same message over and over—being me was okay. They nourished the hunger in my heart, while I unsuccessfully attempted to nourish the rest of my body.

But the long-set pattern of starving, eating, purging, exercising was an old friend. The outpouring of affection from Aggie and her family was not sufficient to fill my inner emptiness. Anorexia and—though never officially diagnosed—bulimia continued to distract my mind and to destroy my health.

My weight plummeted back down to 71 pounds. Each night, my prayers sent a new message skyward, *"Please, God. Don't let me die tonight!"* And opening my eyes each morning, I breathed a sigh of relief and prayed, *"Please, God. Let me live through today."*

Chapter 15

Angel Tears

"Cindy, are you okay?" Aggie leaned across her kitchen table and grabbed hold of my hand.

"Y-e-e-s-s, I-I think so," I replied slowly. We had been sitting around the kitchen table talking. Earlier in the evening, we had gone out to dinner. When we had returned, I headed for the bathroom.

I struggled to focus on Aggie's face, but her features blurred, and I laid my head down on my folded arms. *What's happening to me?* Limp and semi-conscious, I heard Don call for an ambulance, while Aggie and Jack worked to arouse me. Something was terribly wrong, and the words swirling around in my brain, wouldn't come out my mouth. *I must be dying. This must be the end.* And I fought to stay awake . . . to stay in touch . . . to stay alive.

Sirens in the distance became louder and an ambulance pulled into Aggie's driveway. Her tiny kitchen was a bustle of activity as several medics quickly strapped me onto a gurney and just as quickly, loaded me into the waiting ambulance. Aggie scrambled in next to me. "I'm a nurse," she explained brusquely, "and I'm staying with her."

One of the medics placed an oxygen mask over my mouth, and seemed puzzled as he checked my erratic pulse. "Can you give me some background information on this young lady," he asked. I breathed in and out, struggling to maintain consciousness.

Aggie gripped my hand. "Hang in there, sweetie," she whispered. "You're going to be okay." She quickly filled the emergency crew in on my medical history. "My God! Can't you even put the sirens on! This girl has anorexia and has had heart complications in the past. Can't you see she's in trouble!" Despite the haziness and the mask over my mouth, I managed a weak smile as Aggie barked orders to the ambulance attendants. We sped toward the hospital, the sirens now roaring, and I felt safe, reassured by Aggie's take-charge attitude.

Upon arrival to the hospital emergency department, the medics wheeled me into a treatment cubicle with Aggie close behind them. "You better check her potassium level," she demanded of the emergency doctors who quickly surrounded us. One of the residents stuck electrodes to my chest. "She has anorexia and takes potassium supplements." Aggie leaned over, and reassuringly squeezed my hand. "Dr. Stevens is being notified."

I pushed the oxygen mask down around my neck. "Oh, no, Aggie!" I protested weakly. *"Please!* Don't call him at home. It's so late!"

"Cindy, he's your doctor and he has to know."

"But, Aggie," I whimpered, "I don't want Dr. Stevens to be mad at me!"

"Cindy, Dr. Stevens isn't going to be mad at you. He would be more upset if we *didn't* call him."

That wasn't very reassuring, but the matter was out of my hands. A lab technician came in, swabbed my arm with alcohol, and withdrew several tubes of blood. Finished, she gathered up her supplies, leaving Aggie and I to wait for someone, *anyone,* to tell us what was going on. Aggie sat down on a chair besides my bed, still holding onto my hand.

"Aggie?"

"Yes?"

"Are *you* mad at me?" I asked timidly.

She stood up and gathered me in her arms. "Oh, Cindy! I could never be mad at you! I love you! I just want you to get better, that's all."

"I love you too, Aggie. Some day, I'll be better. I promise!"

"Get better for yourself, Cindy." She brushed back my long tangled hair from around my face, and planted a gentle kiss on my forehead. "Don't get better just for me, because I will always be here for you. Get better for yourself."

A physician joined us. "Well," he said to Aggie, "you were right. Cindy's potassium level is only 1.4." The doctor looked over at me. "That's not even halfway normal. We're going to put an IV in your arm in order to get your potassium level up as quickly as possible. I want to keep you here for the rest of the night, and then we'll see how you're doing in the morning. I just got off the phone with Dr. Stevens. He'll be by to see you around ten in the morning. The two of you will decide what to do at that time." He smiled down at me and patted my shoulder. "This was a close call. You're a lucky young lady to have a friend like this woman. She got you here in time to prevent this from turning into a more serious problem."

A close call. Seems like I've been that route before.

A nurse removed the oxygen mask. She hooked me up to an IV and left the room. Aggie leaned over and gave me a hug. "Honey, do you mind if I go home and try to get some sleep? Will you be okay by yourself? Or do you want me to stay with you until Dr. Stevens comes by in the morning? Or rather," she chuckled ruefully as she examined her watch, "later *this* morning?"

"I'll be okay. Go home and rest. You must be exhausted." I watched her walk towards the door. "Aggie?" She stopped and turned around. "Thank you," I mouthed.

She hurried back to my side, and gave me one last hug

before heading for home. "I'll call you in the morning. If Dr. Stevens says it's okay for you to leave, I'll bring you back to my house."

I settled back onto the stretcher bed and watched the slow, steady drip of the IV. Would I always end up in an emergency room? What if Aggie hadn't been there? *Would I have died this time?* I turned on my side and watched the activity going on outside of the little cubicle. Would there ever be more than this? Or would I always be on the sidelines of life? *God . . . I'm so tired of being scared!* I was tired of being so alone . . . of being so trapped. *Damn eating!* I closed my eyes, and in spite of the hectic and constant noises surrounding my space, I fell asleep.

"Would you like some breakfast?"

Startled, I awakened to find a hospital worker standing at the foot of my bed, a tray of food in her hands. I shook my head. After the previous evening's events, I didn't trust myself to eat. The fear of keeping food in my stomach was too strong, and my strength to resist, too weak.

"Hi," Dr. Stevens walked in as the food service worker walked out. "How are you feeling this morning?"

"Dr. Stevens, I'm sorry that the hospital called you during the night," I apologized.

He pulled up a chair next to the stretcher bed and sat down. "Cindy," he said, brushing my apology aside. "I am your doctor. I *want* to be called when you are in trouble. And, my friend," he added gently, "you *are* in trouble. Things haven't been going too well, have they?"

"No." Tears slid down my face. "Dr. Stevens, I don't want to go back into the hospital. Please," I begged, "don't put me back in! I don't think I can do that anymore."

"Cindy, it's up to you. Do you think you can keep yourself well enough to stay out of the hospital?"

I nodded my head somewhat dubiously. After all, my track record hadn't been too successful so far.

He studied my face for several moments. "Cindy, if the

doctor here says you're okay to be discharged today, I will agree to it on one condition." He paused, making sure he had my complete attention. "If I see that you're heading for trouble again, I want it to be our agreement that you will be admitted onto the Behavioral Unit for treatment. Is that a deal?"

"Why can't I be admitted to the unit I always go on? I don't think I want to go on the Behavior floor. I hate those behavior programs! They don't help me, Dr. Stevens!"

Dr. Stevens shook his head. "It's not working on the other unit either. Look at how many times over the last several years you have been on the same floor. I'm sorry, Cindy. But if you are admitted again, it will have to be on the Behavioral Unit. No," he insisted as I continued to protest. "I could have you admitted there today, but I'm not. Can we shake on this agreement?"

I shook his hand, and reluctantly agreed to his terms. Over the next few weeks, I tried to make good on our agreement. But each time I sat down to eat, the fear of gaining weight rose and overpowered my good intentions. Unable to see beyond that fear, or to understand its irrational hold, I was not ready to let go. I had been at the mercy of anorexia for fifteen years.

I stood in front of my living room window, and watched the sky above darken and grow ominous. In minutes, the rain began in earnest. The torrid sheet of raindrops pounded against the windowpane, not unlike the tears that fell from my eyes. As a child, grandma had told me that when it rained, it meant that the angels were sad. Raindrops were their tears. I walked over to the kitchen area of my small apartment and checked a pot of boiling pasta. While spaghetti sauce simmered on another burner, I removed a tray of chocolate-chip cookies from the oven. For three hours, I devoured the food in an effort to appease my hunger. The behavior was automatic. No thinking involved. No feelings involved.

The cycle that had begun years ago continued unbroken.

"Cindy, I'm very concerned about you." Dr. Lazareth, my

internist, studied the latest lab reports. "Your electrolyte levels are not good, and you've lost another three pounds."

I fidgeted uneasily. In the two weeks since the emergency department visit, I had not been able to keep up my end of the agreement with Dr. Stevens. As much as I wanted to get better, I wanted to be thinner more. I knew I shouldn't be losing weight, but its implications continued to elude me. Why *couldn't* I be healthy without gaining weight? Didn't Dr. Lazareth understand that once I started gaining weight, I'd *never* stop?

"Cindy, if you aren't able to eat and put on some weight within the next couple of days, I'm going to have to put you back in the hospital."

I jolted upright. I *couldn't* go back into the hospital! "Please, Dr. Lazareth," I begged. "Don't put me in the hospital."

"Cindy, you are sick. I can't take the risk of something happening to you. I've tried everything that I can think of to help you gain weight, and none of it is helping. I really thought the liquid supplement would work, but it hasn't."

I wrinkled up my nose. Disgusting stuff! It was a thick, milky, nutritional supplement in which even the flavor additives could not mask its medicinal taste. Of course, the taste didn't matter anyhow. I threw up everything. And I was too ashamed to admit to Dr. Lazareth that I didn't know how to *not* throw up. I didn't even have to use my fingers to bring up the food anymore. It happened automatically. I simply bent over and my stomach contents regurgitated—spontaneously.

"Cindy, have you ever heard of hyperalimentation?" Dr. Lazareth asked. I shook my head. "Okay, let me explain what it means, and why I'm bringing it up now. Hyperalimentation is a way of administering total nutrition through an IV. We often use it for patients with cancer or other stomach disorders who are unable to eat. If we can't get some nutrition in you in any other way right now, I believe this is our next step. I would like to put you in the hospital, on one of the medical units, for a possible course of hyperal. It will at least give you a start and, I hope, keep you out of intensive care. I'm very worried about you. You are extremely malnourished."

At least he wasn't talking about the behavioral unit. I *definitely* did not want to go on the behavioral unit. Maybe he was right. Maybe this hyperalimentation would help turn things around.

"Dr. Stevens? I think Dr. Lazareth is mad at me." I pulled my sweater tighter around my chest. It was so cold in Dr. Stevens' office.

"Cindy, why do you think that?" Dr. Stevens reached over and turned off his air conditioning unit.

"Well, I think he might be mad at me because I'm not better yet."

"Dr. Lazareth is not mad at you, Cindy. I talked to him earlier today. What you are probably sensing is his frustration at not being able to help you more than he is right now. He is very worried about you . . . and so am I. We both agree that hyperalimentation is necessary. Do you understand that if we don't get nutrition into you, you can die? Cindy, we're not going to give up on you. Is that what you're afraid of?"

I nodded, and my eyes flooded with tears. If they were mad at me, they would leave.

"Cindy, haven't I always told you that you are a strong person. If you weren't, you never would have survived this long."

"Don't say that to me!" I yelled. "I hate it when people say I'm strong. If I'm so strong, why am I still sick?"

"Cindy, being strong does not mean that you're not sick, or that you *don't* hurt. It means that in spite of how awful you feel, you don't give up. You're hanging in there."

I left his office not at all convinced that strong was good. After all, if I was so strong, than I *should* have been able to get over anorexia by now.

The next morning, I received a call from the hospital admission's department to come in that afternoon. I walked over to the living room window and looked down onto the parking lot below. The bright, hot August sun beat against my face as I watched some neighborhood children play among the parked cars, and long ago memories of another summer afternoon emerged from deep inside of me. The loneliness, the desperation, and the sadness from many years past were still present. That beginning still had no end.

Wearily, I packed a suitcase and called my mother. As I broke the news of yet another hospitalization, I sensed her weariness with this endless, devastating battle. She tried hard to hide her discouragement, but it came through the phone lines anyway. Her helplessness was as great as mine was. But Mom had long ago resigned herself to the fact that, if this was how I wanted to live my life, then there was nothing she could do about it—except to let me know that she loved me. In the face of yet one more hospitalization, she did just that.

I said good-bye, and her, *"I love you,"* echoed in my ears as I picked up my suitcase and glanced around the bedroom one more time. *Whiskers!* I snatched up the little stuffed tiger from his place on the bed. I had almost forgotten him. After twenty-two years of ownership, he was as bedraggled and as threadbare as I. Whiskers and I had been through so much together that there was no way I could face another hospital stay without him. I opened the suitcase and tenderly nestled my little friend against a nightgown. We were both worn out and in need of gentle care.

For the next two weeks, hyperalimentation poured life into my veins as anorexia drained it out.

"Miss Nappa?" Groggily, I sat up in bed and looked over at the hospital-room door. A tall man in a white coat walked in closely followed by over a dozen other white-coated people. *Morning rounds already?* They circled my bed. "Miss Nappa, I'm Dr. Morris, and these are third-year medical students. May we talk with you?"

"Yes."

"Miss Nappa is here because she has anorexia nervosa,"

Dr. Morris explained to the students. He sat down on the edge of the bed. "Do you mind if I listen to your heart?"

"Uh-uh."

Dr. Morris pulled back the bedcover and the students gasped. At a skeletal 70-pounds, I laid delicately upon a lambswool pad. A pillow, wedged between my thighs, cushioned those sparrow-like limbs, as I could no longer bear the pressure of any part of me touching me. My bones ached. My entire body ached. And my skin, in spite of a summertime tan, was gray, parched, and thickly covered with fine, downy-like hair.

"Can you tell us, when you binge—how much do you eat and what do you usually eat?" asked Dr. Morris.

Embarrassed, I mumbled vaguely in low tones, his questions stripping away the little dignity I struggled to maintain. I couldn't even talk about those issues with Dr. Stevens. And this man expected me to answer with all those people gawking at me?

Dr. Morris realized my discomfort, and pulled the blankets back up. The white-coated crowd turned their heads away from my vividly exposed anorexic adventure. Their effort to afford me a privacy I no longer felt was mine. Or maybe they were afraid to see I was more than a specimen with a pulsating heart. I cradled Whiskers against my chest. "It's okay," I whispered as they filed out of the room. "What do they know, anyway."

After another week of vein-fed, life saving fluids, I was, nutritionally, on more stable ground. Even so, Dr. Stevens and Dr. Lazareth strongly agreed I was definitely not out of the woods. I was to be admitted to the Behavioral Unit as soon as a bed became available. In the meantime, I was discharged to wait at home.

For the next five days, Dr. Lazareth had me return to the hospital for blood levels. Even over the weekend, he had me come into the emergency department for continued monitoring. On Sunday, I rolled down my blouse sleeve and prepared to return home, when one of the emergency room nurses sat down next to me, a lab report in her hands. "Cindy," she said gently. "I was just talking with Dr. Lazareth and Dr. Stevens. Your potassium has dropped significantly. They would like you to be admitted to the hospital today. In fact, there is a bed available on the Behavior Unit. Your doctors asked that we let you go home to pack a suitcase. Will you come back if we let you do that?"

I shuddered as she delivered my sentence. "I don't want to come back into the hospital! I can't do this anymore!" It hadn't been a good week. I had binged and purged incessantly. Because I knew this day would eventually come. And *they* would make me stop soon enough. And I didn't want to. Not yet.

She patted my hand. "Cindy, you are very sick. Your doctors want only to keep you safe. You really do need their help. The sooner you come into the hospital, the faster you can get better and go home. Do you understand?"

I sighed. Didn't she realize how tired I was of hospitals? Couldn't she see that I was too tired to fight anymore?

Why couldn't I see that I was the only person doing this to me? Left on my own, I always returned to starving or vomiting.

I had no choice. I went home, packed a suitcase, called my mother to let her know where I would be, and made a tray of sugar cookies before I left for the hospital. Once there, I settled quickly—too quickly—into the very familiar hospital routine. A behavior contract was drawn up, I signed my name reluctantly, and the pressure to gain weight was, again, strictly enforced. Within two weeks, I gained five pounds and could not continue. At 70 pounds I was safe. At 75 pounds, I was not. I couldn't do this. Just like I had tried to tell the emergency room nurse. Why could no one understand that the more they wanted me to gain weight, the more I could *not*.

So I resorted to gaining weight in the only manner I could tolerate, by drinking water—*tons* of it. An hour before weigh-in, I sneaked into the bathroom and began what soon became an agonizing ritual—drinking *gallons* of tap water to the extent that I rendered myself speechless, because if I opened my mouth, water would have spurted out. And as soon as I stepped off the examination room scale, I ran to the bathroom to vomit and pee it all out. Even though the line on the weight graph indicated success, and the staff loudly applauded my efforts, my body remained frail, my face stayed bloated, my mind felt tortured. Could nobody see the game we all played?

When had my reflection become theirs?

The early morning deception was exhausting, and my guilt, increasing. I wanted desperately to stop this way of life. Yet the threat of anorexia's absence—and isn't that what gaining weight meant?—was the most frightening of all. It was all I had. It was all I was. I couldn't possibly let it go.

At night, I curled up on the hospital bed and wrote in a journal. It was part of my treatment. Dr. Stevens said that maybe it would help me get in touch with my feelings.

Saturday. . . Okay. Here I am—again. I don't know why I have to keep this stupid journal! How is writing supposed to help? I don't believe my life will ever get better. This is how it has been for fifteen years! So why should it change now? I could just sit here and cry. The sadness hurts so much that my insides just ache. Lonely. I don't even have one friend.

I feel so fat today! I am afraid to gain even one pound. Doesn't anybody understand that? I AM VERY WORRIED ABOUT EATING AND GAINING WEIGHT!

I'm confused about this stupid eating. The vomiting is pretty bad and I can't seem to change it. I don't even recall vomiting anymore. How has it become so automatic and so much a part of my character that I am not even aware of doing it anymore?

Tired. So tired. Will I ever be normal?

I slammed the notebook shut and threw it to the floor. *No. I was never going to be like everyone else.*

Mom, her husband, Dick, and my Aunt Vera came to the hospital to help celebrate my thirtieth birthday. A milestone in many a normal person's life but, for me, a signal of something more—a distant memory. They brought a cake and sang happy birthday. Aunt Vera hugged me while Mom and Dick passed out slices of cake. "Honey," she whispered, tears in her eyes. "You have to eat so you can build up your strength and come home. You look like a skeleton. How could you let your body decay to nothing?"

"But Aunt Vera, I weigh 72 pounds. I'm not a skeleton." Why couldn't she see that I was fine?

"Cindy, you have suffered for years! Look at you honey. You are a prisoner in your own body!"

"I'm going to be okay, Aunt Vera. Look, I'm having a piece of my cake." I smiled valiantly, and put a forkful of the moist, chocolate cake in my mouth. Surely my efforts were to be admired. But as soon as they said good-bye and stepped onto the elevator, I wasted no time; I headed to the bathroom and threw it all up.

Mom and Aunt Vera cried all the way home. They knew the cake would not stay down. The years of pain were not mine alone. They had watched helplessly as I wasted away before their eyes. The reasons and causes of this behavior no longer mattered. They wanted only to have the Cindy they knew me to be, healthy and alive, back again.

Hours after they had left, I readied for bed. Yet sleep would not come. I was thirty years old and all alone. I turned over on my side and huddled under four white cotton blankets. "God," I prayed, "what's happened to me? Is this all there is ever going to be to my life?" I fumbled under the bedcovers until I felt the rough yarn fibers of Whisker's body. I pulled him close. "I feel so old, God! There's so much I want to be able to do, and I'm running out of time!"

I thought back to that first hospitalization in Philadelphia, and Kathy, the older woman with anorexia, the one who I was not going to be like. The one who had been so old . . . at thirty. The distant memory flooded my consciousness. I was thirty. I still had anorexia . . . I wasn't better. I was no different than

Kathy. My life hadn't changed at all. Time had passed by without me.

I went into the bathroom, snapped on the light, and stood in front of the vanity mirror. Gaunt, hollow-eyed, thin. *What price has anorexia cost me?* I stared into the mirror. Baby-fine hair, yellowish skin that cried out for hydration, and sunken-in cheeks. Dental problems that had resulted in the loss of all my teeth. And with no teeth to hold onto, my jawbone was reabsorbing at an alarming rate. *What monster have I become?* What, and who, had I been searching for all these years? How had I gotten so lost? Did it even matter anymore?

I climbed up on the toilet seat to get a better view. The skinny body that had once been comforting was now only confusing. *Why? Why am I so sick? So stuck? Why is thin not making me happy?* My eyes rested on the plastic water container. Who had I fooled these past few months?

I stepped down from the toilet and headed back to bed, but stopped first to pick up my journal. I settled back against the pillows and started writing.

Friday . . . Okay, Dr. Stevens, I'm facing my feelings. Just like you keep telling me I need to do. I'm angry, and I'm scared, and I want to run away. I'm just so damn trapped.

I've lost so many years of my life. Is it too late for me to get better?

I know I'm still keeping you at an arm's distance. And I feel so alone because of it.

The bingeing and vomiting has actually gotten worse since coming into the hospital. It is going to kill me; of that I'm certain. My eating disorders are no better. I don't feel that the hospital is going to make any difference. I don't know what to do anymore.

Dr. Stevens, I'm writing this to you because this is what I have been trying to say: I'm scared because I'm only going in circles. I'm not getting better. The sadness is growing inside of me. It just keeps getting bigger and bigger. I want so much to be that little girl I used to be, but I lost her, and I don't know how to find her. I'm afraid to grow up. But it happened anyway—time moved on without me. I can never get back what I lost in my life, time or people. I'm afraid I may have to die, because I don't believe anybody will ever love me. You say I'm strong, but am I strong enough to survive these feelings?

I wish I could go back to my beginning and start over, but I can't.

When had my body become a paper cutout of life?

I put down my pen and closed the notebook. Facing my feelings was one of the hardest tasks I had ever done. Throughout the next month, and the rest of the hospitalization, I said nothing to Dr. Stevens about what I had written.

After four months of hospitalization, and a few days before Christmas, Dr. Stevens announced that I was ready to go home. I had come in at 70 pounds, I was leaving at 73. I had lied and cheated the entire time. In spite of those earlier realizations of what I was doing to my body and my life, I was sure of only one thing: I was never—*ever,* going to return to the hospital again.

Chapter 16

Another Way to Get There

"Cindy," Jon hesitated. "Umm, make sure you write when you have time."

"I'll write, don't I always," I joked. "The question is—will you write back?" We both laughed and went back to our respective thoughts.

I gazed out the car window and reflected on the past two weeks. What a surprise it had been when Jon showed up at the hospital the day I was discharged. He had come home for a holiday visit. His career had recently taken him to California, and he had brought a lot of exciting and interesting news to share. We had a wonderful time those two weeks, and I found myself already longing for his next visit. It was strange, but Jonny seemed patient and kind of at peace with me and my illness—a calmness that had not been present for many years. For the first time since anorexia had entered our lives, there was no tension, no stress in our interactions. Laughter had returned to our relationship.

"Cin?"

"Yeah?"

Jonny hesitated, his internal debate obviously continued.

"Nothing," he finally mumbled. Apparently, whatever he wanted to say, it must not be that important.

Dick turned into the airport parking lot. We unloaded Jon's suitcases and walked to the terminal. Mom and I stood inside, chatting quietly while Jon and Dick waited in line to check Jon in.

"Cindy," Mom said. "It's going to be so hard to have Jon leave."

I nodded, afraid to say out loud how much I was going to miss him. We had spent his entire visit together. We went shopping, to the movies, played games, and went to the video arcade. And in the process, we rediscovered the close bond we had shared as children. It was still there. And as a result, his departure became that more difficult. I sighed. Would I ever get used to people leaving?

Jon and Dick walked over to us and pointed at the security gate. *Time to go.* In less than ten minutes, Jon would be gone.

"Flight 1016, departing for Los Angeles, will be delayed forty-five minutes. Flight 1016, departing for Los Angeles will be delayed forty-five minutes. Boarding time will be at one-thirty."

"Why, Jon, that's your flight!" Mom exclaimed. "Oh, good! We have thirty minutes. Why don't we all go sit in the coffee shop and wait?" It was agreed all around, and we headed in that direction.

The coffee shop was packed with waiting passengers, but we spotted four empty seats. Only problem—they weren't together. Two were on one side of the room, and two were clear across on the other side.

Mom turned to me. "Cindy, why don't you and Jon go sit at the counter. Dick and I can take the ones on this side of the room. That way, you can spend some more time with Jon. Okay?"

"Sure." And we went over and sat down at the counter. I glanced over at the wall clock. Twenty minutes until departure. God, it was going by too fast.

"Cindy?" Jon fidgeted with his paper napkin, folding it

over and over into a tiny triangle.

"Yes?" Hadn't we just gone through this same scenario in the car?

He cleared his throat. Whatever he was trying to tell me was taking a lot of courage.

"Cindy, I want to tell you something. And I'm afraid you're going to think I'm crazy when I tell you. But don't say anything, just listen . . . okay?"

I nodded curiously, and glanced up at a wall clock above the counter—one-twenty. We had ten minutes. Whatever Jon wanted to say, he better say it in that time.

"Cindy," Jon bit his lower lip anxiously. "You know it has been a struggle for me in trying to get my career started in L.A. Things were pretty rough for a while, but I found this little church out there and started attending its services. And you know . . . I found it really helpful. I guess what I'm trying to say is that I lost a lot of faith in God—what with all that you and our family has been through. Well, I discovered a lot of strength and faith in that little church." He paused, not sure if I was still listening.

I was. I just wasn't sure what he was trying to tell me.

"A couple of months ago, I was talking with Mom. She told me that you were in the hospital again. Well . . . what with everything I was struggling with, and then to hear that you were doing poorly . . . well, I got *really* discouraged. I was terrified that you were going to die. And I didn't know what to do. So when I hung up the phone with Mom, I got down on my knees and started praying—*hard*. I just prayed and prayed to God to please help you, because I didn't know how to help you anymore," Jon said, and he fidgeted with the now shredded napkin. "Cindy, God talked to me. He told me that you're going to be all right. He said that you are going to win your battle and be healthy again. Cindy, I had the most incredible, *wonderful*, peaceful feeling run right through me. It was so strong. And you know," Jon looked straight into my eyes. "I trust it—Him. I know it sounds crazy, and you probably think that I have really flipped my gourd this time. But,

Cindy, I'm not scared anymore. Do you know how many *years* I prayed for you to get better? And that I never believed before that you would? But not anymore, Cindy. Not since that night. As weird as this all sounds, please believe me when I tell you that you are going to be okay." Jon stopped, unsure of my reaction to his bizarre tale. "Cindy, there is something else that I believe."

"Flight 1016 is ready for boarding. All passengers for Flight 1016, please prepare to board."

"Cindy, I know how important Dr. Stevens is to you, and how much he has helped you. But there will be more in your life than just doctors and hospitals some day. I'm not sure when, and I'm not sure how, but some day, Cin, you will have what you want for yourself."

"Flight 1016 is ready for boarding. All passengers for Flight 1016 to Los Angeles please prepare for boarding now."

God talking to Jonny? Is he nuts? Besides, if God really did love me than why had I suffered all these years?

Mom and Dick approached us, and pointed at the clock—one-thirty. I shook my head in an effort to clear out Jon's words, and followed everyone to the boarding gate. Jon and I hugged each other tightly, and then he was gone.

"Cindy, are you okay?"

"Hmmm? . . . Yes," I muttered. Mom's question barely penetrated my deep, uneasy silence. And for some reason, I said nothing, keeping Jon's strange message to myself.

Crazy. My brother has just gone crazy.

I returned to Rochester, still having said nothing to anyone of Jon's strange conversation, and settled into the familiar daily agenda of day hospital—Dr. Stevens' and the hospital staff's decision that this was all I could handle. The biggest concern on my mind: how did I keep up the weight pretense? How did I continue to keep fooling everyone? I certainly could not keep drinking water—*that* was much too painful. Just the memory of those early mornings weigh-ins sent shudders down my spine. *Maybe I could go back to tying pennies around my waist?* No, that wouldn't work either. I'd have to carry all those pennies around all day, and what if I got caught? The idea of faking weight gain was no longer appealing. The effort to keep up the game had become too draining.

For over a week, I followed the routine of day treatment hospital: mornings making craft projects, afternoons meeting with Dr. Stevens. On the tenth day, I sat in the craft room and looked around at my fellow participants. Some talked amongst themselves, but the majority worked on projects. I looked down at the needlework in front of me, and considered which colored thread to use.

Which color thread to use? Was this what my life had boiled down to? *Was this all I could show after almost seventeen years?* I watched a man across the table struggle to glue a tiny blue ceramic square onto a small iron trivet frame.

Dammit! What am I doing here? And then something— deep inside my soul—stirred. And then it gurgled, as if swallowing air. As if it hadn't breathed for a long time, years—seventeen years.

One of the program counselors noticed my lack of activity and walked over to me. "Cindy, do you need some help?" she asked, as she looked from the unfinished needlepoint to my worried face to my clenched fists.

Help? Help? How in the world is needlework going to help me get my life back? I shook my head and picked up the needle. Satisfied, she moved on. *There has to be more to life than this. God! There has to be more to me than this!* I set down the needle and glanced at the clock—one o'clock. Time for my afternoon session with Dr. Stevens. I pushed back my chair, the needlework all but forgotten, and left for his office.

And the something deep inside grew, and gathered strength, and its force jet-propelled me down the hall. Whatever was happening, I did not understand and I did not question.

I set my shoulders in a straight line, marched into Dr. Stevens' office, and planted myself firmly in front of his desk.

Dr. Stevens looked up from the papers he had been working on, surprised by my unannounced arrival. It was the first time
in all our years together that I had not waited for him to summon
me from the waiting room.

"Dr. Stevens," I began firmly. "I have something to say,
and I'm afraid you're not going to like it." My legs grew suddenly
shaky. I took a deep breath and sat down in a chair. "I cheated the
whole time I was in the hospital. I really didn't gain any weight at
all." *Oh my goodness! Where had that come from?*

Dr. Stevens sat straight up, his eyes wide behind his horn-
rimmed glasses. "Cindy, you *lied* to me?"

"Yes!" I blurted out, truthfully. *Oh, dear! What was I doing?* And the words I had always thought about, but could never
say out loud, burst forth now. "I want you to know that being on
that behavior floor was the most awful experience. I absolutely
hate those programs. I will *never—ever* do that again! I can't worry
about getting weighed anymore!" The words spewed out. And I
couldn't stop them. "Dr. Stevens, I *want* to get better. And I have
never wanted it more than I do right now. But I want to do it my
way." *Desire.* The something deep inside of me was desire. "With
no behavior programs, no threats, no punishment, no *having* to
gain weight every day. I *never* want to go into the hospital again."

Determination. It was desire and determination.

"I'm sorry that I lied to you, but I can't get better under
those conditions." I stopped abruptly, unsure if I should say more,
or if I should wait for Dr. Stevens to throw me out of his office. I
had, after all, failed him.

Dr. Stevens sat there, stunned, not quite sure *how* to respond. "Cindy," he said finally, "I'm very sorry that you feel you
had to lie to me. All those months in the hospital!"

"Four months, Dr. Stevens. And I can't do it anymore. I
cannot live by those rules anymore. If I only want to weigh 75
pounds, then that is my right. I can't worry about someone telling me how much to eat, how much to weigh, or how to be! If I
weigh 95 pounds, it will be because *I* want to weigh 95 and not

because somebody else keeps telling me I *have* to weigh that much. And maybe you don't want to be my doctor anymore." *Oh, dear God! I didn't mean to say that.* But it was my worst fear, and having spoken the words out loud, I couldn't take them back.

Dr. Stevens, his face grim, was silent for several minutes. "Cindy, I'm not sure what I'm going to do." He was obviously still stunned. "I'm not sure if I *can* continue to be your doctor under these conditions. Maybe it would be best if we both think about this, and then talk more about it at tomorrow's appointment, okay?"

"Okay," I agreed, not at all sure what I had just done, or what I had just said. And I walked out of his office, not even sure if I would be welcomed back. Later, at home, I replayed our conversation a trillion times over. And each time I knew that I couldn't have said it any different. Because what I had done was to tell him that I refused to deal with my weight. *God!* I only hoped he understood that I meant under the terms it had always been under. After all, Dr. Stevens had been a caring doctor and a trusted friend for eight years. I smiled to myself. *I trust Dr. Stevens. He has stood by my side through so much of anorexia's illness. Can I trust that he will stay by my side now? Or will I lose, once again, another friend?*

The next morning, I went to the day program and tried, unsuccessfully, to concentrate on the needlework. *Shit!* I laid the needle down.

Margaret, the program counselor, again came over and sat down next to me. "Cindy, are you okay?"

"Margaret, I can't come to this program anymore." I blurted out. "I'm going to go to . . . to . . . college." *Oh, dear God! Now where had that come from?*

Margaret nodded sympathetically, took me by the hand, and led me to the back room. She closed the door and motioned for me to sit at the table. She sat down across from me, and folded my cold hands into her own warm ones. "Cindy, you can't go to college right now. You are *very* sick. You need to be here. You need to let us help you."

"Margaret, people have been telling me for a long, *long* time that I'm too sick to do anything. Hell, maybe it's what *I've* been telling me too! As long as I'm sick . . . anorexic . . . bulimic—" *There, I said it. I finally admitted to the vomiting*—"I can't do anything. I can't go to school . . . to work . . . nothing! Well, maybe I *am* too sick, but I have to do this. I have to try." I withdrew my hands from hers, and stood up. "I want so badly to be *somebody*. I want more than what I have now. I want to *be* more than I am right now. And I don't know what else to do anymore. All I know is that if I'm going to die, than I want to die trying—not waiting." I walked out of the room. It was time to face Dr. Stevens.

I sat down in his waiting room and thumbed through a magazine. *God, I'm really scared. What if Dr. Stevens says no?* And suddenly I knew if I had to get better without him, I would. I would depend on that feeling . . . that desire inside of me.

"Hi, Cindy. Ready?" Dr. Stevens walked towards me, smiling. I nodded, not at all ready. *Maybe his smile is a good sign?* I couldn't tell. Dr. Stevens was *always* smiling. I followed him to his office and sat down.

Dr. Stevens' face grew serious. "Cindy, I've put a lot of thought into what you told me yesterday. I was very disappointed when you admitted that you lied and cheated during your hospitalizations, but I think I understand. I'm sorry you felt you couldn't trust me enough to share these feelings while you were in the hospital. I have thought about it a lot, and, well, I'm not about to give up on you now." My heart leaped into my throat. "I'm willing to let you handle your own weight if . . . and I mean *if* . . . you promise to, *at least,* let Dr. Lazareth help you from a medical standpoint." He smiled. "Otherwise, I would not be a very responsible doctor, and I would worry about you."

I let out my breath. *Dr. Stevens is going to remain my doctor! Thank you, God. Oh, I do want to take charge of my life.* Dr. Stevens had always been there to pick me up when I stumbled and fell, and he was still going to be here. But I had to make sure.

"No more programs, Dr. Stevens?"

He grinned. "No, kiddo. No more programs." Then, on a more serious note, he added, "Cindy, no matter how much I have wanted for you to get better, and no matter how much I have wanted for you to have what *you* want in your life, it wasn't enough. *You* had to want those things for yourself. And *you* had to recognize that you are the only one who can give them to you."

"It's kind of like the first step, isn't it, Dr. Stevens? I mean, I always wanted to be healthy, or I guess I *thought* that I wanted to be healthy. But maybe 70 pounds isn't really healthy after all. It's just that I thought I could *do* anything and *be* anything by weighing 70 pounds. But 70 pounds isn't working. It's funny, but I've tried all these years—since I was fourteen—to have a life being skinny! And now I'm *thirty!* But the only life skinny has given me is one of sickness. I keep waiting for things to get better—to *be* better. But it's not happening. My life is never going to be more than this," and I waved my hand in the air, indicating the hospital, "if I don't at least try. I guess I believed that it would just happen, that *somebody . . . you . . . my parents . . .* yes, I know," I admitted a bit sheepishly. "Even though I didn't want any of you telling me what to do, or *especially* what to weigh. I guess I still thought that *somehow* other people would make things better. But you can't. My family can't. Nobody can. I'm the only one who can make things—*me,* better." I looked around the room I had come to know so well. "I guess I want to *matter.* I mean, I want my *life* to matter, to be important, to *mean* something."

My 73 pounds of determination looked straight into Dr. Stevens' eyes. "I know it's not going to be easy, and I don't know how long it's going to take. In fact, I'm terrified. All I know is that I want to have what everyone else has, and I want to be like everyone else—just a regular person."

Chapter 17

Changing Direction

"**D**r. Lazareth, this may sound strange but, I don't know *how* to eat." *God!* I couldn't say that to him! *Everybody* knows how to eat! I stood in front of my bathroom mirror, and rehearsed how to admit that I didn't know *what* or how *much* to eat in order to be healthy again. "Dr. Lazareth," I began again, "how do I eat?" *Shit!* That sounded stupid too! All I had to do was just start eating, right?

Wrong. I was so used to eating whatever I wanted in such massive quantities, that I had forgotten what a normal meal-size or a normal serving-size was! Somehow, I had to learn how to recognize when I was hungry and how to eat in response to it. And I had not a clue where to begin!

Two hours later, I sat in the lobby of the hospital. My checkup with Dr. Lazareth had revealed no weight gain—but alas, no weight loss—and Dr. Lazareth's suggestion to try eating frozen prepared dinners. I glanced up at the wall clock, twelve o'clock. *Hmmm . . . lunch time. Maybe. . . .* And I headed towards the hospital cafeteria, stopping long enough to buy a newspaper and a diet Coke. I settled in at one of the empty tables and spread out the newspaper. Two women immediately sat down across from me. I sipped my soda and studied their plates. A sandwich—*looks like tuna fish*—tomato soup and an apple on one tray. Macaroni and cheese—*God, that looks so good*—and broccoli, on the other. *How did they do that? How did they know what to eat?* I turned a page of the paper and pretended to read. That was an improvement, at least I wasn't pretending to eat.

A third lady sat down, and I eyed her tray—a juicy hamburger on a wheat roll, a small dish of buttered sliced carrots, and a slice of chocolate cake. *How in the world could she eat all of that?* I drained my soda, watched the women eat, and took notes.

Later, at home, I prepared a baked chicken breast, broccoli, and rice. I filled my dinner plate and stared at it—for several minutes. I forked a piece of the chicken and raised it to my mouth . . . quickly . . . before I lost my nerve. I swallowed. *Oh shit!* "It's okay, Cindy. It's going to be okay." I scooped up a spoonful of the rice and broccoli. I closed my eyes. "I just want to be healthy. I just want to be healthy," I chanted, not at all convinced. "I don't want to be fat. I just want to be healthy." Tears slid down my face. *This is soooo hard!* I struggled through another bite of the chicken. And the fear of eating, of getting fat, tripled—*quadrupled,* with each mouthful. The tears flowed steadily, mingling with the food on my plate. *Chew, swallow, cry. Chew, swallow, cry.* There was no other way to do it. I had to face this fear and see what would happen.

An hour later, I laid down the fork, the plate in front of me empty. Almost immediately, my stomach muscles tightened and prepared to repel what I had just laboriously ingested. Vomiting was reflexive and normal. *"No! I mustn't!"* I gritted my teeth, and forced the food to stay down. And the little voice in my head went through its taunting routine: *Throw up, Cindy. Throw up! If you throw up, you can have more to eat. You can eat those cookies you baked the other day. You can eat WHATEVER you want, and how MUCH you want. And you won't BE FAT!*

"No! I can't . . . I *won't!* I want to be healthy. I'm *going* to be healthy. Shut up!" But the voice tormented my good intentions. *Cindy, if you don't get rid of the food in your stomach, you shouldn't eat. You can't eat.* "Shut up!" I screamed. "I will be okay. I *must* be okay!" I grabbed my jean jacket out of the closet and stormed out of the apartment.

Two hours later, I returned, exhausted more by fighting the voice and the fear, than the nine blocks I had circled—twice. But I hadn't throw up. For the first time in sixteen years, I had eaten a normal meal without vomiting. I smiled ruefully. *One day at a time, one meal at a time.* Obviously, finding me was going to take a bit longer than I had anticipated.

The next morning, I slipped out of my nightgown and stepped onto the bathroom scale. The dial stopped at—77. *Shit! I gained four pounds!* One meal and I had gained four pounds! This was *never* going to work! I was *never* going to be able to do this! *Forget it!* The old fear was back in the driver's seat.

"No!" And I *willed* the fear into the back seat. *"Please . . . let my desire for wellness be stronger than my fears."* I *had* to rely on myself. Nobody else could do this except me.

I scrambled two eggs for breakfast and tried to forget that morning's weight. "Don't focus on the numbers, Cindy." But how else could I judge if I was getting better? The scale had controlled my life, for over half my life. How could I *be* without that guidance? Yes, I had managed to eat one complete meal without restricting or vomiting. But would I ever manage to eat *three* meals without running to the bathroom?

I sat down at the kitchen table and scrutinized the eggs before me. My resolve weakened. *"God,* I'm so hungry!" Changing my behavior would be impossible, if I couldn't change the feelings that went along with it. I needed to try and understand anorexia and bulimia. Maybe if I could, then I would be able to understand how to break free. *I'll go to the library and do some research. Maybe I'll find some answers.* I pushed the eggs aside—so much for being healthy—drank some orange juice, and left for the library.

My search produced several different books. I signed them all out. Surely there would be an answer somewhere within those pages. And at my appointment with Dr. Stevens on the following day, I brought one of the books, positive that I had found what I was looking for. "Dr. Stevens, what about lithium? This book says that it has been shown to help control bingeing that it helps decrease cravings. Can we try it?" I asked, the book opened in my lap.

"Cindy, didn't the Philadelphia hospital try you on lithium way back in the beginning?"

"Yes, but I wasn't *really* bulimic *enough* back then. Besides," I added knowingly, "they only tried it for a short time. I'm sure it was nowhere near long enough. I think we should try it again."

Dr. Stevens smiled at this budding persistence. "Okay," he agreed. "But only if Dr. Lazareth monitors your course on it. After all, you are still in poor physical health. Four pounds has been a start, but you are still a long way from healthy."

Dr. Lazareth approved, and with his medical eye keenly overseeing this new direction, lithium therapy was started. Within a couple of days, the cravings to binge and purge lessened, and I increased meals to three times a day.

One meal . . . two meals . . . three meals . . . four days. I was eating, not vomiting, and working hard to *not* increase my exercise. But I chastised myself for becoming lazy and gave in to long bike rides rather than return to vomiting. My stomach felt full constantly, and I was *positive* that my body had expanded to incredible proportions. Walking around in such a state was awful. Lithium couldn't help with everything.

I hid the bathroom scale in the back corner of a closet and stopped weighing myself every day. Out of sight, out of mind. Maybe it would be better *not* to look at the numbers. Finally, with Dr. Lazareth's medical okay, I resumed daily walks. As long as I undertook some type of exercise, the daily weight increase was not as upsetting.

After a week of lithium therapy and no vomiting, my clothes became uncomfortably tight. I pulled the scale from its hiding spot and stepped up on it. *"Eighty-six pounds!"* I was horrified. *I had gained thirteen pounds in one week! This was terrible!* I raced to the telephone. *"Dr. Stevens! I gained thirteen pounds!"* I cried into the phone. "You *promised* me that I wouldn't get fat! This is much worse than the weight programs!"

"Cindy, it's okay. It is quite common to gain what seems like a lot of weight in the beginning. Don't forget . . . you have been restricting nutrition and calories from your body for a *long* time. As a result, your body is going to grab onto everything you ingest and hold onto it. Remember how your body always swelled up from the IV fluids? Well, this is the same thing. As far as your body is concerned, it has no idea when it will get fed again. Only by eating consistently will your body stabilize. This weight gain will slow down and become less as time goes on. You have been pretty dehydrated, my friend. You can't expect your body to start metabolizing and processing normally when it hasn't done so for years. You have to give your body time to readjust itself . . . and it *will.*"

"But I'm *never* going to stop gaining weight!" I whined, not at all reassured. "I just know it!" It was my biggest fear come true.

"Cindy, you *will* stop gaining," Dr. Stevens repeated calmly. "Remember, getting better *means* gaining weight. You know that. You told me yourself that you want to be healthy. So, how can you be healthy if you don't gain any weight?" His words worked hard to soothe my terror. "Cindy, you can't spend years abusing your body and then expect it to recover in one week. Your metabolism has slowed way down. What you need to realize is that cutting back on calories and nutrition to the extent that you did forced your metabolism to slow down considerably. Right now, you are gaining weight on what seems like a very small amount of food. But as you continue to gain, and as you continue to eat without purging, and if you exercise *appropriately,* your metabolism will speed up again. Of course, the other factor for this large weight gain could be the lithium. Fluid retention is a common side effect of that drug. Cindy, you have to trust *me*. You are not going to keep on gaining. Your body will stabilize."

I wanted to trust him. I wanted to trust me. If I was to truly overcome these disorders, I had to get past this point. And yet in spite of my good intentions and Dr. Stevens' words, the weight proved too threatening. Eating three meals was, again, too scary. I stopped the lithium. I went back to vomiting. I needed to know I could still lose weight.

I lost nine pounds—back down to a weight of 77 pounds— and went back to the books. There had to be other answers.

"Dr. Stevens, I read that anti-depressants have been shown to help with bingeing. The literature says that vomiting can cause an increase of serotonin in my brain and that's why I feel so good. Maybe we should try anti-depressants so that I can feel good by another means." I was unyielding in my efforts.

Dr. Stevens patiently pointed out that I was *already* taking an anti-depressant. In fact, I had been taking it for ten years.

"Yes, well . . . maybe we should try another kind of anti-depressant. It says here," and I looked down at the sheet of paper in my hand, " . . . *tricyclics have been shown to help diminish the craving to binge."* I looked up at his smiling face. "Can't we try one of those?"

"Yes, Cindy. We can try another kind of anti-depressant. Just keep in mind that what those studies are referring to is that most people with bulimia also suffer from depression. It is believed that by relieving the symptoms of depression, it will help reduce the need to binge. And we *have* been treating your depression—for quite a while. But," he continued as discouragement clouded my face, "I'm willing to try another type of drug to see if another kind might be more helpful."

Once again, we tried a chemical solution. Several more weeks passed with no decrease in my bingeing and Dr. Stevens put me back on the Sinequan. Guess I would have to learn how to overcome those binges and purges by myself.

I started again. For breakfast, I ate a poached egg on a slice of wheat toast, a small glass of orange juice, and coffee. Lunch was a small carton of yogurt, an apple, and six saltine crackers. Then came a three hour binge and vomit session in the afternoon, a brief break, and then a dinner of chicken or fish, vegetables, a baked potato or rice, and skim milk. I ate nothing after six o'clock.

Slowly, in spite of still vomiting, in spite of the fear still in the pit of my often bloated stomach, my weight inched upward . . . 80 . . . 83 . . . 88. And the terror that had seemed insurmountable, weakened. The merry-go-round was slowing down; the lure of its music was quieting.

"Dr. Lazareth, what if the pounds just keep coming?" I was *very* worried. I had just weighed in at 90 pounds. I hadn't weighed that much since I was twelve years old.

"Cindy, everyone's body has a natural set-point. I believe yours is around 105 pounds. Once you reach a more normal weight, your body will automatically maintain it, give or take a few pounds either way. At that point, you'll need to learn how many calories you'll need to stay at that weight. Of course, if you continually overfeed your body, you will gain."

Calories in, calories out. A balancing act. It sure was easier when I just ate whatever I wanted and then vomited.

"By the way, how is the vomiting?" Dr. Lazareth asked. "Your latest potassium level is within a normal range. Of course, the potassium supplements you are taking are probably helping with that."

Reluctantly, I admitted to that continued struggle. Though I no longer had all-day marathons, and in the overall scheme of things that was something to be proud of, I knew it would be a triumph *only* when I could go all day without vomiting—even once. For now, I accepted any small steps as big accomplishments.

"Cindy, how about hopping up onto the examining table so I can do a quick exam." He walked over to the table and placed a clean gown on top of it. "Holler when you're ready." He left the room.

A bit anxiously, I stripped off my jeans and sweatshirt, and put on the thin cotton gown. It was my first physical in two months, a time in which my body had undergone some surprising changes. Boy, was Dr. Lazareth going to be surprised. "Okay, Dr. Lazareth, I'm ready," I called out.

Dr. Lazareth knocked on the door and came back in. He slipped the gown down from my shoulders, and listened to the beating of my healthier heart. Instead of just skin and bones, I now had muscles. As the pounds had come on, my breasts blossomed, my hips widened, and my periods arrived monthly. I *definitely* did not have the figure of a pre-pubescent child anymore.

Dr. Lazareth finished the physical exam and stepped back. I pulled the dressing gown back up. "Cindy, it looks like your body is going through puberty. You are developing the way a young girl does as she grows up. Would you like to talk about it? Do you have any questions to ask me?"

I grinned shyly at my doctor. Instead of being embarrassed and angered by my womanly body, I was curious and awed by its development. I was finally becoming adult-sized. For whatever reason, it didn't scare me like it had at age fourteen. Now when I looked in the mirror, I was starting to recognize that long ago person I had lost. With each pound I gained, the pull and desire to lose, lessened. The further away from 70 pounds I got, the more I wanted to see what I was going to look like at 80 pounds, at 90 pounds, and soon—*maybe*—100 pounds. The roses in my cheeks had returned, my hair was bouncy and shiny, the sparkle in my eyes was back.

Oh, how I had missed me!

All those years of running away and hiding. I was so busy worrying about what others thought of me, of what I weighed, of what I looked like, that I had lost touch with this sense of me. I had forgotten who I was—and what I was. But Dr. Stevens, Dr. Lazareth, Aggie and her family, the nurses, the staff at the hospital, and my own family, had all tried to help me see that I was a person, a *good* person. A person who could be happy, who could be sad, who could be angry, who could be lonely, and who could be joyful. A person with all kinds of feelings and that it was okay. That I was okay! Being Cindy was more than okay, it was *all* right!

The journey back had begun. I was learning to try. Because as long as I tried, I was not a failure.

In nine months time, I finally reached 100 pounds. I no longer felt the pull, or the need, to be thinner. And I felt less tortured, less controlled by the voice—the thoughts—in my head. Because that's what that taunting voice in my head was: my own thoughts, my own fears. Coming to grips with the fear of eating, meant coming to grips with the fear of my own self and realizing that *who* I was, was *not* dependent on a number on the scale. The funny thing was that when I reached 90 pounds, the weight no longer *felt* threatening. When I looked in the mirror, I didn't even *look* fat to me. And I couldn't even explain why. But Dr. Stevens did. He said that believing I was fat at 70 pounds is part of the physiology of being at such a low weight. "The other part," he explained, "is psychology." That it was all mixed in with my low opinion of myself, with my depression, with my not being able to express my feelings, with my inability to separate myself from my family, and my not knowing how to cope in any other way. At 70 pounds, and way back at 59 pounds, no one had been ever able to convince me otherwise. It took weighing a healthier—and heavier—weight to actually help me to understand anorexia's effect on me. But most of all, I had to allow myself to change my attitude about me, to challenge my thinking, in order to see beyond the number on the scale.

"Mom, don't use the water, I'm going to take a shower!" I yelled from her guest bathroom. Mom and Dick had invited me to spend a couple of weeks with them. Earlier in the day, Mom and I had gone shopping. It was a new experience to walk into a store and be able to buy clothes right off the racks from the women's department. For years, they had been way too big. But not anymore.

I dried myself off, wrapped a towel around my body, and ran a comb through my wet hair. Several loose strands fell into the sink. *Why am I losing hair?* Since I had started eating more, and had retained more food, my hair had become thicker. "Cindy, it's okay. You're hair is fine," I reassured myself. But I peered anxiously into the bathroom mirror, anyway. My hair *was* noticeably finer and thinner. "Mom!" I ran out of the bathroom.

"Cindy, what's wrong?" Mom asked, alarmed, as she met me in the hallway.

"Mom, my hair's getting thin! I can see my scalp!" I shouted hysterically. *"I'm losing my hair! What's going on?"*

"Cindy, your hair looks fine."

"You don't believe me! Something must be wrong. I *shouldn't* be losing my hair!"

"Cindy, calm down. I'm sure it's nothing. We all lose hair." She ran her hands through my wet hair. "Your hair doesn't look or feel any different than it ever has." I skeptically accepted her reassurance, and trudged back into the bathroom.

Later that evening, I was reading in bed when Mom knocked on the bedroom door. She came in and sat down beside me. "Is that a good book?" she asked. I set it down. "Honey, I just wanted to let you know that I'm so proud of how hard you're working to get better. You look so much better." She gave me a big hug.

But my weight hadn't been the only thing to improve over the past year. Mom and I had also worked hard on our relationship. Dr. Stevens had taught me over and over that I couldn't change anyone but myself. What I hadn't realized was that changing myself could, in effect, cause others to change as well. Mom and I didn't argue like we had in the past. Maybe it was because I didn't feel I had to keep defending my beliefs, my body, or myself. In the process of gaining weight, I had learned to trust myself. Mom, as well, seemed to develop a stronger trust in me. And it had allowed her to let loose of the reins she had held so tightly. As if she sensed that I didn't need her like I had when I was so sick, or when I had been so young. After all, she had never meant to control my life—only to save it. Anorexia had been the wall between us as I struggled to become my own person, and she struggled to let me. As I worked to break free of anorexia's chains, I also worked hard to become healthier in my interactions with her and with others. I no longer accepted responsibility for their problems or their happiness. I had learned to listen to my own self, and tried hard to not be so self-doubting.

"Cindy," Mom asked now, "what made you all of a sudden turn things around? Your sister, your aunts, your uncles, your cousins, *everybody* keeps asking me. Honey, what happened that made you want to be well?"

Her question caused me to ponder. Had I gotten better because of Dr. Stevens, and his helping me to believe in me? For years, he had listened to my fears and never once judged me. Was it because that support had proved he was someone who would not go away? Or had I gotten better because of that day in the airport when Jonny shared his conversation with God. After all, nothing seemed to be getting through to me before then. And in the long run, there had been an awful lot of prayers said over the last seventeen years. Maybe God did have a plan for me, and this anorexic journey was one piece of it. And maybe it *was* only He who could let my desire become stronger than my fears.

Or had I gotten better simply because my life had become so full of nothing, and I was scared . . . *terrified, actually* . . . of always being stuck in a hospital, with no friends, with no life. I had never meant for that quest for a better me to be so life-long, so life-isolating, so life-destroying. Yet it almost had. And I was so tired of fighting a battle that I wasn't winning. Maybe it was all of these reasons, or maybe it was none of them. Maybe it was best not to question why, and just accept that it was.

I had never told Mom or anyone of that crazy conversation with Jon in the airport. My face softened at the memory of that year-old scene. Crazy as it seemed back then, I no longer questioned its meaning. *Maybe it was time to say something.* I took a deep breath. "Mom, last January, Jonny said something to me that I never told you before. I don't know if it's *the* answer to your question or if it's even a *portion* of the answer. But I think I should tell you, and then you can decide for yourself. Do you remember when we were sitting in the airport coffee shop? Well, while we were waiting for his plane, Jon told me about this conversation he had . . . with God," I began, and Mom listened quietly while I shared that strange afternoon.

" . . . Of course, I never said anything to you, because it sounded pretty bizarre, even to my ears," I finished fifteen minutes later. "I don't know, Mom. I don't really understand what it means." I hugged my knees and rocked back and forth. "I mean . . . I've been in therapy with Dr. Stevens for *nine years!* The last four of which I've seen him *every single day and still do!* If that doesn't account for any of this, nothing does!" I paused as we both reflected on my words. "Mom, maybe Dr. Stevens *and* God, *together,* played a big part in helping me get to this point."

Mom nodded, her face thoughtful. "Cindy, Jon has been getting reports from me about how well you're doing. He had never said a word about what happened at the airport either. But when I was talking to him the other night, he told me the same story you just did. At first, I found it hard to believe, but you're telling me the same thing." Mom smiled. "Cindy, I asked God so many times to please protect you, to keep you safe . . . to keep you alive. You know, honey, I cried so many tears, I had no tears left, and I just didn't know how to help you anymore. I finally had to accept that if being anorexic was the way you wanted to live your life, than I had to accept that. All I could do was to turn you over to God, and ask that he keep you safe. Maybe He really *has* been listening to our prayers. Maybe we just have to believe." We sat there in silence, and wondered over the power of God, the power of a doctor's care, the power of hope, and the power of my own determination.

I spent a week with Mom and Dick, then returned to Rochester with a routine I was finally comfortable with: breakfast and dinner without any problems, and vomiting for *just* two hours a day. I was getting better.

But better was all relative. I had gained weight by eating *safe* foods. Chicken, turkey, fish, vegetables, fruit, baked potatoes, poached eggs, juice, skim milk, diet sodas, and bread—two slices a day—were the mainstay of my diet. The diet books I had devoured as an anorexic were as deeply ingrained as the vomiting. Cookies, cakes, pies, fried foods, candy, steak, hamburgers, pizza, and pasta remained forbidden *and* binge foods.

Better was still a compromise.

Chapter 18

Detour

I woke abruptly from the middle of a sound sleep, and winced painfully as I turned over on my stomach. *My breasts really hurt.* I went into the bathroom, unbuttoned my pajama top, and examined my breasts in the mirror. Other than being swollen, they appeared fine. It was probably nothing to worry about. I buttoned the pajama top and went back to bed.

Over the next couple of months, my breasts became noticeably more painful and other symptoms soon began to emerge. My monthly period, which had been sort-of regular for several months, had suddenly become irregular. I went through a cycle every three weeks. And my hair *was* increasingly thinning in accordance to that cycle. In addition, I *craved* carbohydrates, which made the bingeing and vomiting harder to control. On top of all that, my tolerance dropped, and my frustration and irritability increased.

What the hell was happening to my body?

At my next appointment with Dr. Lazareth, I went through this puzzling new list of symptoms. "I can't explain it, but something is wrong." Learning to have a healthy body, meant recognizing when it wasn't.

"Cindy, I'm not a gynecologist. Do you have one?" Dr. Lazareth asked.

"No. Can't *you* help me? Is it something that I'm doing, or not doing, that's causing this? I don't need to gain *more* weight do I?" I maintained a weight of 100 pounds, and I had no desire to gain more.

"No, your weight is fine." He was thoughtful for a moment. "Let me consult with the gynecology group here and I'll try to find out what might be going on." The gynecologists concluded that it was just my menstrual cycle, and prescribed Motrin for cramps.

"Dr. Lazareth, I don't really have bad cramps," I insisted vehemently. "That is *not* what the problem is. And what do they mean its *just* my cycle. I never had this problem before!"

"Cindy, your hormones will stabilize and straighten out in time. Don't forget . . . you went many years without a regular cycle. It's going to take time for your body to regulate itself. We can try putting you on a birth control pill to see if that will help control some of the bleeding."

I left his office discouraged, but with a prescription for Motrin and birth control pills. I would try anything if it would help balance out my periods.

But the pills didn't help. And neither did my sessions with Dr. Stevens. "Dr. Stevens, I don't think I can take this anymore!" I cried, frustrated with the doctors' inability to come up with an answer. The initial excitement of winning anorexia's battle lessened as my menstrual cycle worsened.

"*What* can't you take anymore?" Dr. Stevens asked gently.

"*This . . . this. . . .* I don't know! I don't know *what* I can't take anymore! I just know I can't take it anymore!" The gynecologists had insisted there was nothing abnormally wrong. That my body was recovering from anorexia and just needed time to stabilize. A realistic observation, but one I had trouble accepting. Mostly because I would be fine for a couple of weeks and then, suddenly, the bottom would drop out. I could tolerate *nothing*, and I cried constantly for no apparent reason. In spite of what the other doctors said, *that* did not feel normal to me.

Puzzled by this strange turn of events, Dr. Stevens increased my anti-depressant to its safest maximum dosage. It didn't begin to touch the growing depression. Neither did our therapy.

"Dr. Stevens," I yelled angrily, after another frustrating session. "How can those doctors say there's nothing wrong with me! *Dammit!* Is it because I had anorexia? Is that why they don't believe anything is wrong? Do I have to become anorexic again in order to make this stop?" Anorexia had been my solution to problems before, why not again? Dr. Stevens listened helplessly. As a psychiatrist, he could listen and help me understand my feelings. But these feelings made no sense. "I want to go to college!" I sobbed openly. "How can I go to college when I don't know what's happening to my body!" Exhausted, I slumped in my chair. The vomiting, which had been holding its own, worsened with each coinciding cycle. And the cravings, which had been manageable, became *un*manageable, and my efforts to overcome that behavior went right out the window. "Dr. Stevens, I want to go to college. How do I do that?"

"There's a vocational counselor here at the hospital that you probably want to see." Dr. Stevens was thrilled to have me focus on something else. Maybe it would help distract me from the discomfort I felt. "His name is Greg Walker. If you want to go to school, he's the guy who will know how to make that happen."

Within a few days, I had an appointment with the vocational counselor. It was with great anticipation, and some dread that I knocked on his office door.

"Hi, Cindy. Come on in and sit down." Greg ushered me into his tiny, corner office and offered me one of two chairs. I sank, somewhat rigidly, into a dark brown, well-worn leather recliner. Out of the side of my eye, I studied the person whom I hoped would make college a reality for me. A dark-haired, handsome man in his mid-thirties, he was nicely dressed in khaki slacks and a multi-colored sweater. His pleasant manner was apparent from his friendly greeting, the relaxed way he sat, and the warm smile on his face. Though this was our first formal introduction, Greg had already heard reports about me while I had been in the hospital day program. Apparently, I had a reputation of being extremely rigid, very controlling, and set on one course only: to lose weight.

"I want to go to school," I began nervously, not at all aware of the reputation that had preceded me. "I'm not sure what I have to do to start. All I know is that I *really* want to go to school."

Greg nodded. "Okay, Cindy. If you want to go to school, I can help you with that. But let me explain that I have a lot of people walk through my door and tell me the same thing, and then nothing ever happens. I can tell you what you have to do, and make recommendations. But nothing is going to get done, unless you *want* it to get done." Greg smiled. "College won't be easy, but if we work on this together, we can make it a reality for you. Do you have an idea what you would like to study in school?" I shook my head. He scribbled some information down on a piece of paper and handed it to me. "Here's the name and phone number of a person I'd like you to see for some vocational testing. It will give us a baseline of your interests and skills. We'll go from there." I left Greg's office with another appointment in two weeks. Yet even as school became more of a reality, so did the extent of the still nameless symptoms.

I walked home from the bus stop after yet another discouraging appointment with Dr. Stevens. The wind picked up and whipped my shoulder-length hair sharply across my face. Irritated, tears blurred my vision. "Damn wind!" I muttered angrily. I hurried into the apartment building, and ran up the stairs to my apartment. I recognized the beginning symptoms of another cycle.

I slammed the door, and angrily threw my purse across the room. *"Goddammit!"* I screamed to the empty apartment. *"I can't take this anymore!* What is wrong with my body? I just want to be healthy! *Please.* . . . . I just want to be healthy." Crying hysterically, I crumbled into a sobbing heap on the kitchen floor.

I winced in pain, turned gingerly on my side, and tried to get comfortable. But my sore and swollen breasts prevented any comfortable sleeping positions. *Would this pain never go away?* I finally gave up, went out to the living room, and phoned my mother, even though it was two o'clock in the morning. "Mom? I don't think I can deal with this," I cried when she sleepily answered. "I wish I knew what was wrong. My breasts hurt so much! I'm crying all the time, my hair keeps falling out, and I don't even know why!"

Mom listened to the anguish in my voice as my fear carried through the phone wires. These middle of the night phone calls had become too familiar. "Honey, what do the doctors say?"

"Oh, Mom! The birth control pills aren't helping with the bleeding. My periods keep coming every three weeks. I've been taking the Motrin, but it's not cramps that are the problem! Cramps I can deal with. It's all these other things. I know something is not right with my body! Why doesn't anybody believe me?" But Mom had no answers. She could only offer her love and reassurance that it would get better.

"Mom, I fought so hard to get control over anorexia and now—*this?*" I whimpered. "Do you think it's the anorexia that is making this happen?" *Was this the price I had to pay for being afraid to eat all those years?*

"Cindy . . . honey, I don't know. Maybe your body is just readjusting to having periods again. After all, it *has* been a long time since you have had a regular cycle. Maybe, in time, it will straighten out on its own." And I started crying in earnest at those words. Maybe I really *was* to blame for this current distress.

"Mom, I want to be well! I want go to school. . . ." I choked on my sobs. "I'm scared, Mom. I'm scared it's never going to happen. I'm thirty-one years old! I thought that when I gained weight, everything would be better. But it's not! I lost, didn't I? I lost, and so did my body."

"Honey, it hasn't been that long since you started eating again. You were malnourished for a pretty long time. God only knows what damage could have been done over the years. Your body needs time to heal itself. I'm sure it's going to straighten out. If the doctors are telling you it will be okay, listen to them."

I hung up and went back to bed, but sleep was not to be a reprieve. Insomnia was the newest symptom to add to the growing list. *"Dammit!* I'm going to find out what is wrong with me . . . even if it kills me!"

The next day, I sat, crying, in Dr. Stevens' office. "And to think there was a time when I had no tears," I joked weakly. Dr. Stevens smiled. My feeble attempt to make light of the seriousness of the situation was encouraging.

"Dr. Stevens?" I looked at him wearily. "I want to ask you something . . . and . . . I'm a little afraid to ask you." I took a deep breath. "In all the years you've known me, I have never—*ever*—asked you directly, to put me in the hospital. Well . . . I'm asking you now. Would you please put me in the hospital?"

"Cindy, why do you want me to put you in the hospital?" Dr. Stevens asked, surprised by this request. "Is it because of what we have been talking about during the last few sessions?" We had started talking about people leaving . . . Janey . . . Sandy . . . Rob . . . my family. If I was to get beyond my eating disorders, I would need to free those stored up feelings and memories.

My tears began again, in earnest. "Dr. Stevens, I know I have to face some painful feelings. And yes, that's scary. But it's more than that. I'm scared for *me*. I stood at the top of the stairwell in my apartment building today, and I thought how easy it would be for me to jump. But Dr. Stevens, I don't want to die. I don't even want to hurt myself!" I stopped, and stared at him. "Dr. Stevens, I know that my eating disorders are one problem, and my periods are another. But together, I can't sort out what's what. All I know is that when I had anorexia, I didn't get a period, and I didn't have to go through this every month. I don't want to be anorexic again, but I don't know how else to make this stop. I need more help. *Please,* Dr. Stevens . . . help me."

Dr. Stevens sat back in his chair. "Okay. If it will help keep you safe, I'll admit you."

A little more than a year had passed since Jonny and I had sat in the airport coffee shop. The road back to health had proven bumpy and unpredictable. I had hoped to never return to the hospital again, except—*maybe*—to have a baby.

I boarded a bus for home and sat at the first empty seat I spotted. I leaned my head against the bus window. Gaining weight had only been the first step. I had many more to take before I reached my goal. The fight wasn't over.

Dr. Stevens admitted me into the hospital, and the first week passed uneventfully as I settled into the hospital routine. At the beginning of the second week, I went in the day room of the inpatient unit, and joined another female patient as she worked on a crossword puzzle.

"Do you mind if I ask why you're here?" she questioned. "It's just that you look so *okay* . . . and so *normal.*"

Normal. It was exactly how I wanted to be. But I wanted to be normal *outside* of a hospital, not inside of one. "I'm here because I'm having some problems with my menstrual cycle; a lot of strange symptoms."

"Why aren't you on a medical floor, instead of a psychiatric floor?"

"That's a good question. I guess it's because no one really seems to believe that there is anything terribly wrong with me. Maybe because I feel like I'm going crazy every month." I laughed sarcastically. "Maybe that's why I'm here."

The woman was puzzled. "What kind of symptoms are you talking about?"

I hesitated to answer. She'd think I really was crazy if I told her. Oh what the heck, even if she did, at least she would know I was on the right floor after all! I described what I had been going through for the past year.

"You know," she said wisely, "you should talk to Deedra. It sounds like you and she have the same problem."

"What do you mean the *same* problem?"

"I think she's here for the same reasons you are. Guess they thought she was going crazy, too. Anyway, she's got this doctor now, who's helping her. Maybe you should talk to her." She gave me the other patient's name and room number, and I immediately went looking for her. *Please, God let it be true!*

I knocked on her door. A very pretty black woman, who appeared to be in her early thirties, looked up. "Deedra? I'm sorry to disturb you, but I *really* need to talk to you. I was just talking to another lady, and well, one thing led to another. The point is, I'm having a lot of the same symptoms with my period as I'm told you are. Can we talk and compare notes?"

Deedra listened as I recounted how it had been over the last several months. Time and again she interrupted, exclaiming, *"Gawd,* honey! That's exactly what's been happening to me! Did anybody tell you what's wrong?"

I shook my head mournfully. "The doctors think it's just my needing to get used to having a monthly period again."

"I thought that I was going crazy, too. But I'm not and neither are you. They put me on this psych floor because my family didn't know what else to do. My doctor got me a referral to Dr. Blake. Dr. Blake told me I have PMS. That's *premenstrual syndrome.* Maybe you ought to see Dr. Blake, too," Deedra added knowingly.

"Okay, Dr. Stevens," I mused as I left Deedra's room. "You tell me to trust my feelings. Well, my feelings are telling me that maybe Deedra is right. Maybe I need to see this Dr. Blake." When I saw Dr. Stevens the next day, I repeated my previous day's conversation with Deedra. Dr. Stevens agreed to make the referral to Dr. Blake.

Several more days passed before arrangements were completed. *"Please,* God," I prayed frantically on the morning of his scheduled visit. *"Please,* let Dr. Blake be able to help me."

"Hello . . . Miss Nappa? I'm Dr. Blake." A tall, white-haired, soft-spoken man knocked on my open door and entered my room. He offered his hand and sat down on a chair while I sat nervously on my bed. "I hear you have been asking to see me," he said, his words eloquently laced with the faintest British accent. "Would you like to tell me what has been going on for the last several months."

For the next hour, I shared not only the strange symptoms, but also my long battle with anorexia and bulimia. Maybe if I told him everything, he would find the answer somewhere in the middle of all of it. "When my periods first started up again, I was happy. Because, to me, it was a true sign of my body returning to normal. Even though they weren't exactly regular right from the beginning, I guess I figured that in time they would be. But it's hasn't happened yet. If anything, it seems to be getting even worse. I don't know, Dr. Blake. I'm beginning to feel as if I'm going crazy."

"Cindy, you are not going crazy. And I don't believe that you have to go through this agony every month. I believe I can help you."

He can help me? But I didn't think anybody even *believed* me! I resisted the urge to throw my arms around him. "Dr. Blake, I was really afraid that I would have to lose weight again. Not because I want to be anorexic, but because I know I have to make this all stop, and it's the only way I know how to do that." I smiled, relieved. "What happens now?"

"Hormone tests first. I would like to get some levels on you and proceed from there."

The tests revealed an extremely low estrogen level, which could be corrected by an estrogen supplement. Within a week, I was discharged. Now that my body was receiving the hormones it needed to stabilize itself, I could, once again, focus on college.

Three weeks later, I awakened with severe cramping throughout my abdomen. "What in the world?" I gasped, and clutched my stomach. I made my way to the bathroom and discovered that my period had started. I wasn't sure whether to be happy or worried. It was the first time in months that I had no premenstrual symptoms. It was also the first time that I had ever experienced such horrible cramps. I returned to bed. "Gosh, it feels like I'm in labor!" I joked. The pain didn't let up until several days later, when my period stopped.

At my next appointment with Dr. Blake, I described the pain, jokingly comparing it to a woman in labor—for a week.

"Cindy, I want you to stop the estrogen pill. You shouldn't be having pain like that," he cautioned. "Until we know what is going on, I don't want you taking anymore hormones. I believe that it would be best if I do a laparoscopy—a test where I would make a small incision in your navel and insert a scope to look at what's going on." I left his office with the test scheduled, not at all pleased with giving up the medicine that had worked so well.

The next day, I baked a batch of oatmeal cookies, and then sat at the kitchen table eating the warm, gooey cookies . . . one by one. Bingeing and purging still worked for coping with uncertainty and fear. Even though I maintained 100 pounds, most everybody—including myself—believed I had recovered completely. It was at if gaining weight meant everything was better.

Three weeks later, I had the laparoscopy. The day after the test, Dr. Blake shared the results with Mom, Dick, and myself. He said I had a severe case of endometriosis. "And," he said, "this diagnosis immediately cancels any continuing help from hormones. Estrogen will only make the endometriosis worse. Cindy, I have to tell you that I never saw such extensive damage from endometriosis before. Endometrial tissue is growing not only over your reproductive organs, but also into your muscles." Mom grabbed my hand. "If you were married," Dr. Blake continued, "I'd suggest that you get pregnant. That often helps control endometrial problems. But I'm not sure you'd even be able to *get* pregnant. However, we do have to stop your periods. That can be done either by taking a hormone called Danazol or by having a hysterectomy. If you take Danazol, understand that the longest you can take it will be nine months. At that time, you will again have to make the decision whether or not to have surgery. You must understand that this hormone treatment is only a short-term solution to eventual surgery. The most it will buy you is time." His face was serious as he delivered this news.

A *hysterectomy?* I was only thirty-one. I was too young—wasn't I? I had to grow up first! I had to go to school. I had to get married. I had to have my own family some day. And what about the anorexia? Had all those years of being without a menstrual cycle, disrupted not only my hormones, but also prevented an earlier diagnosis of endometriosis? And the bulimia? Every time I purged, I placed my hands on my abdomen and pushed *hard*... kneading . . . pushing. For seventeen years, I had pushed on my stomach. Had that, plus the vomiting, been contributing factors?

"Cindy, I don't want you to make a decision today. Go home, think it over. Talk about it amongst all of you. If you have any questions, call me. Give yourself time to make this decision. The important thing to remember is that you feel comfortable with whatever decision you make."

We were a subdued group leaving his office. I spent the next few days at my mother's home, discussing the pros and cons of each of the given options. In the end, I kept coming to the same conclusion: I just wanted to be healthy. Taking hormones to stop my periods would only bring me to this same point in nine months. Dr. Blake had been quite blunt. I really had no choice. Surgery was inevitable. The sooner I had it done, the sooner I would be back on the road to health. Besides, I had to go to college in September.

I made my decision.

"Mom, can we talk?" I walked into her bedroom and closed the door behind me. She stopped folding laundry and sat down on the bed. "Mom, I always wanted a little girl . . . just like me," I said, and went over to the bed. I sat down next to her and grabbed her hands, squeezing them tightly. "But Mom . . . I've been sick for a year because of these periods. I'm exhausted, physically and emotionally. Even though estrogen supplements help with that, Dr. Blake says that I can't take them because of the endometriosis. Mom, even if I don't have surgery, he believes that I may never be able to have children. Besides, what good would it be for me to have children if I'm not well enough to take care of them?"

"I know, Cindy," she agreed softly.

"Mom, I don't even have a life of my own. Maybe if I were married, I would feel differently. But Mom, I don't know where I'm headed. Wherever it may be leading, I'll never get there if I can't get past this hurdle." Mom wrapped her arms around me, and rocked me gently, just like she had when I was a little girl, and one of my adventures had turned scary.

I pulled away and looked into her eyes. "Mom, maybe I will never be able to give you a little Cindy. But maybe I will be able to give you me . . . the *real* me." Tears welled up in my eyes. "I've been sick for more than half of my life, and I really miss me! I want the person I know myself to be. And I can't let this detour stop me from finding me." I took a deep breath. "I've decided to have the hysterectomy."

We sat there, mother and child, our arms entwined around each other's body, and cried. Our tears were for the children I would never have, and for the person within me that I still struggled to find. The decision had been made.

The journey was far from over.

Chapter 19

When a Door Closes, A Window Opens Elsewhere

"Hi, Cindy. My name is Mary, and I'm going to be your nurse today." I was in the hospital awaiting surgery. Once I had told Dr. Blake my decision, the surgery was quickly scheduled in an effort to avoid my having to go through another cycle. Now, the day before surgery, I had come to the hospital alone. Mom and Dick would be there in the morning.

"Come out to the nurses station when you change out of your street clothes. I need to get your weight and height." Ten minutes later, I walked over to the scale, and stepped up on it— a feat that was no longer threatening.

"One-hundred pounds and," Mary raised the measuring bar, "five-feet, one and a half inches tall."

I had grown an inch and a half? How could that be? I was just months shy of turning thirty-two, too old to still be growing. But the numbers weren't lying. Along with the gained weight, I had gained height. *Could my body really be picking up from where it had left off at age fourteen?*

That evening, I slept soundly—courtesy of the sleeping

pill Dr. Blake had ordered. The next morning, Mom and Dick arrived early. When the surgical orderly arrived to take me down to the operating room, I hugged them both and scooted onto the waiting stretcher. The next time I saw them, it would be all over.

I opened my eyes, yawned, and turned over on my side. Outside the hospital room window, the warm May sun shone brightly. I sat up, and a knife-sharp pain ripped through my abdomen. "Owww!" I doubled over, and instinctively folded my arms across my stomach. I took a deep breath, then slid gingerly to the edge of the bed. I hung one leg over the side. *So far, so good.* Very carefully, I slipped my other leg out from under the blanket, spasms tore across my lower abdomen. I gasped, waited several minutes and then—*very slowly*—laid back down. *Maybe I'll just stay in bed.*

"Hi, Cindy." Dr. Stevens knocked on the opened door and walked in. *"Well . . .* I see you're finally awake." He smiled broadly. "How are you feeling?"

"Dr. Stevens! I was wondering when you were going to stop by and see me," I winced, and sat up—slowly. Three days after surgery, and the haziness from the pain medication was finally lifting.

"You don't remember, but I did stop by the day of . . . and after . . . surgery. You were asleep, but I talked to your mom."

"Dr. Stevens, she'll be here soon. So will my sister, Debbie. She's visiting from Florida. Do you know that it has been three years since I last saw her? Do you think you could stick around to meet her?" I asked. "She's heard so much about you. . . ." Voices from outside the room, interrupted, and my family descended into the room.

Debbie stopped mid-sentence as she laid her eyes upon me. *"Oh . . .* my God!" she gasped. "I can't believe it! It's my sister! *Cindy* . . . it's you again!" She rushed over and threw her arms around me. Laughing and crying at the same time, she sat down on the edge of my bed, and clung to me. "Look at the roses in your face!" She touched my cheeks, my nose, as if to reassure herself that they—*I*—was real. "Cindy, you're back! You look just like you did before you ever got sick!" Debbie looked around the room, and spotted Dr. Stevens as he tried to slip out of the room. She jumped off the bed and ran over to throw her arms around him. *"Thank you,* Dr. Stevens. Thank you for giving me my sister back."

And one of my aunts, who visited later that week, had the same experience. "Cindy," Aunt Martha whispered in my ear. "It's so good to have you back with us. We missed you."

And so had I—missed me too. Anorexia was no longer standing in my way. I had learned that as long as I searched for "thin," everything else got pushed aside. It had come before friends, before family, and even before myself. It was a destroyer of relationships, a destroyer of health, and a destroyer of life. And yet, even though my obsession with food and weight had over-shadowed every aspect of my personality, anorexia hadn't won. I was fighting back.

After ten days in the hospital, and two weeks recuperating at my mother's, I was ready to go home. I packed my suitcase, and glanced around the guest bedroom to make sure I hadn't forgotten anything. My eyes rested on three old model horses still holding a place of honor on a bookcase shelf. I walked over and picked up the Golden Palomino. *Sandy.* The memory elicited a sad smile. "Cindy," I gently scolded. "Are you *never* going to be able to forget that your friend is gone? That was a long time ago. It's time to let go and move on." *It's time to grow up.* I placed the prancing steed gently back on the shelf, zipped the bag closed, and lowered it carefully onto the floor. My abdomen was still sore.

"Cindy! Breakfast is ready."

I joined Mom and Dick at the breakfast table, and accepted a portion of scrambled eggs and two crispy strips of bacon. The stitches and pain allowed for little appetite and—no energy for purging. It hurt too much. I pushed aside a nagging worry—would the bulimia return when the pain was gone?

I had a huge stack of mail waiting when I arrived back in

Rochester. One of the envelopes was from the college I had applied for admission. I tore the manila envelope open. *"Dear Ms. Nappa, It is our pleasure to offer you admission to the fall semester at Monroe Community College. . . ."* I had done it! I was going to college!

By the end of that summer, my sessions with Dr. Stevens were reduced. School would be starting soon, and maybe—*just maybe*—my life and health were finally stabilizing. At 100 pounds, my body seemed to finally be at a point—a setpoint—where I could eat and not keep gaining. The calories that I had consumed to gain the weight were now maintaining that weight. Just like Dr. Stevens and Dr. Lazareth had said would happen. But I had to see it for myself. I had to experience that I *really* would stop gaining. I now knew how much to eat to be healthy, and I wasn't panicking. At times, I still felt a little shaky and scared. But in spite of the fear, I kept my weight stable. I was giving myself a chance—a chance to try life differently. And it was working. In one year's time, the numbers on the scale no longer dictated the script I had to follow. It was a slow process, and I wasn't doing it perfectly, and I stumbled often. *But my desire never wavered.* It still remained stronger than that fear. Going back to college would be scary, but not as scary as facing those fears. If I could let go of anorexia, everything else paled in comparison. Sessions with Dr. Stevens focused more on feelings, and less on the numbers, because the numbers were less of a worry. *And because gaining weight was not a cure-all,* the issues behind it, underneath it, surrounding it, needed to also be conquered. True recovery meant acceptance of all of me.

"Dr. Stevens, do you think I'll ever be able to love anybody?" That question had been on my mind for a very long time.

Dr. Stevens' face was thoughtful. My continued search for answers often caught him off-guard. "Cindy, why do you believe that you will never be able to love anybody?"

"Well, look at the problems I had with Rob. I think he left

me because I couldn't love him. But Dr. Stevens," I insisted. "I *did* love Rob . . . *really* . . . I did!" After ten years of not being able to talk about that experience, I was finally ready to acknowledge it.

"Cindy," he smiled gently. "You were a very sick and scared young girl. Even though you were unable to express yourself in a more direct way, you dealt with your feelings as best as you could back then. It didn't mean that you didn't love him. You weren't ready to commit to a marriage back then. Deep down, you knew that, and you stopped it the only way you knew how. You didn't have the knowledge or the tools to express that in a healthy manner, but you did the best that you could."

"Dr. Stevens, I still love him, you know. Sometimes I dream about Rob and it's always the same dream."

"And what dream is that?"

"Where he comes back, and he wants to marry me," I answered softly. "And in my dream, he still loves me. But when I wake up from that dream, I feel *really* sad. The same sadness that I felt for so many years." My lower lip trembled. "It never really went away, you know. Even though I've gained weight, it's still there . . . in the background. It's the sadness of all I lost. Rob, Mary Jean, Sandy . . . even Janey, isn't it?" And in spite of my best efforts, the tears came. By saying the words out loud, I lessened anorexia's strength and tore down its wall, brick by brick. I had to face those feelings. I had to say them out loud, and acknowledge their reality. "I hated my dad for leaving me, too. When he got so sick, I was so mad at him! I wanted him to be strong like he always had been. I needed him. I didn't want to be strong for him . . . or for my family. I felt like the most horrible person. It's like I could never do enough to please them. And yet I thought if I could only be the way that everyone wanted me to be, then everything would be fine, and maybe everyone wouldn't have left. I guess I binge to fill the loneliness, don't I, Dr. Stevens?" I said sadly, and the pain of that admission gripped my heart, my empty heart. We both knew that answer.

"Cindy, you are grieving your losses. This is part of your healing. You have tried to bury these painful feelings for more than half your life. Anorexia kept you so preoccupied, so out of touch, so numb, that you could almost forget you had feelings. Yes, Cindy, the loneliness is a big part of why you are sad, and why you binge. You always felt that you were never good enough. You weren't a good enough friend, you weren't a good enough daughter, you weren't a good enough lover, you weren't a good enough person. What I have been trying to show you—*teach you,* over the years, is that you *are* good enough. *Just the way you are.* But anorexia and bulimia kept you from seeing that. Just as they kept you from growing, experiencing life, and learning healthy coping skills. But," Dr. Stevens added, "you didn't know how to cope in any other way. At the same time those disorders were slowly killing you, they were keeping you alive. *All* these feelings that you talk about are normal. The problem was that you did not *perceive* them as normal. Emotionally, you couldn't handle what they represented. My challenge was to keep you alive, and at the same time, help us understand *who* you were and *why.* Throughout that whole process, I needed to get you to trust me—so you could trust yourself. But more importantly, I tried to help you *see and accept yourself* as you."

"Dr. Stevens, I'm really afraid that I'll *never* be able to love anybody . . . *ever!*" I insisted. "Maybe I'll always be alone. And all I'll have are memories of people who *used* to love me." I stopped abruptly, and studied the books lining his bookcase shelves. "Did you read all those books, Dr. Stevens?"

He smiled patiently. I wasn't really interested in his books. "Yes, Cindy. Over the years I have. So, tell me more about the loneliness."

I sighed deeply, my mournful brown eyes glistened with tears. "I can't stop dreaming . . . about Rob. And I can't stop thinking of him. It's *really* crazy, Dr. Stevens. I mean . . . I know he's probably married. And that he probably has *tons* of kids. But I still love him, and I don't know how to stop. It hurts. These feelings really hurt." I stopped abruptly and again, stared at the bookcase. "When I eat and throw up, I don't feel the sadness or loneliness. I'm afraid if I stop, all that will be left is this *huge* emptiness inside of me." I paused, and looked back over at Dr. Stevens. "Going to college has helped. To my classmates, I am no different than they are. But," and I hung my head hopelessly, "I'm still bulimic . . . and I still love Rob."

"My friend, look at me," Dr. Stevens encouraged gently. I raised my woeful face. "Cindy, it is okay that you still love Rob. Nobody says you have to stop that feeling. There will probably always be a corner of your heart that will hold a special place for Rob, and that's okay. There is plenty of room in your heart to love others." He smiled. "But right now, you are mourning the loss of something you wanted, but never really had. We all tend to look back at our past and only remember the good times. You are hanging on to a memory you always wanted . . . had *needed* . . . but it had never really happened. It is human nature to forget about the pain. I will remind you again—for the first time, you are discovering who you are, what you want, and you are going after it. Some day, you will meet a special someone who will fill the emptiness inside your heart. Just because it hasn't happened yet, does not mean it never will."

"But will someone be able to love *me*, forever? Everybody that I loved—left. I don't want people to keep leaving. How do I make that *not* happen? Is it *me*, Dr. Stevens? Is it because of who I am that people leave?"

"Cindy, you are not responsible for everyone's actions or feelings. You always believe it is *your* fault when other people hurt you, that you must have done something wrong. That is not true. You don't control the way other people behave. Nor do you control the way they *feel*. Just like nobody controls your behavior or feelings. You have a great sensitivity about you, but it often works to your *dis*advantage—you doubt yourself. As your self-confidence grows stronger, and you become more sure of yourself, your feelings, your decisions, you will be less impacted or influenced by other's behavior. Being Cindy is good enough, and it is *all* right," he emphasized. "You are considerate, compassionate, intelligent, and *okay!* You are a very strong person, Cindy. You would never have made it this far if you weren't."

Strong. I used to hate it when people said that to me. I thought it meant that I *shouldn't* be bothered by the events in my life. That I *shouldn't* be angry . . . that I *shouldn't* be sad . . . that I *shouldn't* be lonely. I thought it meant that I should have no wants or no needs, and that I was supposed to accept every hurtful thing that ever happened. "Strong is good?" I had to be sure.

"Yes," Dr. Stevens confirmed. "Strong is *very* good. It means you are a fighter, not a quitter. It means there is something in you that says '*I will survive. I will not give up.*' It means that when you fall, you get back up. Strong is you, Cindy."

"Dr. Stevens, Rob just up and left and I shut my heart. What happened ten years ago, still feels unfinished. How do I end it inside of me? How do I let go of it?"

"You could call him," he stated simply. "Or call his family."

Call him? Call his family? "I could *never* do that!" I protested.

"Why not? You always said you liked his family and that they liked you. There is nothing wrong with calling to say hello and ask how everyone is."

"But Dr. Stevens!" The mere thought sent me into a panic! "They wouldn't even know who I was! It's been *ten years!* They wouldn't remember me. People don't remember me . . . *remember?* I can't *just* call them! I mean, what would I say—hello, remember me? I'm the girl who broke your son's heart and in turn, he broke mine!" I shuddered at their imagined reaction. "Be real, Dr. Stevens. I can't do that!"

He shrugged his shoulders. "Well, write them a letter. I don't care. All I'm suggesting is a way to conclude that chapter in your life. It's up to you if . . . and how . . . you do it. If you don't, that's fine too."

Call Rob's family? And risk being rejected, or not being re-membered? Well, I'd think about it.

Despite my budding confidence and Dr. Stevens' sessions, my daily binges had increased to three hours. Weekends were another matter. On those days, I was mostly confined to the kitchen and bathroom. School had broken my isolation, but I still kept to myself when at home. Anorexia's cycle had been broken, but would I ever be able to do the same with bulimia?

Dr. Stevens' earlier suggestion continued to haunt me. There was absolutely no way that I could pick up the phone and call Rob, or write him a letter. The years had been too many. I couldn't intrude on his life, especially if I brought unhappy memories. But what if he hadn't married? What if he still loved me? I walked over to my desk, and flipped through the pages of an old address book. I still had his parents phone number. Did I dare? I picked up the phone receiver and quickly set it back down again. *No, not yet.*

For the next few weeks, I constantly wondered, should I call? *Just call. For once and for all, finish a part of your life.* I took a deep breath and picked up the receiver. I dialed Rob's family.

"Hello?" A man's deep, resounding voice answered. It was Rob's father.

"Mr. Polinski?" My voice shook—my entire *body* shook! "You probably don't remember me, but this is Cindy . . . Cindy Nappa."

"Why, I don't believe it! This is wonderful! My dear, how *are* you? How have you been? It's been so long since we've talked to you!"

"I'm sorry that I haven't called before this," I apologized. "I was sick for a pretty long time, but I'm all better now." *Liar. You're still bulimic.* "I've been thinking of *all* of you, for quite a while. . . ."

"Cindy," Mr. Polinski interrupted. "There is no need to explain. We have talked about you often, wondering how you were doing, *what* you were doing. You have been the topic of many of a

229

dinner conversation here." He paused and then added, "I know you had a lot of things you were struggling with, Cindy. But I always believed you would overcome them some day. I am very happy for you, everyone will be." We talked for over an hour, about my family . . . his family . . . my going back to college . . . but nothing about Rob.

I eyed the clock and took a big gulp. I had to ask. "How's Rob doing? Is he married now?" I asked nonchalantly, and prayed for courage to accept whatever he said.

Rob's father must have sensed how hard it was for me to ask, for he answered gently. "Yes, Cindy. Rob is married. He has been married for several years. He has a little boy."

Married? A little boy? My heart sank. "I'm happy for him. I wish him well." My voice trembled. "Please, tell Rob for me." We talked for several more minutes, promised to keep in touch, and said good-bye. *Rob is married. He has a child.* Just because my life had stopped, was no reason to think his had too.

And for the next few months, Rob haunted my nights. Only now—in my dreams—he had a wife. And—in my dreams— he left her for me. Rob still loved me—in my dreams.

"Shit!" I massaged my jaw then attempted to eat the baked chicken breast I had prepared for dinner. I bit down again, and my extremely loose lower denture pressed painfully against gum tissue. Over the last several years, root canals gave way to extractions until none of my natural teeth remained. I went into the bathroom and padded the partials with cotton; a technique I had resorted to for the last few years. It worked. The soft cushioning allowed me to continue to eat.

My next dental exam revealed that my jawbone was reabsorbing at an alarming rate, a result of the loss of all my teeth and the current ill-fitting partials. The dentist's recommendation: bone grafts in my upper and lower jaw, which would allow more surface area for the dentures to rest on.

"Cindy, how is it that you lost all your teeth? You are not

that old." The oral surgeon my dentist had recommended was puzzled. I was only thirty-three years old.

My face reddened. "I have had a lot of problems with my salivary glands over the years. My left parotid gland was removed when I was only twenty-two." I didn't mention the vomiting. Admitting that the vomiting was responsible would be the same as pointing a finger at myself and declaring, *"It's your fault, Cindy. This is the destruction you have brought on yourself."* I already blamed myself for the loss of my reproductive organs. I wasn't ready to admit responsibility for the loss of my teeth.

A week later, I returned to make arrangements for the bone grafting. The oral surgeon pulled up a chair beside me and sat down. "Cindy, I've been studying your situation in great detail, and I've come to the conclusion that bone grafts are not your best solution here." I stared at him wide-eyed. "Cindy, you need to understand that bone grafts will only work for the short-term. In time, they too will reabsorb, and then you'll be back at square one again. I don't want to put you through surgery if, in the end, it won't give you what you really need—a more permanent answer. Actually, dental implants would be a better option for you."

It was a most discouraging discussion. I had thought for sure that bone grafts were going to fix the problem with my mouth and jaw. I called the oral surgeon whom had been recommended, Dr. Mason, and made an appointment for the next morning.

Dr. Mason came to the same conclusions. "Due to the loss of your teeth, your lower jawbone has reabsorbed to about the width of a cigarette." He held up his fingers and demonstrated the size—slightly more than a quarter of an inch. "That's pretty thin. But there is enough bone for me to place implants . . . titanium posts . . . into your jaw. These implants, if successful, will generate new bone and anchor themselves," he explained. "This is called bone integration. Six months after this initial post placement, I will then add another piece to the implants called abutments. These come up through the gum line and a permanent prosthesis is screwed onto them. So, essentially, you will have as close to real teeth as you can possibly get. This is what we call *fixed dentures*. They are permanently attached to the implants. The most encouraging part of all this is that the implants will help slow the bone from reabsorbing."

Why that is better than bone grafts! I would have permanent teeth again! No more sores in my mouth, no more pain, no more bone loss! But even more importantly, I wouldn't have to take the stupid dentures out of my mouth every night; a most unpleasant and embarrassing side effect of my search for thin. *Ohhh!* This was wonderful! "Okay," I agreed quite enthusiastically. "I want to have these implants. What do I have to do?"

"Well . . . the dental implants are rather expensive. Insurance does not cover their cost."

"How much is it?"

"The total cost, including all the outpatient work that will need to be done, is ten thousand dollars," he answered quietly.

Ten thousand dollars! I didn't know whether to laugh or cry. But tears quickly clouded my eyes, and I struggled to speak past a lump in my throat. "Dr. Mason, I was sick for a long, *long* time. The only income I have right now is social security disability. I live in government subsidized housing because I don't have enough money for rent. I buy my food with food stamps, and walk or take a bus everywhere because I can't afford a car. *Hell,* I don't even know how I'm going to pay for this consultation. But I can tell you one thing," I said firmly, "maybe I don't have any money today, but some day I will." Dr. Mason listened without comment. "I know that my oral health is not going to get any better, if anything, it will continue to deteriorate. I don't want to lose any more bone or," my voice shook and I choked on the words, "any more time."

Dr. Mason nodded sympathetically. "Cindy, I wish that this procedure was covered by insurance but, for now, I can only hope that some day it will be." His words were of little comfort. The bottom line remained the same: I couldn't afford the treatment that was needed.

After talking it over with my mother, she offered to finance the implant surgery. A small inheritance from her mother, who had died a year earlier, would cover the cost. Six months later, I underwent the first of two surgeries. The lower jaw would have to be broken, and then be pushed back—about half an inch— before implants could be placed; a result of the receding bone structure that caused the upper and lower jawbones to no longer line up. The second surgery—implanting of the posts—would follow ten weeks later.

On the night before the first surgery, I settled back in the hospital bed with Whiskers safely in my arms. He was still by my side; our journey was far from over.

"Cindy, are you awake?" Mom whispered softly in my ear.

Groggily, I turned towards her voice, and tried to open my medicated-laden eyes. Piercing pain encased my entire head. "Mmmm iiii hhh uuuu?" *Mom, is that you?* "Mmmmm fffff, uuurrrsss!" *My face hurts.*

"Shhh, don't try to talk, honey." Mom placed her cool hand on my painfully swollen face. "Dr. Mason is here."

Dr. Mason gently patted my shoulder. "Hello, Cindy. The surgery went very well. There were no complications. I did not have to wire your jaw as I thought I might have to. I used screws in the joints to hold your jaw in place. Please don't try to talk because you can't open your mouth more than a quarter of an inch."

"Aa wwwnntt mma mmmrrrr lllllsss." *I want my mirror please.* I gestured towards the nightstand by the side of the hospital bed. Mom placed the tiny mirror in my hand. I held it up to my mouth and squinted at my lips. They were black and blue, almost hidden by the immense swelling of my face. But my lips matched; the lower jaw no longer protruded outwards. "Uu ddd uh ggdd jjbb." *You did a good job.*

Four more days in the hospital, and I left to recuperate at

my mother's. I could not talk clearly or ingest anything other than liquids or blender food. Chewing was impossible. The screws did their job. They held my jaw secure and allowed for little movement. Recovery was difficult and painfully slow. I checked the bathroom mirror daily to see if anything looked like my own familiar face. Each day, a little more of me emerged. And as my face became more normal, so did my appetite. Two weeks after surgery, I was starving. Baby food was just not cutting it. I wanted steak, cookies, potato chips, pizza . . . I was so hungry! I opened the refrigerator freezer and spotted a familiar package—chocolate marshmallow ice cream! But of course! Why hadn't I thought of this sooner. Mom had stocked the freezer with a couple of half gallons of my favorite ice cream. I grabbed the container, slammed the door shut, and ladled generous scoops into a bowl. I wolfed down two large dishes of the sinfully, *wonderfully* tasty treat. And then, I did what came so naturally—I went to the bathroom, leaned over the toilet, placed my hands against my abdomen and pushed *hard*. In seconds, the cold thick mass reversed its route and gushed out.

And my mouth never opened more than a quarter of an inch.

I walked over to the bathroom sink and rinsed out my mouth. I looked up, and met my pale, swollen face in the mirror. "Oh, Cindy. What have you gone and done?" I chastised. But the disgust was short-lived. I had managed to out-smart the limitations of my jaw. Bulimia had won another round.

Seven weeks later, eleven posts (six in the upper jaw, and five in the lower jaw) were implanted. I started my second year in college, just ten days after surgery. Still in pain . . . still eating soft foods . . . still bingeing and purging.

I *still* had a long way to go.

I stood in front of my bathroom vanity mirror and brushed back my shoulder-length hair. Eight months had passed since the implant operation. I held a small hand mirror up to the side of my face, and studied my profile in the larger mirror. My lips met perfectly, but what had once been a strong jaw line was now a short one, and my chin drooped slightly. Moving the lower jaw-bone back had required removing a piece of bone. And the process had subtly changed my whole profile. Between the facial bone loss, the drooping chin, and the short jaw, the true damage of anorexia and bulimia was more than I wanted—or was willing—to accept. "Shit!" I threw the hand mirror across the room, and it hit the bathroom wall, shattering into several pieces. "Oh, *great!*" I groaned. "Just what I need—seven years of bad luck." I dropped down on my hands and knees and picked up the broken pieces and threw them in the trash. "A flat face! I have a *stupid*, flat face! Even my hair doesn't look right!" I picked up a hairbrush and yanked it down my long tresses, which in themselves seemed only to exaggerate the new shallowness of my face. *Would I ever feel at peace with my body?*

I sat in Dr. Stevens' waiting room, drummed my fingers nervously against the wooden armrest, and tapped my foot anxiously. Impatience got the better of me, and I walked over to a picture hanging on the wall. Its gray background allowed a vague glimpse of my once shoulder-length hair, which had been replaced by an above-the-ear, cropped hairstyle.

"Hello, Cindy." Dr. Stevens walked into the waiting room. *"My* . . . look at you! You got a new haircut!"

Nervously, *very* nervously, I followed him into his office. "What do you think? Does it look okay?" The short boyish cut was one I had spotted in a magazine. On the model, it was adorable. But then—*she* had a great jawline.

"Turn around, let me see the back." I anxiously obliged. "It suits you perfectly," he approved.

"I wasn't sure if I would look okay in short hair."

"Cindy, do you remember the last time you cut your hair short?" Dr. Stevens asked, smiling. "Do you remember what all the nurses said?"

I groaned, and nodded my head at the memory. It had been during a horrible summer hospitalization years ago, when my wrists were not all that I had lashed out at. In a fit of rebellious anger, I had another patient in the hospital cut my waist-length, gorgeous hair all off. After their initial shock, the nurses had loved it. They had said I looked like a pixie. "I guess that means you like it?"

"What it *means*, is that you can wear your hair any way you want to. And . . . you don't have to be angry to cut it." Over the years, I had often expressed my anger by lashing out at my body *and* my hair. Sort of like controlling my weight. Hair and body—both an unspoken symbol in this struggle of self.

"Dr. Stevens, can I ask you a stupid question?"

He chuckled affectionately. "Cindy, your questions are *never* stupid. You may ask me anything you'd like."

"Dr. Stevens, do I still look like me?" I worried. After all those years of self-abuse, I wasn't sure I hadn't destroyed myself, the person I saw in the mirror.

Dr. Stevens smiled ever so gently. "Yes, you still look like Cindy. Don't you realize that no matter *how* you style your hair, or what kind of clothes you wear, or how much you weigh, you will *always* be you."

"Can I ask you one more thing?"

"Just *one* more?" he teased.

"Dr. Stevens, I'm *serious!* This is important!"

"Cindy, *everything* you say is important. And *yes,* you may ask me one more thing."

I took a deep breath. *God! How did I say this without sounding so stupid?* "In another couple of months, I'll be getting the permanent teeth attached to the implants, and, well, I'm scared that I won't look like me or be me," I blurted out. "I mean . . . I miss me! I want me back, and I'm afraid that it's never going to happen!"

"You really are scared, aren't you?"

I nodded slowly and tears filled my eyes. "Dr. Stevens,

nobody knows . . . *not even you* . . . that no matter how much I try to understand, or how much I try to accept the damage that eating disorders have done to my body, I am reminded every single time I look in a mirror." The tears spilled over and flowed down my cheeks. "Do you know what it is like to look in a mirror . . . and not recognize yourself?" Dr. Stevens shook his head. "Well, *I* do. I look in the mirror and I don't see my face as I have always known it to be. This isn't about being skinny. It's about reality." I paused, and took a deep breath. "It's weird, but the body image I had of myself was so distorted that I never could see the way I really looked." I smiled sadly. "I wish I could have seen myself then, the way I see myself now. I would gladly trade that skinny body for my jawbone."

"Cindy, yes, it's true. You *have* done a significant amount of damage to your jaw, but it is not as awful as you feel it is. You are *still* you, inside and out. Hey, we all change as we grow and get older. Look at me," he smiled, and touched the top of his balding head. "I used to have hair!" His tone grew serious again. "My friend, you are right. This *is* your reality. But you are still basing your self-worth on the picture in the mirror or rather, the picture of who you believe you *should* be. Don't be so hard on yourself. You are struggling to accept you for *who* you are and *what* you are. I see Cindy, when I look at you. I always have, and I always will."

I glanced over at his bookcase then turned to face him once again, my eyes twinkling. "Well," I grinned impishly. "I may not have a pretty face any more, but I have a *wonderful* personality!"

Chapter 20

Impact!

"Dr. Stevens, will I ever get over bulimia?" I rocked back and forth in one of the office chairs, and waited for his reply.

"Cindy, I think you may be able to answer that better than I, though I do believe that your bulimia has become habitual, like an addiction. After all, it has been a part of your life for over . . ." his eyebrows puckered as he thought back. "How old are you now?"

I groaned. "Thirty-five, almost thirty-six."

He smiled at my grimace. "Over nineteen years. That's more than half your life. That in itself would make it difficult to give up this behavior. Addiction is a funny thing. Part of it is chemical, which is why you are taking an anti-depressant, and part of it is, well, simply a habit. It makes you feel good. The bingeing and vomiting increases the hormone, serotonin, which is why you get such a peaceful, contented feeling. Apparently, you still feel the need for the purging. Even so, when you are ready to let go of it . . . just like you did with your anorexia . . . I believe that you will. Understand that I'm *not* saying it will be easy, because I know it won't be. What I'm saying is that you will do what you need to do in order to change that behavior."

Was I still striving for perfection? Was that why the bingeing and vomiting continued to play an active role? Had I only substituted one behavior for another? "Dr. Stevens?" I took a deep breath. "I've been seeing you for almost thirteen years. For the last couple of years, I know I have been seeing you once a month. But I would like to decrease it even more, and see you every few months or maybe, only when I really need too. It's not like I have a *lot* of problems anymore, you know?" *Just bulimia.*

Dr. Stevens nodded, grinning broadly. "Cindy, I think that's a wonderful idea."

I sat back, a bit more relaxed. "I know bulimia is still an issue but I *have* decreased it down to only one hour max a day." *No problem here. Vomiting your guts into a bowl sounds pretty normal to me.* "That's the best I've *ever* done so far. It's not hurting me like it used to. I mean, I know that I still take potassium supplements, but I'm keeping myself healthy." *Of course, if I stopped the potassium, I'd have to stop the vomiting. Otherwise, I'd end up back in the hospital with screwed up electrolytes. And as long as I wasn't in the hospital—I must be doing okay.* "I know I'm the only person who can truly make it stop. And I know I would like to be able to say I don't need it anymore. But this doesn't mean I don't want it enough, or that I'm not trying . . . right?"

Dr. Stevens leaned forward in his chair. "Right. And you are the only person who has a hard time giving herself credit for trying."

Even though bulimia remained a strong foe, I maintained a weight of 100 pounds. And now that I was healthier, I had the energy to return to an old love—bike riding.

"Hi, Cindy. Going for another bike ride?" Ellie, my neighbor from down the hall, called out as she headed towards the laundry room at the end of the corridor. I waved hello and passed by, half-wheeling, half-carrying my bike down the six flights of stairs and out the lobby's front door. The brilliant summer sun beat down as soon as I stepped outside. I adjusted my Walkman radio headset around my ears, glad that I had decided to wear a sleeveless tank top with my shorts. Although it was only ten o'clock in the morning, the temperature was already a hot and muggy 84 degrees.

I rode out into the morning traffic and pedaled the familiar route that would take me to a bike trail three miles away. Cars zoomed past on the busy city street and I turned onto a quieter, less hectic neighborhood side-road. *Now, where is that street I use as a shortcut? Oh yeah . . . there it is . . . up ahead and to the left.*

I looked in front of me. *No cars.* I peered back over my left shoulder. *No cars coming from behind either.* I took a last look straight ahead. *No cars.* Humming to the music flowing through my headset, I turned the front bike wheel sharply to the left and glanced up. *A car! Oh, my God! Where . . . I think I'm going to get hit. . . .*

And everything went black.

The light was so white and brilliant that it hurt to look at it. And somebody was screaming in my ears. I struggled to turn towards the sound, and then slowly . . . painfully . . . I opened my eyes. *Who is this woman holding my head, and why is she patting my face with paper towels?* "Are you okay?" she screamed in my face.

I can't move. My body remained in the crumbled position it had landed in. *My head.* My head hurt horribly. The blackness overtook me again.

"Are you always this tired?" I opened my eyes and stared into unfamiliar faces. *Who are these people? Why are they asking me questions?*

"Do you remember what you ate for breakfast?" A strange man bent over and shone a light into my eyes. "Do you know what day it is?"

What did I eat for breakfast? "Eggs," I responded faintly. *Liar.* I couldn't remember what I had eaten that morning.

"Do you know what happened, or where you are?" The man with the light waited.

"No," I whimpered softly. *Oh, God! My head hurts!*

"You were hit by a car and you're in the hospital. Do you know what day it is?"

Questions! So many questions! "Wednesday?" The man with the light nodded his head. *Good, I got that one right.*

"My head hurts. *Please,* my head hurts," I whispered. One of the faces from the crowd leaned over and patted my shoulder gently. "Yes, we know. We are going to take pictures of your head now." And they pushed the stretcher I laid upon, down a long hall.

"Hold her head." Hands grasped the top of my anatomy. *Oh, shit! I'm going to be sick!* I fought to retain consciousness and lost.

The x-rays showed no broken bones. *Thank God.* The CT scan and the physicians' exam revealed contusions to the right side and back of my head, fluid and increased intracranial pressure and hemorrhaging to the left side of my brain.

"Are you always this tired?"

I tried to keep my eyes opened. "No," I answered groggily. The strange faces walked away. I closed my eyes. *God, I feel so sick!* I turned my head to the side of the stretcher and threw up. The blackness overtook me again.

"How are you feeling?" The man with the gentle voice was alone. He looked at the pillow. "Did you get sick?" *Oh God, I did something wrong!* I nodded painfully.

The man with the gentle voice watched me thoughtfully. "You've been here for several hours. You have a head injury . . . a concussion. We want to see if you have any trouble walking. Do you think you can get up and walk for me? Here, let me help you," and he released the side rail of my bed, helping me sit up.

The room swam. The man with the gentle voice had strong arms. He wrapped one strong arm around my waist and the other strong arm around my shoulders. I stood up and swayed unsteadily.

A strange lady in white, stood on my other side and together they guided me across the room and back again. "Cindy," the man with the gentle voice helped me back onto the bed. "We are going to let you go home. Do you know someone who can come pick you up? Is there someone who can stay with you tonight? You really shouldn't stay alone."

"Ernie," I whispered. Ernie was a neighbor who lived in my apartment building. My stomach did flip-flops, and I struggled to keep from throwing up. "Renee." A friend I had made from an eating disorder support group I had attended a few years ago.

"Cindy, I would like you to go for follow-up treatment. Do you have a doctor you can go see?" The man with the gentle voice and strong arms scribbled on some papers in his lap.

I looked at him blankly. "Dr. Blake." Dr. Blake, my gynecologist.

"Good." He scribbled some more. "I want you to make an appointment and go to see him in about a week, okay?" He handed a couple of the papers to me. "These are instructions on head injury. If you have any questions be sure to call us. I'm also giving you a prescription for a painkiller, for your head." The man with the gentle voice and strong arms helped me down from the bed and over to a wheelchair.

I looked down at the papers. The letters and words bounced all over the pages—I couldn't read them. "Okay," I said obediently.

"Cindy, you look terrible!" I lifted my head painfully, and forced a smile at Ernie. I had been sitting for more than an hour. The nausea rose from the pit of my stomach, and I slumped further down in the wheelchair.

Ernie rushed over and gave me a hug. "Shit! Not for anything, Cin, but you look like a truck hit you! Are you sure you're okay to go home? Have you looked in a mirror?" The right side of my face was black and blue and swollen. The blood vessels in my right eye were broken.

Ernie settled me carefully into the front seat of his car. "Geez, Cin," he joked wryly. "Not for anything, but you look like shit! What happened?"

I grabbed onto the dashboard as he slowly backed out onto the road; my head and stomach competed for my attention. "Could you not drive so fast please," I whispered.

"Cin, if I go any slower, we wouldn't be moving. Man, are you sure you're okay?"

"Hmmm." It hurt to talk. It hurt to move. The ten-minute ride took forever. I don't care what Ernie said. He was driving too fast.

But he wasn't. I was nauseous. My entire head throbbed in pain. And the confusion wouldn't go away. By the time Ernie pulled into our apartment complex, my memory of the emergency department had become distant and blurred.

"Cindy, why are you walking so funny?" Ernie reached out a steady hand and walked close behind me as we climbed to the third floor. "Are you sure you're going to be okay? *Shit!* Why the hell did those people let you go? Don't they know you live alone?"

Why was Ernie talking so much? My head hurt. What the hell was he talking about? What people?

We walked down the hall to my apartment, unlocked the door, and went in. I looked around my orderly kitchen. I walked into the living room and stood there.

Ernie shook his head. *"Boy,* are you acting weird!"

"Ernie, where's my bike?" My tone rose frantically. "Where's my bike, Ernie?"

"Do the police have it?"

"Why would the police have it?"

"Cindy, was this accident reported to the police?"

"No . . . I don't think so. *I . . .* I was left lying on the side of the road."

Ernie's eyes widened in disbelief. *"You were left lying in the road?* Cindy, you *have* to report it to the police. We'd better call them right now," and he hurried over to the phone.

"Do you think somebody . . . s . . . *stole* my bike, Ernie?" I sat down on the couch. "Ask the policeman if he knows . . . where my . . . bike is."

Ernie nodded, relayed the information, and hung up the phone. "They're sending a cop over to fill out a report. *Shit!* I can't believe nobody reported this accident!" He lit a cigarette and paced back and forth.

Why was Ernie so upset? What accident? Where was my bike?

The ringing of the door security system startled both of us. "Wow, the cops sure got here fast!" Ernie ran to buzz the person in. It wasn't a cop; it was Renee.

I stared at her uneasily while Ernie updated her and then left. *Why is Renee here?* What was going on? Why didn't somebody explain what was going on?

Renee set down her overnight bag. "Cindy, are you okay?"

"I was riding my bike. I got hit by a car." I answered flatly. "I was left . . . lie . . . on the side of the road. A cop is coming . . . so that I can . . . rr . . . report it. Somebody stole my bike. I'm going to . . . get . . . to bed." I left Renee standing in the kitchen, and went to my bedroom. It had been a long day. I was tired. I was *very* nauseous, and *nobody* was explaining what was going on.

The doorbell rang again and this time, it was the cop. Renee summoned me from the bedroom so I could give my version of events.

"Uh huh. And what happened next?" He scribbled in a small, spiral-bound notebook.

" . . . and I was left lying in the road," I finished.

"Uh huh. And were you taken to the hospital?"

"No, I don't think. . . ."

"Yes, she was," Renee interrupted.

I looked at her, perplexed. "Yes, I was in the hospital." How did she know what happened? What was going on? *Where was my bike?* "Where is my bike?" I asked. Renee and the cop's faces blurred together, and the room started spinning. I sat down abruptly—on the floor. Renee and the policeman stared at me. "I'm okay. Where's my bike?"

"I'm not sure," the police officer replied. He closed his little tablet. "I'm going to go back to the station and fill out a report on this. I'll give you a call."

He left, and I didn't move from the floor.

"Cindy, do you want to go back to the hospital? You don't look good," Renee worried. "Should I take you back?"

"I think I'm going to go to bed." Renee helped me back to the bedroom. Without another word, I fell on top of the bedcovers and everything went black.

Renee tiptoed into my room throughout the night to make sure I was still breathing; wondering if she should take me back to the hospital.

I was; she didn't.

The policeman called in the morning to say that the driver had reported the accident. I had *not* been a hit and run victim. Ambulance and police had responded immediately. There was a police report already filled out. My bike was at the station.

Renee left for work though my strange behavior still worried her. But a phone call from my mother earlier that morning had reassured her I would not be left alone. Mom had returned home, after being on vacation for a week, and found a message on her answering machine from the hospital. She immediately called my apartment and talked to Renee. As soon as they hung up the phone, she and Dick were on their way to Rochester.

When they arrived at my apartment two hours later, they were more puzzled than reassured. The change in my behavior was dramatic and quite scary. My speech was incredibly slow, and I slurred my words. The nausea was so great that I spent most of the day in a reclining position. The pain in my head extended down the entire right side of my face. Even though I would not admit to it, I had trouble following Mom and Dick's conversation. And I was angry. Only I didn't know why. And I yelled at Mom and Dick, because I couldn't control the anger. And *that* was very *much* unlike me.

"Mom, tomorrow I'm . . . supposed to . . ." *word, what was that word?* " . . . go for . . . school." I had graduated that past May from the two-year college and planned to continue on for my bachelor's degree at a local state university. I was supposed to attend registration for incoming freshman and transfer students.

Mom and Dick shared a worried look. "Cindy, maybe it would be better if you registered next week. Is it possible that you could call the school to explain about your accident?" Mom asked hesitantly, afraid to upset me further than I already was.

"No! I have to. . . ." *Damn!* "Sign up tomorrow. There's nothing . . . wrong with . . . me. I am . . . going to go to school. There is nothing . . . wrong . . . with me," I repeated.

Mom was doubtful. "But honey, how are you going to get there?"

"Bus. Just like I . . . always . . . have when I have . . . to go . . . somewhere."

But Mom and Dick weren't convinced that I would be able to navigate on my own, so they offered to drive me to school the next day. Dizzy, confused, and nauseated beyond belief, I laid down on the back seat of their car for the entire trip up and back the following morning. The large crowd of boisterous students irritated and hurt my head. Registration was a blur, but I left the campus with a full course load.

The road to health took a sharp turn to the left. Not even I knew the direction I was headed.

After a week of feeling nauseous and dizzy, those symptoms began to fade. Yet the ensuing weeks were horrible. Reading, watching television—normal daily activities—had become incredibly difficult. I couldn't concentrate or focus on what I was reading or watching. Conversations with others went right out the window. I was forgetting—losing?—words. What else do you call it when you are talking, and all of a sudden, your mind goes blank—erased. Like a blackboard. Like somebody wiped the day's lessons from your brain. Maybe something was wrong with my eyes? I made an appointment with an eye doctor only to receive a verdict of: "The broken blood vessels are healing, Cindy. I'm not finding anything permanently damaged. Your eyes are fine." *Great! I was back to being crazy again.*

And the confusion stayed confusing. But more terrifying— sometimes I couldn't remember if I had eaten, or thrown up. And so I was afraid to eat again, only this was different, and yet the same.

"Dr. Stevens, what is wrong with me?" I sat in his office, confused. "Why do I have to see you again?"

Dr. Stevens sighed. He had returned from a two-week summer vacation to find me, once again, on his weekly schedule. "Cindy, you got hit by a car and hurt your head. That is why you are having trouble right now," he explained patiently.

"Well, why didn't you tell me this before?"

Dr. Stevens smiled. I asked that question every time I saw him. "I *have* told you before. You don't remember. In fact, I've been telling you over and over for the last few weeks that you injured your brain."

"Oh . . . well, why do I have to see you again?" In spite of his answer, I was still puzzled.

"Because I'm trying to keep you safe while you are recovering and help you understand what is going on."

Keep me safe? Now I was really confused. "I just want to ride my bike, that's all. I have a helmet now."

"That's what I mean. It's really best that you don't ride right now. Your judgment is not where it should be. It's hard enough for you to understand your own thoughts, let alone ride safely. Be patient my friend, you will be able to ride your bike again."

I left his office not fully convinced. But only Dr. Stevens

understood that I would be back the next time, asking the same questions.

Over the next few weeks, I moped around my apartment. Dirty dishes littered the kitchen counter, old newspapers laid strewn across the living room floor; I hadn't read in weeks. Every time I did try to read, I couldn't focus on the words. And even the television remained off as I found its noise irritating and intrusive.

I sat at the kitchen table, and glumly laid my head down on my folded arms. I was so tired all the time. "God, what is wrong with me?" I muttered into the hard surface. After several minutes of feeling sorry for myself, I headed to the refrigerator. Within minutes, I had the ingredients for chocolate-chip cookies—a recipe I knew by heart—spread out on the table. I measured and mixed the stiff batter in between shoving spoonfuls of the gooey mass into my mouth. *Remember, Cindy. You're eating.* Because I needed to remember. Because I was scared I would forget.

I stood in front of Greg's door, and took a deep breath. I knocked and stuck my head in his office. "Hi . . . is it okay to come in?"

Greg swung around in his chair. "Cindy, hi. Sure, come on in."

I sat down hesitantly. "Greg, I . . . I think I . . . mmm . . . mmm . . . might not do so . . . good in school this . . ." *Damn!* ". . . this . . ." I gave up.

Greg's smile faded as he witnessed my struggle to talk. "Cindy what happened?" he asked gravely.

Slowly and with much difficulty, I relayed the previous month's events. "And . . . I . . . don't think I'm going to get . . . all . . . good grades in school this fall."

Greg grew more frightened as I filled him in on the details of the accident. My slow speech was accompanied by a flat tone. There was no emotion in my voice or on my face. My usual upbeat, personality—always present in our interactions—was no-where to be seen. The person he knew me to be was not the person sitting in front of him.

"I . . . I . . . I just wanted to . . . let . . . you know," I finished blankly.

"Cindy, have you had any type of rehabilitation?"

I shook my head. "What do you mean?"

"Cindy, unbeknownst to you, I also work with people with head injuries. Most people who have sustained a head injury often benefit from different types of rehabilitation. There's speech therapy, occupational therapy, and physical therapy. I bet that you could really use one or more of those. Especially the speech therapy. The difficulty you are having in talking is called *word finding*. It's very common and very normal to have trouble recalling words after a brain injury. People, who are trained in this kind of reha-bilitative therapy, would be able to teach you how to deal with these kinds of problems. In fact, there's services right here in Rochester that specialize in helping persons with brain injuries." Greg scribbled a name on a piece of paper. "Here, maybe you might want to check these out." He handed me the paper. "Talk to your doctor and ask him about these places. In the meantime, why don't we plan on you *not* starting school this semester. You need to give yourself time to recover more fully from this injury. We can re-evaluate where you stand in a few months, in January. And Cindy, I want you to start writing things down. It will help you retain things in your memory. Here," Greg handed me a stenog-rapher notebook, "this is a present from your vocational counse-lor. Use it as a logbook."

"But what do I write in it?"

Greg smiled. "Anything you want to remember. Write down what we talked about today, if you like."

I clutched the notebook in my hand. "Will . . . I really be able to go back to . . . school in . . . January?"

"Let's see what happens. Try not to worry about it. Take one day at a time."

I left his office, discouraged. *Great, one day at a time. Seems like I've been down this road before.* Damn head injury! It may have knocked me down, but I *had* to get back up. I just wasn't sure when . . . or how.

I called my new internist, Dr. Davidson, who I had recently started seeing when Dr. Lazareth moved out of state, and he made a referral to a neuropsychologist for testing. The results would determine my next steps. But before the testing could begin, Mom and I had to meet with the clinical psychologist who would interpret the tests. "Cindy, how has your eating been lately?" The young doctor asked at our first meeting with her.

What did my eating have to do with this? I glanced at my mother. "My eating's fine," I answered curtly.

"Cindy, it would be understandable if you start having problems with your eating, and your weight again. We don't want to see your anorexia become a problem for you. If you see that happening, make sure you let us know how you're feeling, okay?"

"Sure." *Like hell.* As if I'd share that issue with her—a stranger.

"Joyce, I know Cindy doesn't live with you, but have you noticed any changes in her since the accident?"

"Yes, I have. I've noticed that she sometimes becomes confused when she's talking, and her speech seems slower than it used to be. She also is having difficulty making decisions. And, I'm afraid, Cindy is becoming more withdrawn from people again." Mom reached over and patted my hand. "She just has been so *different* since this accident."

"Hhhmmmm." The psychologist wrote in her notebook. "Cindy, are you depressed?"

"I'm *not* depressed—I'm *angry!*" I snapped at her. "Wouldn't *you* be angry if this had happened to *you?*"

She smiled, closed her notebook, and didn't answer my question. "Well, that's it for today. I want to thank you for coming in. When I finish with the test findings, I'll schedule a meeting to discuss the results." She stood up, extended her hand to

251

my mother, and then to myself. "If you have any more questions, please feel free to call me."

Three weeks later, Greg joined me for the doctor's evaluation of the testing. We listened as she explained her interpretation of the tests. And it made no sense. Something about cognitive (the way I processed my thoughts) dysfunction, something about it being normal in persons who have injured their brain. The slowed, slurred speech, the memory difficulties, the reading problems, even my withdrawing from people, were all part of my brain injury.

She shuffled through the papers, shared my test scores—none of which made any sense to me—and made her recommendations. "Cindy, I think you would benefit from a short duration in our Cognitive Remedial Program here. I believe it would be helpful if you worked with our speech therapist and our occupational therapist. They can help you learn some effective strategies in the areas you are having problems with."

"Will I be able to go back to . . . school?"

"Yes. It may be a little difficult at first, but you should have no problems."

"Can I go . . . back in . . . January?"

"Why don't you wait until after you go through the program here and then plan on returning to school."

"Can I start this . . . program right away? It's . . . already . . . November. If we hurry, maybe I can still . . . r . . . r . . . go to school in January."

"We'll try to hurry the paperwork along," she promised. "In the meantime, call me here if you have any further questions."

And so I waited. The November rain turned to December snow. The acceptance letter finally came—in *January*. My shoulders slumped in discouragement. "God, I am so sick of all of this!"

Even the detours were sprouting roadblocks.

"Dr. Stevens, I don't think the people at rehab are helping me," I complained. I had been attending speech and occupational therapy, twice a week for three months.

"Oh? Why is that?"

Frustrated, I rocked back and forth in my chair. "Because I've been going for three months, and all they keep having me do are *tests!*"

"But Cindy, your speech *is* much better now. It's not as slow, and you don't seem to be having as much difficulty with word finding. Have they not helped you with that?" Dr. Stevens asked, puzzled by my accusation.

"Dr. Stevens!" I exploded, and almost toppled over in my chair. "If I'm getting better, it's because *eight* months have passed since the accident. *Time* has helped me improve! *Nobody* has explained or taught me *anything.*"

"Cindy, they're not doing *anything* to help you?" Dr. Stevens could not believe *nothing* was being done.

"Dr. Stevens," I said patiently, as if to a small child. "If sitting in front of a computer and playing games is helping—then I'm getting helped. If talking about *wanting* to go back to school while the speech therapist listens is helping—then I'm getting help. If talking to the social worker and telling her that I have an apartment, I have medical insurance, I have a nice family, is helping—then I'm getting help. If telling you that I'm not getting help is helping—then I guess I'm getting help."

Dr. Stevens laughed, and threw his hands up in mock self-defense. "Okay, okay! I believe you. So what are you going to do?"

"*I* am going to help me," I said determinedly. *I had helped myself get over anorexia, why not a brain injury?*

"Dr. Stevens, I made up my mind. I'm going to school."

"Oh? And how are you going to do that?"

"I'm applying for a scholarship." I had read an article in the newspaper about scholarships for women. "There's one in particular that I want to try for."

"Cindy, I think that's wonderful. You should try for it."

The detour was over. I was back on course.

*　　　*　　　*　　　*　　　*

I sat down at my desk, turned on the computer and stared at the blank word processing program. For the next two hours, I attempted to get the words out of my head and onto the screen. Those efforts produced one sentence. *Two hours to write one sentence!* I leaned my head against the screen, and sobbed. Words had never been lost to me when I had dreamed of being a journalist. At this speed, it would be July before I finished! I winced at the thought. The letter had to be submitted by July fifteenth and it was already the first of April. "I don't want life to be so *hard* anymore," I cried, frustrated by my newest challenge. "All I want is to be *somebody*—somebody who has a life! Somebody who goes to school or goes to work or . . . or just a somebody!" I was so *tired* of struggling. I was so *tired* of trying.

I was so tired of being me.

Chapter 21

Cindra Meets a Fella

Day in and day out, I worked diligently on the scholarship letter. I labored over the keyboard, and forced the words out of my brain. The results: three paragraphs in three months! I groaned and continued tapping. Yet putting words on paper forced me to look at how far I had traveled: I no longer fell asleep at night worried that I would die before morning. Climbing stairs, walking—across the room, to a store—were no longer activities beyond my capability. I could sit at a table and eat normally—well, at least one meal—in front of others. The anorexic thoughts in my head had dissipated; they no longer demanded all my attention, my preoccupation. It had happened so slowly that I could not say exactly when the critical inner voice had softened, when the scale and the mirror had stopped ruling my world. The process of recovery: I was finding my own way back. Cautiously, one step at a time, discovering the person within and giving her a chance to try life differently. Trying and learning to not let my body be the measure of my self.

My stomach growled. I stretched my arms and glanced at the clock, two o'clock. *Time for a break.* I went into the kitchen, and ate and purged six tuna fish sandwiches, a large bag of potato chips, a box of twelve sugar-powdered donuts, and three cans of diet Coke.

All better? Had I now accepted bulimia as normal?

"Ellie, I wish I could meet someone." My neighbor and I visited over a cup of coffee. An older woman, in her early 60's, Ellie had become a kind friend. During many of our coffee chats together, she talked often of her own daughters and their relationships, which only further intensified the lack of such in my own life.

"Cindy, why don't you try and answer a personal ad," Ellie suggested now. "That's how my daughter met her boyfriend. He's an architect."

"Oh, I could *never* do *that!*"

"Why not? It wouldn't hurt to just try answering an ad. I know my daughter met some nice people that way." We finished our coffee and Ellie left, but her suggestion lingered in my mind. *Answer a personal ad?* My family would absolutely flip if I did anything like that!

And the something inside that had nudged once before gave me a swift jab. *Okay, maybe I'll try.* I got out the morning paper and opened it to the personal section of the classifieds. *Single, white male, 40 years old. Loves adventure, romance, and eating out.* "Oh, God! I can't do this! These guys are probably all weirdoes, or perverts, or something." Yet the seed had been planted. It was up to me to make it grow. Maybe—*just maybe*— there was someone out there who would like me for just being me.

"Hi, is this Cindy? My name is Phil. You answered my ad."

My heart pounded in my ears as the voice on the other end of the phone identified himself. *I shouldn't do this. I know I shouldn't do this.*

"I read your letter and would like to meet you," he continued. "Is there a restaurant you'd like to meet at?"

A restaurant? But I didn't have a car! *Think, Cindy, think!* "Tootsie's," I answered. Tootsie's was a small sandwich shop on the corner of my street. It shared the same parking lot as my apartment complex. I could watch for his arrival from my window.

"Tomorrow afternoon, say . . . around three?" Phil asked.

Tomorrow? At three? Maybe this isn't such a good idea after all. "Sure. That sounds fine."

"In the *parking lot!*" Ellie exclaimed. I had phoned Ellie as soon as I hung up with Phil. "Why in the world would he meet you outside? Why don't you meet him where a lot of people will be around?"

"I shouldn't be doing this, should I?"

"Just make sure there are people around," Ellie cautioned.

"It was *your* idea! Maybe I shouldn't have answered that ad!" I groaned. "Should I call him back and cancel?"

"No, don't do that. He could be a nice guy. You have nothing to lose."

Nothing but my life. The guy could be an ax-murderer or something.

The following afternoon, I felt differently though—kind of excited. It had been a long time since I had sought out a new adventure. I peered anxiously out of the living room window. *Relax. Take a deep breath. It's not quite three yet.* I took a deep breath, and peeked out from behind the curtain. A red car drove into the lot. *Phil said he would be driving a red car.* I breathed deeper, and went down to the parking lot.

I approached the car. The driver's window rolled down and a round jolly-looking face popped out. "Hi, are you Cindy?" he asked, his voice boomed across the lot.

He looks harmless. "Yes, I am," I replied. *Maybe this won't be so bad.*

"I'm Phil," he announced loudly, and motioned for me to come closer to his car.

Cautiously, I walked over until I stood several inches away. Phil had dark brown hair that reached to his shoulders, a handle-bar mustache, and he wore a black leather motorcycle jacket. He looked to be in his mid-thirties, but it was hard to tell. His eyes remained hidden behind mirror-reflective sunglasses.

"Can you open your coat?" Phil requested.

His question caught me off-guard. I unbuttoned my cor-duroy jacket. "Why?" I asked, even as I opened my jacket.

"Great! You really do weigh what you say. You'd be sur-prised how many women said they weigh a lot less than they re-ally do. But you didn't lie."

"Well, take off your glasses," I ventured, growing a bit more confident. "I can't see your eyes."

Phil willingly obliged. "See," he smirked. "Aren't I as cute as I said I was?"

I groaned inwardly. *Great! Just what I needed, an overgrown, adolescent man!*

"Would you like to see what I do for a living?" Phil opened up his car door and stepped out. He was tall, lanky, and wearing black vinyl jeans. He squeaked when he walked.

Shit! Now, I'm in trouble! "Why don't you just tell me what you do," I suggested, and took a couple of steps backwards as Phil strolled toward me.

Phil laughed at my obvious display of nervousness. "Sure. I sell women's perfumes." He walked past me and went around to the back of his car. "Come here, I'll show you." He opened up the trunk, rummaged around, and emerged with two cologne bottles. "Here," he held them out, smiling broadly. "What kind do you like?"

I walked over and glanced into the trunk. No axes, no chains, no guns. Just boxes of different fragrances piled through-out.

"Here." Phil handed me the bottles. "Have them both. I like you. Do you want to go out?"

"Well. . . . " I breathed a little easier. Phil seemed okay, but something just didn't *feel* quite right.

Phil slammed the trunk closed. "Look, wouldn't you like to go to the movies Friday night? It would be fun." He walked around and opened the passenger side of his car. *"Brrr!* It's cold out here." The April wind had picked up. "Come on. We can sit inside my car and talk." He held the door open, invitingly. I hesitated, and then got in. Phil slammed the door and hurried around to the driver's side. "See, I'm not going to bite you," he teased, and climbed in beside me.

I laughed nervously and clutched the cologne bottles.

"Look," he said brusquely. "You're a cute girl. I'm a cute guy. We will look pretty good together. Is it really going to hurt you to go to the movies with me? Afterwards, we can go to my place. I bet you really live in this neighborhood, don't you?" he said abruptly, changing the subject. He looked around the parking lot, disdainfully. "Only poor white trash people live here. What's a nice girl like you doing living in a place like this?"

Oh shit! I shifted uneasily on the vinyl-covered car seat. "How do you know that I live here?" I moved a bit closer to the door. "And what makes you think I want to go to your place?" I asked nonchalantly.

"Look, I'm not going to ask for much from you. All you have to do is give me a little kiss every now and then, at the movies, my place . . ."

"I'm sorry," I interrupted hastily. "But what makes you think I want to go to the movies . . . or kiss you?"

Phil glared. "Look, it won't kill you. We'll hold hands, and all you have to do is give me one kiss. Why don't you think about it, and call me later tonight."

"Why should *I* call *you?*" I asked, put off by his brazen ways.

"Because I like to have women call me. I like my women to be strong and dominant."

Cindy, say anything! And get out of this car! "Sure Phil." I opened the door, and scrambled out. "I'll give you a call."

"And Cindy, my friends call me *Sweet P* . . . get it?" he roared, amused with his own wit. *"Byeee!"* Phil gunned the motor and took off.

"Was *that* a close call!" I laughed weakly, and attempted to calm my racing heart. "I'll bet that his bedroom comes equipped with whips and chains!" I walked back inside. That guy's too weird! Next time, I'll try to listen to my feelings." I breathed a sigh of relief. Next time, I might not be so lucky.

"Cindy, I know the perfect ad you should answer!" Ellie spotted me in the laundry room and waved her newspaper in the air.

I groaned. *Not again!* "Ellie, I think I better stop answering ads." That experience with *Sweet P,* was not one I cared to repeat.

"Oh, Cindy! Just read it. I know this one's perfect for you! He's a professional, an engineer, thirty-five-years old. . . ."

"Ellie," I interrupted. "This is not going to work."

"Cindy, now where's your faith. How will you know unless you try?" she admonished, throwing my own philosophy at me. "It won't hurt to just answer one more. And don't wait till the last minute," Ellie advised as she left the laundry room. "I bet this guy gets a lot of responses."

I laughed at her insistence. "We'll see." I finished folding clothes and went back to my apartment. It was time to finish the scholarship letter. Several hours later, I sat back, and stretched my fingers. "Finished! Only three months to write two and a half pages. I can't imagine how long it will take me to write my papers in school!" I saved the document, switched off the computer, and spotted the morning's paper. *You won't know unless you try.* I opened the paper, and quickly scanned the personal page. *Ahh! There it was.* "THE specs aren't quite stable yet . . . but! Single white male, engineer, 35 6' planning for a professional, goal-oriented, non-smoking female. Let's spend summers enjoying the lake, winters skiing the mountains & travel, theater, fireplaces, & each other year round. Stable, open, charming personality a must. Prefer unattached, educated, 24+, with multiple interests. Of course, no drugs! Petite, trim/fit, headstrong & valid passport desirable. Photo not required but appreciated."

I set the paper down. "I don't know about this." *Cindy, just answer it. One more time isn't going to hurt you.* I went back to the desk, and dashed off a response before I could change my mind. It had been a long day. I changed into my pajamas and went to bed. "Okay, God. This is it. I truly believe there is some-one out there for me. I don't know who he is . . . or where he is. But I know YOU will make it happen . . . when the time is right. Maybe I need to stop questioning so much, God, and just learn to accept my life, like I'm learning to accept myself. Maybe I just have to trust YOU, and believe that things will work out."

I tried to sleep, but sleep would not come. I tossed and turned restlessly as racing thoughts kept me awake. "God? I'm not sure if I should mail that letter tomorrow. But if I do, it will be the last time. And then I'm going to put this out of my mind. And if that guy does call, I'm going to just look at it as an oppor-tunity to make a new friend." *There. I wasn't getting my hopes up.* My mind at peace, I fell asleep.

"Hello, Cindy? This is Tom. You answered my ad."

Yikes! The passport guy! It had been a week since I had mailed out my response, and never once had I thought he would *really* call. We talked for about an hour, and shared bits of infor-mation of who we were. Tom had an easy-going phone manner, and he seemed friendly and harmless—at least he did over the phone. Our first encounter was already more pleasurable than the one I had had with Phil.

"I know it's short notice, but would you like to go out to dinner tomorrow evening?" Tom asked.

"I'd love to," I replied without a moment's hesitation. *It feels right. My gut feels good.*

"Would you like to meet me at a restaurant, or would you

like me to pick you up at your home?"

"You can pick me up," I answered confidently. Ellie was right. If I didn't try, I would never know.

I spent most of the next day trying to decide on the right outfit. "What'll I wear?" I groaned, and pawed through my meager wardrobe in vain. I finally settled on a dark-green cotton skirt, a white blouse, and an ivory-colored cotton sweater.

I gave myself two hours to shower, wash my hair, put on my makeup, and get dressed. I ran a comb through my hair and glanced at my watch nervously. *Almost time.* I went over to the window and peered down at the parking lot. A sport utility vehicle pulled in, parked, and a handsomely dressed gentleman stepped out. My heart skipped a beat.

The door buzzer rang. I took a deep breath, and pressed the speaker button. "Hi, Tom. I'll be right down." I gathered up my sweater and purse and locked the apartment door behind me. I resisted the urge to race down the hall. *Cool it, Cindy. First impressions are very important.* I slowed my pace, and tried to be as ladylike as possible. And when I stepped into the lobby, Tom's eyes lit up approvingly.

"Hi, you must be Cindy," he greeted, and extended his right hand. "I'm Tom." I smiled, and accepted his hand. Tom was just as he had described himself, only much more handsome. His brown eyes sparkled behind iron-rimmed glasses and matched his brown hair, which still glistened from a recent shower. His stylish, obviously expensive, business suit hung smartly from his nearly six foot frame. His manners were impeccable, and I sensed that the evening was going to be different, special.

Tom had chosen an upscale restaurant whose fine-dining atmosphere was a new experience for me. Tom laughed, kindly, at my naiveté over which fork to use and when. We lingered over wine, and conversation flowed non-stop; both of us, seemingly comfortable in the mutual sharing of ourselves. And for the first time in years, I felt pretty and womanly. In a couple of quiet relaxing hours, I learned that Tom was an engineering manager at

Xerox Corporation. I told him I was a student and not too much else. The time passed quickly—too quickly— and then it was time to leave. "Would you like to see my boat?" Tom asked as he helped me back into his Blazer truck. "It's such a pretty night." He, too, seemed reluctant for the evening to end.

"I'd love to," I said, and chatted easily while Tom drove to the marina where his boat was anchored.

" . . . And then I couldn't believe . . . *oh."* I stopped, mid-sentence. Tom was driving down a dark, unfamiliar, heavily wooded incline. "I guess you must be taking the back roads to this marina?" I said, and tried to keep my tone neutral, but failed as my voice squeaked at the end. *Oh shit! Cindy, what have you gotten yourself into this time? This was worse than Phil. There was no way out of this one!* I gripped the edge of the truck seat and peered anxiously into the dense trees on either side of the narrow road.

"Huh?" Tom looked over at me, puzzled, and then burst out laughing at my worried expression. He said not a word, and turned into a well-lit parking lot. At the end of it sat—the marina. Dozens of boats bobbed along the many slips, one of which belonged to Tom. *Just like he had said.* Still laughing, he parked and helped me out of the truck. I blushed and joined in his laughter. Together, we walked over to his small powerboat, and Tom helped me climb in.

The star-filled sky hung over our heads, and the water lapped quietly against the shore. And when Tom took me home, we planned to see each other again.

Chapter 22

A New Beginning

"So tell me. Are you always this happy?" Tom asked. We were walking along the pier, and enjoying the cool summer breeze off of Lake Ontario. "You're always laughing. I've never met anyone so happy before."

Me? Happy? The adjective threw me. It was the first time in way too many years that I had been labeled so positively.

Tom stopped and faced me. His warm brown eyes searched my own. "You are. You're always laughing. There must be a reason. Come on, there must be more to you than you've been telling me." It was only last night that we had our first date. Tonight was our second one. Tom had called earlier that evening and asked if I would like to go for a walk on our city's pier.

I smiled, and continued walking. How did I tell Tom that in less than twenty-four hours, I had rediscovered a part of me that had been hidden for so long that I had forgotten it existed? How did I tell him of the solo journey—twenty-two years long and not yet ended—that had led me into sickness, poverty, and nearly robbed me of a life that only recently had awakened? Would he—could he—understand the horrible hopelessness, or the despair, which caused me to be more afraid to live than to die? How could I tell him who I was, and why?

"I don't know. I guess I just enjoy life, that's all," I finally answered, and successfully evaded his question. "Come on, let's walk on the beach."

We had met on Sunday. We walked the pier on Monday. We went bike riding on Tuesday. On Wednesday, we watched fireworks light up the sky as Rochester celebrated Independence Day. On Thursday, we spent it apart. On Friday I got a delivery.

I accepted a long, narrow gold box from the deliveryman. My fingers were all thumbs as I untied a red satin ribbon and lifted off the box cover. *Oh, my goodness!* There, nestled in a cloud of tissue paper, was a single red rose. I gently removed the delicate flower, breathed in its soft fragrance, and read the accompanying card. *"Hi. I have thought a lot about you over the past several days. Have concluded that I like this match very much! Your enthusiasm is contagious and your love of life obvious. And I really like knowing that if I like it . . . so will you. I'm sincerely looking forward to continuing to know and understand each other better. Friends first and then we'll see sorta sums it up. Thanks for a Great Week . . . I'm anticipating more to come! Enclosed please find my favorite flower. (Another brand simply wouldn't fit.) A Rose has tremendous depth and beauty captured in a compact package . . . Hmmm . . . sounds familiar. Tom."*

I lifted the rose to my nose and breathed in its fresh sweet smell. *He likes me! He really likes me!*

I stared at the plate of food in front of me and half-heartedly lifted a forkful of spaghetti to my lips. *What's wrong? Why am I not hungry?* I gave up and walked down the hall to Ellie's apartment. "Ellie?" She opened the door.

"I think something is wrong with my stomach." I rubbed my abdomen. "It feels really weird. Like . . . I don't know . . . sort of really strange . . . and I can't eat. Do you think there's something wrong? Should I make a doctor's appointment?"

A slow smile spread across Ellie's face.

"Why are you smiling? I'm really worried about my stomach. I think I'm sick! I've *never* felt like this before!"

"Cindy," she said, amused. "I think you've fallen for this guy."

"Oh no," I protested vehemently. "I couldn't possibly have! I've only known him for *six days!* I think something is wrong with my stomach!"

Ellie shook her head, wisely. "I don't think so, Cindy. I think you are falling for this guy."

Oh, that can't possibly be true! We just met! Sure, we had been having a lot of fun the last few days. And yes, it was the first time in a long time that I had felt so attracted to another person. But *no!* I *couldn't* have fallen for Tom.

"Cindy, I still feel there's a lot more than you've been telling me. Is there?" Tom asked.

We were going to the movies and I shivered though it was a warm July evening. "You keep asking me that, Tom," I said a bit nervously. "Why do you keep thinking that there's more to me?"

"Because there's such an innocence about you, and you're so . . . *so happy!* It just feels like there is more depth to you than you're telling me."

Oh dear! This was getting complicated. *Tom, I can't say anything. Not yet.* Not while I was still afraid of being judged, based on all those horrible years that I called my life. No . . . he would find it—*me*—disgusting, and not want to be my friend. I couldn't risk it. Not yet.

I smiled as we headed into the theater and said nothing.

"Ellie, I think I have to tell Tom about having had anorexia and a head injury." Tom's continued questioning worried me.

"Cindy, don't. I think you'd be making a mistake. It's not important that he knows that stuff. I wouldn't if I were you." But

Ellie wasn't me. And in the nine days that Tom and I had known each other, his questions were becoming more pressing. Tom was not dumb. He had to suspect I wasn't sharing everything. *Hell!* Tom could be thinking that I was an ax murderer or something!

I awoke the following morning with one thought in mind: I had to tell Tom who I was. And I had to tell him immediately. I dialed his office number and we made dinner plans for that evening. Throughout the rest of the day, I thought of nothing else. I had no idea how or what I would say. I just knew that I had to tell Tom. Once again, I had to try.

When Tom picked me up, I climbed into his truck and took a deep breath. "Tom, do you know how you keep saying that there is more to me?" He nodded. "Well, you're right." I glanced out the truck window. "There is more—a lot more." I rubbed my sweaty palms across my lap. "Last year, I got hit by a car . . . while riding my bike. I suffered a head injury. I was supposed to go to college, but instead, I spent several months going for rehabilitation. September will be my first time back to school." I stopped, too scared to say more.

Tom pulled into the restaurant parking lot, turned off the motor, and faced me. He wasn't smiling. "Why didn't you tell me this before?" he asked gently.

"I was afraid," I said, my voice trembled and tears filled my eyes. "I wanted you to get to know me first. I wanted you to know me for who I am, and not for what I had gone through. I guess I was afraid that if you knew I had a head injury, it would cloud your perception of me. I was afraid you would judge me—harshly."

"Cindy, don't you know me at all?" Tom leaned over and gathered me into his arms. "Don't you know by now that I'm not like that. I'm so sorry that you felt you couldn't tell me. But what made you change your mind? Why did you decide to tell me tonight?"

"I don't . . . *yes* . . . I do know. Something inside of me said that I had to tell you—and I had to tell you tonight. You see, someone once told me that I should trust my feelings. Well, my feelings said that I needed to tell you tonight."

Tom helped me out of the truck and we walked towards the restaurant. "You don't know this," he said, his tone subdued. "But I have been going *crazy* trying to figure you out. I felt you were hiding something from me, and I didn't know what it was. I kept waiting for you to say something, *anything*. And I kept trying to give you many opportunities to do so; yet you never did. I finally told my friends that after tonight, I wasn't going to see you any more." He squeezed my hand tightly and held the door open. "I'm glad you told me."

"Tom?" I slid into a booth and waited until the waitress took our order. "There's even more to my story. Maybe we should go back to my apartment after dinner, and I'll share it with you."

Tom hadn't turned away. But the night wasn't over, and neither was my story.

After dinner, back at my apartment, I handed Tom some papers. "Here, read these. It's a scholarship letter that I just finished. I'm mailing it tomorrow, but I'd like you to read it first. It just might answer your question." Tom sat down on the couch and started reading. *"Dear Clairol, . . . My name is Cindy, and I'm no one special, just a regular person. However, being a regular person is* very *special to me, which is why I'm nominating myself for a Clairol Take Charge Award. You see, for over 22 years, I suffered from anorexia and bulimia. I was hospitalized every year, usually months at a time, from the ages of 17 - 31. Normal life, for me, consisted of hospitals, surgeries, therapies, sirens, and prayers. My illnesses isolated me to such an extent that my only friends were the doctors and nurses who cared for me. Some of these doctors believed that my life would never be more than us struggling together to keep me alive. It became a fact of life—I would forever be ill. Yet I hung on, because deep inside of me, I ached to be like other people—just a regular person. I wanted to go to college, to go to work, to go shopping, or just to be able to walk across a room without sheer exhaustion overcoming me. I spent days, months, years, lying on my couch trapped by these disor-*

ders. *I had been sick for so long, I no longer knew what it meant to be well. At the age of 30, my desire for wellness became so strong that I began to believe only one person could make this happen. And that person was me. I had to take back control of my life. With the encouragement of my doctors, I faced the biggest challenge in my life: to "find" Cindy. Just over one year later, I had. I re-gained 35 pounds, re-gained control of my life, and re-gained my sense of self. For the first time since the age of 13, I was healthy.*

During my years of sickness, I often felt I had nothing to offer anyone. But I'm realizing now that my return to health does offer hope and encouragement to others who are still trapped in these battles. If I'm able to help just one person move towards a healthier state of being, than I will have achieved an even greater victory. As I look back to how far I have come in six years, I feel an incredible sense of awe at what I have accomplished since that moment of taking charge. Recovering from my illnesses has not only given me the knowledge 'I can,' but it has instilled deep appreciation, strength, determination, desire, and faith to keep believing in myself and my dreams." Tom, his face thoughtful, put down the paper and said nothing.

I paced back and forth. Not sure what to do, or what to say. *It's over. I know it's over. Maybe it's better that it ends now. . . .* "Cindy?" Tom interrupted my thoughts. He came over and put his arms around me. "Cindy," he whispered tenderly, his words muffled by my hair, "I'm not good enough for you." My knees buckled, and his sheltering arms held me up. Tom had accepted who I was. No more hiding. I was Cindy. And it was okay.

Over the next two weeks, we spent all our time together, and when we were apart, I spent those hours thinking about him. In a short time, he had become very special. *Admit it, Cindy. You've fallen in love with Tom.* Now where did that come from? How could I have fallen in love so quickly . . . so easily . . . so blindly? Could it be because I had never felt this way before? *But I had loved Rob, hadn't I? And if I had, why were these feelings now so . . . so . . . different?* I shook my head to rid the confusion of these emotions, but a new question arose: What if Tom did not feel the

270

same way? Then what would I do?

Later that evening, we watched a video at Tom's house as we snuggled on his couch. "Tom? Do you think it's possible to fall in love with someone in just . . . ummm, ten days?" *I can't believe I said that!*

"Yes, I think so," he replied.

"You do?" I ran my fingers through his hair. "Can I ask why?"

"Because I've fallen in love with you, Cin." My fingers stopped. *Oh, my God!* And suddenly, I knew love. I *felt* love. And I had never felt love like that before. It was right. It *felt* right. Your heart *tells* you when its right.

It was Friday the thirteenth, and my whole world had changed forever—Tom loved me!

I took a pizza out of the oven and set it on the table in front of Tom. He cut a slice and placed it on my plate.

I eyed it apprehensively. I always binged on pizza. I didn't know how to *not* binge on pizza. I took a bite and chewed slowly. I finished the first slice, took a second one, and declined an offer of a third slice. I was comfortably full. I watched while Tom chowed down his fourth slice and felt no compulsion to do the same. I was relaxed and happy. *Was this the connection between my feelings and bingeing?* Was the love I received from Tom filling the hunger I had felt for so long?

"Cin?" Tom leaned forward in his chair. "You know how we have been talking about the long term? Well . . . I'm in this relationship for the long term, and I want to know if you are too?"

"What do you mean by long term, Tom. What are you saying?" I think I did know, but I had to be sure.

Tom squirmed nervously. "Well, I mean *long term*—you know. I'm in it for the long term, aren't you?"

I smiled at his boyish discomfort. "Tom, are you asking me to marry you?"

"Well . . . *yes*. I want to know if you'll marry me. Will you marry me?"

In just three and a half weeks, Tom had become the center of my world. It was what I had always longed for. He loved *me*. He wanted *me*. He wanted to *marry* me. *He* wanted to spend his life with *me*. It was my deepest and longest dream come true.

"Why aren't you answering me?" Tom was worried. I still had not answered his proposal. "What's wrong?"

"Do you know what today is?" I asked instead.

"It's July twenty-sixth. What does that have to do with anything?"

Everything. "One year ago today, on July twenty-sixth, I was hit by a car and my whole world turned upside down. Tom, I never would have believed that, one year later, somebody would ask me to marry them *on that very day*." My eyes brimmed with tears. *"Yes,* Tom. I will marry you." A new beginning. My story had a new beginning.

"Dr. Stevens? I have something to tell you." I all but twirled in the office chair.

"Now, *why* do I have a feeling that you are about to tell me something good?" he teased.

A girlish giggle escaped my lips. "Do you remember how I always asked you . . . how would I know if someone *really* loved me? And do you remember how I always believed that no one *ever really* would? Well," I said, and my cheeks blushed. "Last night, Tom asked me to marry him." I paused as a huge smile spread across Dr. Stevens' face. "And," I added shyly, "I said yes."

"Cindy, that is so wonderful! Congratulations! I am so happy for you."

"Dr. Stevens?"

"Yes?"

"I would like you to be the very first person I invite to our wedding." Dr. Stevens was a trusted friend. He had worked hard to help me understand that just being me was good enough. He had fought to save my life, my sanity, and my dreams. He had shown that someone could care about me and not leave. And even if he were to leave, it would be okay because he had taught me to depend on my own inner strength, that I was responsible for myself and to myself. That happiness had to start from within and work its way out. His words and patient support had shown me that feeling good about myself was half the battle. The other half was realizing that I was not perfect, and that I did not need to be. That it was okay to make mistakes because that was one way in which we learn. And that as long as I tried, I was never a failure. My eyes flooded with tears. I was happy, I was in love, and I was alive.

"Cindy, I would love to come to your wedding. You could not keep me away. Thank you for inviting me."

No, thank you, Dr. Stevens. Thank you for helping me see that I was always just a regular person.

Chapter 23

Friends and Never Less

In August, I moved out of my apartment and in with Tom. In September, I returned to school. And I immediately had trouble. Reading comprehension was difficult, I had trouble following classroom lectures, and I couldn't seem to organize homework assignments. The effects from the brain injury had not just gone away.

Tom tried to help. When my theater class required critiques of plays, he attended with me so what I couldn't remember, he would. We recorded our conversations so I could replay what we talked about. When my brain refused to organize my thoughts, Tom bought a big white-board and hung it on our kitchen wall. He broke down each of my written assignments into steps and outlined them on the white-board. Seeing the words helped me to focus, organize, and know where to begin. He critiqued my class papers, pointed out where words, sentences, and thoughts were choppy, grammatically incorrect, or made no sense.

At Greg's suggestion, I was re-tested by another neuropsychologist, Dr. Sherman. The results confirmed the cognitive problems I still struggled with. I learned something else too—

brain injury does not just *go away*. Strategies to compensate for problem areas could be taught. Unlike anorexia, I would not be able *cure* a brain injury. And this time, I finally received the cognitive therapy I needed from a wonderful occupational therapist, Loni Ferris, who was recommended by Dr. Sherman. With her expert guidance, I finally learned the strategies that I could use at school and at home.

I looked out the kitchen window as the November sky darkened, and wondered if the first snowfall of the season was not too far away. "Tom, I'm going out to get the mail!" I threw a sweater around my shoulders and dashed out to the mailbox. I shivered in the near-freezing temperatures and opened the mailbox. I reached in and pulled out a manila envelope with the return address of Clairol Take Charge Awards. *Oh my God!* "Tom!" I yelled, and ran into the house. *"This is from the scholarship people!"*

I opened the envelope and withdrew a sheet of paper. *"Congratulations on being selected as a Clairol Take Charge Award winner. As you know, the award honors women over 30 who have overcome obstacles and made a positive change in their lives. We at Clairol want you to know that from a field of over 2,000 excellent applicants, only 25 winners were selected as Clairol Take Charge Award winners. . . .* I did it, Tom!" I flung my arms around him. "I really did it!"

And so I had. My persistence had paid off in ways more important than the scholarship money. For the first time, complete strangers had recognized my desperate battles and awarded that fight for life. I had won.

"Cindy, do you want a cookie?" Tom asked, and before I could respond, he headed towards the crowded cookie counter. I shivered as a crowd of holiday shoppers swallowed up Tom's disappearing back. *Oh dear!* Cookies were my biggest downfall! I binged on cookies! As it turned out, falling in love had not turned out to be the magical answer to bulimia. The void in my heart was filled, but I still binged and purged—albeit small amounts—daily. The need had lessened, but the habit was still there.

I smiled weakly when Tom reappeared, the dreaded bag of cookies in his hand. He led me over to a nearby bench and sat down. "Here," he reached in the bag and took out a cookie. *It was enormous!* It was bigger than I was! It was bigger than the mall! It *oozed* with gigantic chunks of chocolate sin and nuts. "Here, have a cookie," Tom insisted and placed it in my hand. He withdrew another from the bag and took a bite.

Oh God! I don't know what to do! I took a tiny bite of the warm cookie. It melted in my mouth. The heavenly aroma of the cookies surrounded us. *Cindy, it's okay. You can do this. It's okay.* I finished under Tom's watchful guise. He squeezed my hand. "Come on, let's finish our Christmas shopping." He crumbled the bag and tossed it into a trash container.

We walked. *I just ate one cookie.* We talked. *I can do this!* We shopped. *I ate one cookie.* We went home. *And I didn't binge!*

I wish I could say that from that point on, I no longer binged and purged. But I can't. What did happen was that slowly and very cautiously, I allowed myself to eat foods that had been *forbidden binge-only* foods. Unbeknownst to Tom, he became my reality barometer. If he could eat it, so could I. As a result, the bingeing decreased from two hours, seven days a week, down to one hour, Monday through Friday and never on weekends. My goal: to be *all* better by our wedding.

"Cin, I'm going to take a nap. Wake me in a couple of hours." Tom kissed the top of my head on his way through the kitchen, where I sat studying.

"Uh huh," I mumbled, engrossed with my reading. Forty-five minutes later, I tiptoed over to the bedroom door and listened to Tom's peaceful snores. I had over an hour until I had to wake him. Just enough time for a quick binge. In the last several months of our living together, Tom's naps had provided the perfect opportunity to binge. While he slept, I ate and purged. I didn't have to worry about him noticing or hearing. After twenty-three years of learning how to hide that telltale behavior, I knew the importance of alone time.

An hour later, I returned to my studying. "Cin!" Tom bellowed from the next room. "Do you know what happened to that pile of papers I had on the dining room table?"

Oh dear! I knew exactly what had happened to those papers—I had put them away. Only problem was, I couldn't remember where. Tom stood in the doorway of the guest bedroom that doubled as our study. "Did you remember to mail those letters that I had asked you to do, *yesterday?*" he asked, somewhat annoyed.

I groaned, and laid my head down on the desk. "I forgot," I mumbled.

Tom sighed. "You didn't write it down, did you? You know that Dr. Sherman said that writing things down helps you to remember. How can I make this *vivid*, so that you'll remember?"

I lifted my head up. "Do you still love me?" I asked in a tiny voice.

"Oh, *Toad*. I'm stuck with you," he kidded, then shook his head, exasperated, "but what are we going to do about your memory?"

I watched apprehensively as Tom approached the desk and reached down to open a bottom drawer. "What are you looking for, Tom?" I interrupted hastily. "I have only school stuff in that drawer."

"Are you sure you didn't put those papers in the desk?"

"I did *not*," I emphasized. "Try looking in your file cabinet. I'm pretty sure I probably put them in there. Or maybe I put them in that box in the garage—the one where I put your other papers."

Tom threw up his hands. "I give up! *You* find them when you're done with your homework." He walked out of the room in a huff.

I sank back in my chair. That had been too close for comfort! The bottom drawer held a secret stash of cookies. If Tom had found those cookies, I had no idea how to explain them.

Not with the truth that was for sure. Bulimia was not something I could share with him. Because if he ever found out, he would leave. Just like Rob.

The following months passed uneventfully. By May, we had most of the wedding plans completed. Only my gown fittings remained.

The ringing of the phone interrupted my studying for final exams. "Hello," I answered a bit impatiently into the receiver.

"Hello," an unfamiliar woman's voice responded. "May I speak to Cindy?"

"This is she." I glanced at the clock. I hoped this call wouldn't take long. I had time for a quick binge before Tom came home for supper.

"Hi, Cindy. I don't know if you remember me, but this is Mary Carson. We went to Liverpool High School together."

High school? The voice and name from my past immediately got my attention. "Of course, I remember you, Mary. You lived across the street from Diane!" Diane, my old school friend.

"Cindy, I'm calling because our twentieth-year reunion is this summer, and your name was on the list of people that no one has been able to find."

"How *did* you find me? I'm not in the phone book."

"I saw an article in the newspaper . . . probably a couple of months ago. It talked of a woman named Cindy Nappa, who had won a scholarship. . . ." *The Clairol Scholarship.* "It mentioned the college you were attending. I thought it might be you, but I wasn't sure. When I couldn't find your name in the phone book, I called the college and they gave me your phone number. I was hoping it was the same Cindy Nappa that we once knew. I wanted you to know about the class reunion this summer." Mary filled me in on the events of her life, and Diane's. *Diane.* My old college roommate. *Diane.* Who had been invited to a wedding that never took place. *Diane.* One of the persons I was going to contact when I was all better.

"How is Diane?" I asked a bit timidly.

"She's great! She's married to a really nice guy and they have a daughter and a son. If you'd like Cindy, I could give you her phone number. I know she'd love to hear from you."

Would she? "Sure. I'd love to have it," I replied, though unsure if I'd have the courage to call. Not after all these years. Not when I knew that I wasn't yet *better*. But even if I didn't have the nerve to call, at least I'd have her number.

I promised to see Mary at the reunion and hung up. I stared at the phone number. *Call her. Call Diane. Mary said she'd love to hear from you.* And before I could lose my courage, or realize what I was doing, I dialed the number.

"Hello," a familiar voice answered from across the miles.

"Diane?" I whispered. "Is that you? Do you know who this is?"

"No? Should I?" She sounded annoyed.

"Diane, it's me—Cindy," I said timidly. "Cindy Nappa." I don't know if you remember me. . . ."

"Oh, my God! Cindy!" Diane screamed in my ear. "Of *course*, I remember you. I *never* forgot you. I have wondered for *years* about you! We all thought you had died. And then Mary called me a few months ago to tell me about an article in the newspaper. We weren't sure if it was the same Cindy or not." Diane told me what she was doing, where she was living—five minutes from my mother. I told her of my upcoming marriage, going to school, living in Rochester for eleven years. We laughed. We reminisced. We shared: Diane, her questions; myself, the answers. We reluctantly said good-bye, but only after promising to get together in a couple of weeks when I went to Syracuse for my next gown fitting. We hung up.

And I burst into tears. Talking with Diane had reconnected me with my past. It was like going back and filling in the blanks. My horrible life hadn't erased me from others' memories at all.

Two weeks later, I followed the directions to Diane's house.

She ran out of her house as I pulled into her driveway. We fell into each other's arms, laughing and crying. Twenty years had not made any difference. We were friends. I had come back.

Our arms entwined, we walked inside for an afternoon of lunch and talk. Over dessert and beyond, I shared my story. I told her all of it, including Mary Jean's turning away and how I had felt. I told Diane of the anorexia, the bulimia, my head injury, and everything in between. I wanted her to know, and hopefully understand, who I was. She did.

"Diane, I never contacted you because I was afraid that I would lose you. Just like I had lost Mary Jean. I was afraid that you wouldn't want to be my friend. That maybe I wasn't good enough," I said quietly, as we lingered over coffee and dessert.

"Cindy, don't you know how silly that is! What kind of friend would I be if I turned my back on you when you most needed me? Don't you know that a true friend would never leave you?"

No, I guess I didn't. But I do now. Diane was right. All those years I had been certain that I wasn't good enough or well enough to be someone's friend, and yet I had one waiting for me. How silly for me to think that people would like me based on how much I weighed, or on what I looked like on the outside. Or that I had to be perfect in order to be accepted. It was just another example of those misperceptions of reality that got me into trouble. I smiled at my newly found friend. "Diane, I'd like to ask you something." I took a deep breath. "I'd like to invite you to my wedding. Would you come?"

Diane's face broke into a huge grin and she leaned over and hugged me. "I wouldn't miss it, Cindy."

Yes. I had finally come home.

Chapter 24

Journey's End—Just a Regular Person

"Toad!" Tom bellowed from outdoors. "Come on, let's get going!"

I looked around the bedroom one last time. The last few weeks had flown by. What with all those last minute wedding things, and my high school reunion a week earlier, I had been afraid of not getting everything done. Our suitcases were packed and in the car. My gown, slip, and shoes were already at my mother's. Yes, everything was done.

I smiled at the warm memory of the reunion. It had been a wonderful and exciting evening packed full of: *"Remember this, remember that,* and *remember when."* How could I have forgotten? The only thing missing was the fear and the worry of not being good enough. Somewhere between the reminiscing and the hugs came the message that I had *always* been good enough. I had just been too scared and too insecure back then to have realized it. If I had opened up my feelings twenty years ago, I might have realized that my friends shared similar fears. It was all part of growing up. I wasn't the only girl who had been afraid of her own body, her own feelings. I hadn't been as different, or as abnormal as I had thought I was. In many ways, I had *always* been like everyone else, trying to learn how to deal with peer pressure, peer acceptance, changes, sexuality, and becoming my own person. Of course, there were the additional factors in my own life that had set me off in a direction that introduced its own unique set of challenges. Yet I really was just a regular person who had taken the long road through adolescence and young adulthood. And now I would continue my journey through adulthood with a life partner. A best friend to share all my adventures with.

The next afternoon, I nervously peered out my mom's living room window. *Where is that limousine?*

"Cindy, it'll be here soon," Mom smiled reassuringly. "We have plenty of time. Try to relax."

I turned away from the window. "I'm not nervous. Really, I'm not!" In less than two hours, I would be marrying the man that I loved, whom I *knew* loved me just as equally. The reality was almost overwhelming.

"Cindy, it's here!"

Thank God! I *had* to get to the church on time!

At the church—its study doubled as the bride's dressing room—confusion reigned. With Renee, my mother, my aunt, my cousins who were in my bridal party, *and* the photographer all crowded in the tiny room, I got dressed. Renee slipped my wedding gown over my head and buttoned the back.

I walked over to the floor-length mirror and stared at my reflection. My shiny, short-coifed hair was perfect. The tiny diamond earring studs—a gift from my mother—sparkled. The gown fit wonderfully. My makeup had been expertly applied. *I felt so pretty.* "Cindy, let me help you put your hat on." Renee placed the white picture frame hat on my head and anchored it in place with a dozen bobby pins. *"Ohh . . .* Cindy! You look *so* pretty!"

"Ohhh! Look at my little sister!" Debbie stuck her head in from the doorway, unable to wait any longer. "Cindy, you are so gorgeous! *You look so beautiful!"*

I shivered from the reality. *I felt beautiful.* It was my wedding day and I was the most beautiful, luckiest, happiest person in the world. *I was me!* And I didn't want to be anybody else but me!

Everyone filed out of the room. One by one, the girls in my bridal party took their places to start the processional. The sudden quietness was as overwhelming as the confusion of moments ago. Only Dad remained in the room with me.

"Hey, Pocahontas," he whispered softly. "May I kiss your nose?" He bent over and lightly kissed the tip of my nose. Dad straightened up. Tears glistened in his eyes. "Is there anything you want to say, or ask me, before I walk you down that aisle?"

I looked at the first man I had loved in life. He had bandaged my scraped knees, protected me from bogey men, rescued me from misadventures, bought me my first bike, my first car, and fought helplessly as eating disorders stole my health, my independence, my personality, and almost my life. Yet, as I had grown, so had he. My struggles had changed both of us.

"It's my day today, isn't it, Dad?" I said quietly, though my heart pounded as the moment drew closer. "Dad?"

"Yes, Pocahontas?"

"I know *now* that I had to go through everything I went through in order to get to this moment. And you know, Dad. I really don't think I could be this happy . . . *this loved* . . . if I hadn't hurt for so long." I paused, and organ music filtered into the room. "Dad?"

"Yes, Pocahontas?" The door opened and we were given our cue.

"Dad, I'm not scared anymore." I smiled, and he put his arm around me. "I'm finally ready, Dad." We walked out into the church lobby and took our places.

The music started and our family and friends stood up, *for me.* My face paled. *All these people!* I looked into the sea of faces and then I saw him, Dr. Stevens, standing head and shoulders above the rest. *"Thank you,"* I mouthed silently. *"Thank you, for never giving up on me."* I placed my arm through my father's, and we started our descent down the aisle. We reached the end and I took my place beside Tom. His eyes shone brightly from his own tears of happiness, as my father lifted my veil and kissed my cheek. "Hold my hand," I whispered to Tom. He squeezed my hand tightly. *And don't ever let go.*

The wedding reception passed in a blur, as did our wonderful honeymoon to the Hawaiian Islands of Maui and Oahu. All the excitement and craziness of the past year's planning was over in no time. As the fall leaves turned to winter snow, Tom and I continued to grow and adjust to each other. The challenges of any marriage were now ours, and we asserted our individuality as well as our unity.

Still, the one constant in my life that had not changed or gone away was bulimia's lingering presence. It had nothing to do with whether or not I was happy. *I was.* It had nothing to do with whether or not my heart was full. *It was.* It had nothing to do with whether or not I felt in control of my life. *I did.* It had nothing to do with whether or not I felt secure. *I did.* It had nothing to do with whether or not I felt fat. *I did not.* The fact of the matter was I loved my life. And I did not *need* bulimia anymore. There was no longer the issue of uncomfortable feelings. There was nothing troubling or standing in my way anymore.

So why didn't I just stop it?

Because I was afraid to lose the part of me that had become so familiar. I still *did* it because it fit so well and felt so comfortable. Like a pair of floppy, old worn-out slippers that no longer served their purpose, but I was reluctant to throw away.

"Cindy, I think we should have Renee stay with us after she has her surgery in a few weeks. What do you think?" Tom asked.

I stared down at my dinner plate. His suggestion was a logical one. Renee lived alone, and would need someone to help her. Yet if she stayed with us, there was no way that I could binge

and purge, *at all*. Renee was too familiar with eating disorder behavior. She would know if I purged. The thought made me uncomfortable. I *had* managed to not purge during our ten-day honeymoon. But if Renee stayed with us, it could be *weeks!* I had
never been able to give up bulimia for that length of time.

But a true friend meant being there when you were most
needed. Isn't that what Diane had said? And Renee was a good
friend. Hadn't she come and stayed with me after my head injury? Hadn't Renee been there for me? *This is your chance, Cindy.
This is your chance to be a friend—a good friend.* I took another
bite of my hamburger. "Okay," I agreed. "Renee will need our
support."

A few weeks later, Renee had her surgery and was discharged to our home. We fixed up the guest room so she would be
comfortable, and encouraged her to do nothing but rest and recuperate. In giving of myself and a little of our privacy, I stopped
bingeing and vomiting.

One day turned into one week, turned into ten days,
turned into two weeks. Renee returned to her own home. I had
no reason to *not* start bulimia's cycle up again. *But did I want to?*
The longer that I went without planning my life around it, the
more time I had to do other things. I felt less stressed by not
having to plan binges. *Maybe I'll just see how long I can go, before
I slip.*

One month passed into two months, passed into three.
By the fourth month, Dr. Davidson said I could stop taking the
potassium. For the first time in eleven years, I no longer needed
that supplement to counteract the vomiting.

Four months stretched to six months, to nine months.
No more panicking after eating. No more worrying if I had eaten
too many calories. No more slave to food. *No more urge to purge.*
No more. No more. No more. I was free.

I had recovered from bulimia. And it had taken more than
changing my eating behavior. It had taken understanding the reasons behind its need. When those reasons were uncovered, dealt

with, and finally put to rest, I had to change one more thing: my attitude . . . about myself . . . every day. I had to stop purging completely. Only then could I really learn how to eat, and learn how to take care of myself and my body in a healthy manner. I was the only one who could take on that responsibility and do it. I had faced that fear of fat and walked through it. It really was the only way to get to the other side. Bulimia wasn't so powerful after all—*I* was.

I had won the war but by having kept it so secret and hidden, I had no one to share the triumph. Only Dr. Stevens and Dr. Davidson had been privy to bulimia's perpetual grip on my life.

Dr. Stevens. I smiled at the memory of my doctor. He had voiced my fears when anorexia's wall had stolen my speech. He had picked me up each time I fell and encouraged me to stand. He had listened to my hurts, my anger, and felt my pain. He had not questioned who I was, but helped me to answer that for myself. He had shared my hopes and taught me how to deal with defeat. He had taught me to trust him, so that I in turn could learn to trust myself. He had taught me that feelings were normal, and that it was my perceptions that were not reality. In the end, I had learned to love and accept all of me, the good along with the imperfections.

It had been over a year since I had stopped seeing Dr. Stevens. It had happened naturally, shortly after my marriage. During that time, I had accomplished milestones. The journey I had started many years ago was completed. I would now continue to travel the road of my life as a strong, independent, and healthy woman. It was time to tell him so.

I sat down in front of my computer and tapped out a long overdue letter.

September 2 . . . . Dear Dr. Stevens, It sure has been a long time since I've written a letter to you. Usually, my letters have been due to concerns of mine. However, this letter is for no other reason that just to touch base and say 'hello.'

Well, I've been married one year. And am I still happy? You bet! It has been a year of adjustment that's for sure. Why did I believe that it would be easy? Tom and I continue to learn more about each other as time goes by. We have had our 'moments' over this past year, but nothing that is not normal for two people still learning. After all, did you not teach me that all feelings, including anger, are okay? Believe me, I have come to have more respect for the word 'compromise!'

Know what I else have come to realize? That Tom is the one I wish to share my thoughts and feelings with now. I guess after all these years, it is so natural to want to turn to you when things aren't setting right with me. Well, it has taken some getting use to, but Tom is my husband, and he needs to be the one I seek out for support, encouragement, comfort, and advice. Yet I know that if I REALLY needed more help than he was able to give, you would be there for me. But only if I could not help myself first.

You see, Dr. Stevens. I can truly say that I am one of the strongest, most stable persons I know (other than my husband). All those years of struggling, hard work, and tears have ingrained incredible strength and optimism in my soul. In so many little ways, you taught me to trust my feelings and myself so well that I know I can depend on me. I am my own main support (isn't that the right way to be?). The happiness within me is real. It continues to grow and bubble over. I have become my own pillar of strength and for my husband too. I like having him turn to me. At times, I find myself repeating words that I so often had heard you speak to me. And just think, the girl who thought she had nothing to offer, has so much to share just by being herself. People who meet me today cannot believe I could ever understand despair, depression, discouragement, or darkness. Isn't it amazing that I am described as a happy-go-lucky type of person? My love of life and of people is one of the most obvious things about me.

This doesn't mean that I don't have my down days or that Tom and I don't have disagreements. We do. But what this says is that I have the skills, the experience, and the ability to recognize the 'nor-

malcy' of it all.

So where am I today? Today I am headed back for my final year of school. It's taking a bit longer to finish due to continued difficulties with reading, memory, and writing papers. Last May, I was nominated to the Brain Injury Association's Board of Directors. I'm very proud of that position. Now, I am working side by side with lawyers, doctors, and other professionals (including Greg!). I am getting incredible amounts of experience and defining more clearly, my career goals.

And something else that I believe only you and Dr. Davidson can appreciate along with me—I ABSOLUTELY, COMPLETELY, stopped bingeing and purging last January! Though I liked to think that I was all better, bulimia stilled played a role in my life. Even if I could go days or weeks without bingeing and purging, I still felt its presence hovering in the background. But last January, I called it quits! Would you believe I now weigh 109 pounds? That is the weight that started me on the plunge into hell all those years before. Except there's one difference now—when I look in the mirror I see me, and I like me very much! Would you believe that I eat anything I want, and that I no longer worry about body-size? It's true!

It's been a long journey, Dr. Stevens. At times, I was so tired and I wanted to quit—or at least take a break! I thank God and thank you for keeping me alive when I couldn't. And now, after twenty-five years, I can honestly say I have completely recovered from my eating disorders. I am healthy!

Well, Dr. Stevens, my life continues. My 'scars' have healed and my heart is full. I love my role as wife and (equal!) partner. Can you feel my happiness from this letter?

Maybe, some time, I'll pass you in the streets. And if you don't recognize me, I'll run up to you, give you a hug and say, 'Hi, Dr. Stevens. It's me—Cindy.'"

The merry-go-round had stopped. I had caught the brass ring. It is called life.

Chapter 25

Epilogue

After completing this book, I realized that a piece of this story still needed to be addressed. Otherwise, it would have no closure. I needed to put an old fear aside and *try*. In order to do that, I had to go back to the beginning.

One evening, I gathered my courage and used it to call the mother of my old friend, Sandy. From her, I discovered that Sandy was married, the mother of two little boys, and living in another state. I got her phone number and address but still, I did not contact her. I was scared; worried that Sandy wouldn't remember me. What was I trying to prove anyway? That nothing had changed?

It took a week of reassuring myself before I finally dialed Sandy's number. On the third ring, a slightly familiar voice answered.

"Hello Sandy," I said. "This is Cindy Nappa. Only I'm Cindy Bitter now."

"Cindy!" Her excitement traveled from across the miles and wrapped itself around me. "My mother told me you were going to be calling. I've been waiting for your call all week. What took you so long. . . ."

We talked for almost two hours, and shared our memories, our stories, and ourselves. We laughed and reminisced about our innocence and our adventures. We were as old as our parents had been; we were as young as *we* had always been. We had grown and changed so much. And yet, we hadn't changed at all. Sandy was still Sandy. And I was still me.

I hadn't lost my friend at all. I had reached out and she was still there. In fact, every time I ever reached out someone had grabbed my hand. Yes, there were some who *had* let go, but it was due more to their inability to see the person beyond the outstretched hand. Guess they were afraid the hand would never stop clinging. But they needn't have been afraid to be a friend because a friend can make all the difference in the world.Since this story ended, I continued to experience life as I had always hoped I might. I earned my Bachelor's Degree, and currently provide vocational consulting services to persons with disabilities—primarily brain injuries and eating disorders. When working, I don't usually share who I am or where I've been with my clients. The focus for me is always on them. But I will never forget one young woman in particular. She was one of the very first persons I worked with. It was she who helped me realize that by sharing my story, I was better able to help others understand, accept, and move forward.

We were driving home after an extremely frustrating day of her struggling to learn and remember her new job tasks. I tried to encourage her by helping her outline her new job routine. I emphasized the importance of writing things down, using her tape recorder. But it was soon apparent: my words were not convincing her that I really did understand her discouragement.

I struggled silently with the dilemma of professional boundaries, and finally decided that here was a person desperately in need of hope. The only way *I* knew to let *her* know I understood was to share my own struggles. I told her I understood what it was like to spend most of your life in a hospital and under a doctor's care. I understood what it was like to suffer a chronic illness, a head injury, and all of a sudden be unable to comprehend life the way you had before. I understood what it was like to feel that life would *never* be better. I understood what it was like to be afraid and unsure of one's self. And I understood how it felt to believe that *nobody* really understood.

Her eyes grew wide. Her silence, as she digested my words, worried me that maybe I had made the wrong decision.

"You really do understand, don't you, Cindy?" she said, and searched my face as she spoke. "You *do* understand, don't you. You know," she added quietly, "everybody keeps telling me that they understand how I feel. But I don't believe them. I mean . . . how *could* they? They never went through what I went through. But you have. You have been there, and you have struggled with the same issues that I struggle with now. You really *do* understand what it's like for me." She smiled, and her whole face brightened. "Thank you for sharing yourself with me. It gives me hope. If you could do it, maybe I can too."

Dr. Stevens once told me he had been a cheerleader in my life. That the best he could do was to watch from the sidelines and cheer me on and encourage me to keep putting one foot in front of another.

Now it is my turn to be a cheerleader. I encourage all of you to let your desires be stronger than your fears. It really is possible to walk away from a carousel of despair and discouragement.

Because as long as you try, you are never a failure.

About the Author

Cindy Bitter has been involved in the area of eating disorders for a total of thirty years. Since 1987, she has educated college students, medical students, and the general public on issues of eating disorders by sharing her personal story of successful recovery. She is active in many organizations that support the education and prevention of eating disorders, and has appeared locally and nationally on radio and TV shows. Her personal experiences with anorexia, bulimia, and brain injury remain the driving force behind her compassion, her sensitivity, and her dedication to providing far-reaching hope and education to as many people as possible. Her supportive outreach has been expanded through the auspices of the Internet, where she has become a familiar voice to those who deal with the issues of anorexia and bulimia.

Cindy holds an A.A.S. Degree in Health Information Management and a B.S. Degree in Health Science from the State University of New York, College at Brockport. She is listed in *Who's Who in American Colleges, 1989* for her scholastic achievements, community involvement, and her personal triumph.

Cindy and Tom continue to be happily married, and thoroughly enjoy the company of the third member of their family, their aging golden retriever, "Corby."

ORDER FORM

Please send me:

Quantity

al book.

s tax.

Total amount Enclosed $

ount to:

HopeLines

P.O. Box 306

Penfield, New York 14526

For further information or comments:

Phone Tel./fax: 585 377-0079

Email cynjoy@rochester.rr.com

www.hopelines.com

HopeLines